First Economics

Also by G.F. Stanlake:
First Economics Answer Book
Introductory Economics
Introductory Economics Workbook
Macroeconomics: an introduction
A Macroeconomics Workbook
Objective Tests in Economics

First Economics

G.F. Stanlake M.A. B.Sc. (Econ)

Longman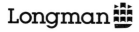

Longman Group UK Limited,
Longman House, Burnt Mill, Harlow,
Essex CM20 2JE, England
and Associated Companies throughout the world.

First published 1982
Fifth impression 1986

Set in 10/12pt Times Roman

Printed in Great Britain by
Richard Clay Ltd, Bungay, Suffolk

ISBN 0 582 22335 0

Acknowledgements

We are indebted to the following for permission to reproduce copyright material: Her Majesty's Stationery Office for an adapted extract from *Financial Statement and Budget Report 1980–81* and Oxford University Press for an adapted extract from 'The Monetary System' by Simon Dawkins from page 16 *British Economy Survey*, Vol 8, 1979.

We are grateful to the following for permission to reproduce photographs: Barclays Bank, page 143 centre right; British Leyland, page 29; Institute of Agricultural History and Museum of English Rural Life, University of Reading, page 12 above; Massey Ferguson, page 12 below; Popperfoto, page 82.
Photographs on page 143 (except centre right) and cover by Longman Photographic Unit.

The bills on page 237 are reproduced from *The London Discount Market*, Gerrard and National PLC, 1981, by permission of the publisher and the following institutions:
Borough of Ipswich; Hambros Bank Ltd and Renault UK Ltd; Barclays Bank Ltd; ICI Finance Ltd and British Gas Corporation; the design of a Treasury Bill is Crown copyright and is reproduced, at less than actual size, with the permission of the Controller of Her Majesty's Stationery Office.

Contents

Preface

I have written this book for O level students, based on my wide experience of teaching at this level and a careful study of the O level examination requirements of the various GCE Examining Boards.

The main aim of the book is to provide an *interesting* introduction to the subject matter of economics. The essential theoretical background has been included, as it is a necessary part of any genuine introductory course and is clearly required by the O level examiners. I have attempted to present it in a realistic manner and to relate it, wherever possible, to everyday experience. To this end I have also included a large number of diagrams, charts and other pictorial illustrations.

To facilitate understanding and to help students check their progress, I have included comprehensive test papers containing a wide range of different types of questions. These should also serve as an important aid to students working on their own.

I must acknowledge the valuable assistance rendered by my colleagues, and especially by Mr B. Harrison and Mr E. Colling.

G.F.S.

1 An introduction to the subject matter

Economics – what is it about?

Much of the language of economics is familiar to us. We know that economists discuss such topics as money, prices, wages, taxes, subsidies, exports and imports. When we listen to economists talking about these things, it often seems that much of what they are saying is no more than a little common sense applied to the problem of earning a living and spending an income. While there is some truth in this, it is a dangerous over-simplification to dismiss economics as no more than a common sense view of everyday life.

The fact that we are so familiar with many of the activities economics deals with is one of the major problems in studying the subject. The things we experience every day are usually the things we take for granted. We rarely, if ever, stop to ask ourselves questions about the economic system we live in. For example, do we know how the money we use every day is created and why it has a value (some of it consists of nothing more than bits of paper); do we, in fact, know what is the most important form of money in use in our own country? Can we answer the question, 'Why is water, which is so necessary for survival, so cheap, while diamonds, which are by no means a necessity, are so expensive?'. Do we know why a book with 100 pages is often more expensive than one with 200 pages? An attempt to indicate the scope of economics by means of a list of questions like these would be a futile task because the list would be endless. But it does serve to indicate the *type* of question which economics seeks to answer.

Since economics looks at the way people behave, it is described as a *social science*. It is, however, only concerned with certain aspects of social behaviour. It studies the way people go about satisfying their *material* wants. Economics deals with the ways in which we use our abilities and the gifts of nature to provide ourselves with food, clothing, shelter, transport, entertainment and other material things. Economists do not make any special study of other features of human behaviour such as our religious practices, or the various social groupings people form like the family, social classes, clubs and societies. It is not directly concerned with the kind of political institutions which people create. These matters form the basis of other social sciences such as theology, sociology and politics. Nevertheless, there is a great deal of overlapping and, in studying the economic features of a society, we have to know something about the religious, social and political life of the people.

Economics is about 'economizing'. This means spending our income carefully and wisely in order to get 'good value for our money'. From the point of view of society as a whole, it means looking at how people set about the task of obtaining the highest possible level of material satisfaction from the resources which are available to them.

Scarcity

One of the great benefits of television is that it enables us to see how the rest of the world lives. We know that in some parts of the world (e.g. Western Europe and North America) people are relatively well off, whereas in other parts of the world (e.g. much of Africa and Asia) millions of people live in miserable poverty. It seems strange, therefore, to learn that the economist refers to scarcity as a *universal* problem – a feature of all societies.

Economics deals with the problem of *relative* scarcity, that is, goods and services are scarce relative to people's wants. It is a fact that economic resources (human skills and knowledge plus the gifts of nature) are insufficient to satisfy all human wants. People's wants always seem to exceed their ability to satisfy them. Even in the developed countries, which have high standards of living, the supply of goods and services falls far short of what people want and there are insistent demands for even higher standards of living.

The point is, of course, that people's wants are not fixed. A rise in the standard of living seems to do little more than raise people's expectations of even higher standards. The common observation, 'the more you have the more you want' does seem to express a reality as far as people's attitudes to material things are concerned. The present average standard of living in the UK is unbelievably high when compared to that of a century ago, but no one would argue that people generally are completely satisfied.

The basic fact of economics, therefore, is that in all societies – rich and poor alike – people's wants cannot be fully satisfied. Scarce goods, then, are those goods of which there are never enough to satisfy people's wants. They are described as *economic goods* in order to distinguish them from *free goods*, such as air, where there is enough to satisfy everyone.

Choice and opportunity cost

Since we cannot have everything we want, we are forced to choose. Every day we are faced with choice; we can have either 'this' or 'that' we cannot have both. With our limited income, we cannot buy everything we would like to have; with our limited time we cannot do all the things we would like to do.

Economists assume that everyone has a scale of preferences. We try to spend our income so as to get the maximum possible satisfaction and, faced with a choice between two alternatives, we choose that commodity which is higher on our scale of preferences, or, more accurately, that commodity which gives us the most satisfaction per pound of expenditure.

This problem of choice leads us to a most important economic concept, that of *opportunity cost*. This is best explained by means of a simple example. Suppose a person with a limited income would like to buy both Good A and Good B, but can only afford to buy one of them. Good A is highest on his scale of preferences and so he purchases it. He has chosen to forego Good B and we regard the sacrifice of Good B as the 'cost' of obtaining Good A. If cost is measured in terms of what has to be 'given up' or foregone in order to get something, then the opportunity cost of a particular article is the next most desirable object which has to be foregone.

The idea of opportunity cost helps to explain a very important reality, especially when it is applied to society as a whole. Since there are insufficient resources to meet all wants, the community, just like the individual, must choose between alternatives. If resources are used to build more houses, the *money* cost consists of the payments made for the land, for the materials and for the labour. But the opportunity cost is the hospital, the school, the office block or other buildings which might have been built with those same resources.

Opportunity costs are often overlooked because they are are not 'paid out' costs. For example, suppose a person has £4000 in a savings account on which she receives interest at an annual rate of 10 per cent. She now decides to use these savings to purchase a motor car for £4000. Now, in addition to tax, insurance, petrol, maintenance, depreciation and other costs of running her car, there is an opportunity cost equal to £400 per annum, because this is the interest she has sacrificed in order to buy the car.

Production, consumption and exchange

There is an infinite variety of economic activities, but the study of these activities can be greatly simplified by classifying them into broad groupings.

Production
In economics, production is defined as any activity which satisfies a want and for which people are prepared to pay a price. If a craftsman worked very hard to produce some article and then found that nobody wanted it, his activity would not be defined as production. In common usage, the word 'production' is usually taken to mean the creation of some physical, tangible object such as a table, a loaf of bread, a piece of pottery or a motor car. In economics, however, the word has a wider meaning because it refers to the production of *goods and services*.

If people create things which other people are prepared to buy, then the activity is defined as production, because if people are prepared to pay a price for something, whether it be a good or a service, then it must be satisfying a want. Thus, teachers, lawyers, accountants and entertainers are productive workers in the same way as cabinet makers or farmers. There is no distinction in economics between 'productive' workers (those who produce goods) and 'non-productive' workers (those who produce services).

This leads on to another important point about production. The process does not end until the good or service is in the hands of the consumer; all the activities which help to get the good or service into the hands of the consumer are classified as production. Thus, the production of a cotton shirt may begin in the cotton fields of Alabama, but it does not end until the shirt is sold to the consumer in the High Street shop. Its production will embrace all the intermediate stages such as spinning, weaving, dyeing, finishing, cutting, sewing, advertising, transport, insurance, banking, wholesaling, retailing and so on.

Consumption

Consumption describes the using up of goods and services in order to satisfy our wants. We are 'consuming' the food we eat, the clothes we wear, the furniture we use, the records we play, the books we read, the electrical appliances we use in our home and so on. Consumption goods are sometimes classified as durable consumer goods and non-durable consumer goods. Durable consumer goods are those which render services and satisfaction over an extended period of time and include such things as the domestic refrigerator, the washing machine and the vacuum cleaner. Non-durable consumer goods are commodities which are used up immediately (i.e. in a single use) or in a relatively short time and include such things as food, soap, tobacco and beverages.

Exchange

In all but the most primitive societies exchange must take place before people can satisfy their wants. Very few people are capable of surviving on the basis of their own efforts; they cannot produce for themselves the things they need. Most of us specialize, that is, we spend our working days producing some small part of a product (e.g. as a lathe operator) or supplying some particular service (e.g. as a shop assistant). In order to obtain the things we want, we have to make use of some system which enables us to exchange what we produce for the goods and services produced by other workers. What happens in practice is that most people sell their labour for money and then use this money to buy goods and services supplied by other specialist workers.

Economics only deals with goods which have an exchange value. Many things are scarce and desirable, for example, personal health and happiness, but such things cannot be bought and sold (i.e. exchanged) and hence are not economic goods. The study of exchange means that we must look at subjects such as money, prices and markets.

Wealth

Economics has been defined as the science of wealth. The first major book on economics was published by Adam Smith in 1776 and called *An Inquiry into the Causes of the Wealth of Nations*. Wealth consists of a stock of goods which have a money value and includes such assets as land, houses, factories, machines and many kinds of personal possessions. It is useful to distinguish between private, social and national wealth.

Private wealth consists of the possessions of households and will include land, houses, works of art and jewellery. Individuals will also include in their personal wealth items such as shares, securities and money holdings.

Social wealth comprises assets owned by the community as a whole and will include roads, schools, hospitals, public parks, libraries and so on.

The *national wealth* is the sum of all the wealth possessed by the citizens of a country whether it is privately or publicly owned and whether the assets are situated at home or abroad. Strictly speaking we should include the skills and knowledge of the people as part of the national wealth, but, if we are trying to measure wealth, it is very difficult to put a money value on skills and knowledge.

The distinction between private wealth and national wealth is important because it is a common cause of confusion. As mentioned earlier financial assets (i.e. shares, saving certificates and money) will be included in an individual's stock of wealth. They are a part of that person's wealth because they can, if the owner so wishes, be converted into tangible or real assets. Shares, for example, can be sold in order to buy a motor car.

If we are calculating the national wealth, however, financial assets such as shares and bank deposits cannot be included. Financial assets are *claims* to real property. Shares represent the ownership of such things as factories, offices, machines, land and so on. Money represents a claim to goods (and services). It would obviously be wrong to take the total value of a company's property and then add to this the total value of the company's shares. Likewise, we cannot count the things which money can buy and the money itself. In other words, when estimating the national wealth we must be careful to distinguish between real wealth (i.e. the physical goods) and claims to wealth.

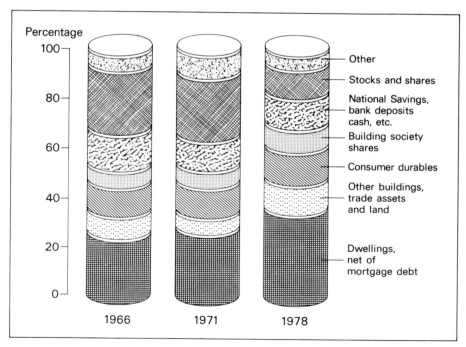

Fig. 1.1   Composition of marketable wealth of individuals, UK

Source: *Social Trends*, HMSO, 1981.

Income

Whereas wealth refers to a *stock* at some point in time, income refers to the rate at which wealth is being produced. Economic activity is a continuous process; production and consumption are taking place all the time. If we are consuming less than we are producing, the national stock of goods (i.e. wealth) will be increasing; if consumption is greater than production, the national stock of assets will be falling.

The continuous production of goods and services can be seen as a *flow* of output and we usually measure the rate at which mines, farms, factories, shops etc., are producing goods and services by taking the value of the total output per annum. This annual value of the national output is known as the national income. The various ways in which the national income is measured are discussed later; at this stage it is only necessary to understand the difference between wealth (a stock of goods) and income (a flow of goods and services).

Value judgements

Economists deal with the problems of satisfying people's wants. They do not ask whether people *ought* to want these things or whether people *should* have them. In economics we study people's wants rather than their needs. If we express views about the things people *need* we are usually making what is known as a value judgement; we are making a statement about what we think people ought to have.

If economics is regarded as a science then statements in the subject should be of the kind which can be proved or disproved by checking the facts. For example, the statement 'In a free market, a shortage of a commodity at the current price will cause the price to rise' is an example of a statement which can be verified by examining what actually happens in the real world. On the other hand the statement 'Incomes are unfairly distributed' cannot be proved or disproved by factual evidence since it is a matter of opinion.

Statements on economic policy are usually value judgements – they express what people think *ought to be done* and we find, therefore, a great deal of disagreement on matters of economic policy. In a subject like economics, which deals with matters which have such important effects on our daily lives, it is very difficult to avoid making value judgements and all economics textbooks contain expressions of opinion as well as of fact.

2 Economic resources

In producing goods and services people make use of an enormous variety of economic resources. Many of these are very familiar to us and have already been mentioned in Chapter 1. Economic resources such as human skills, fertile land, factories, transport systems and communications networks are described as *factors of production*. In order to study these factors of production it is usual to classify them into three or four broad groupings where all the resources in any one group have some common feature. One way of doing this is to divide the factors of production into (a) natural resources, (b) human resources, and (c) manufactured resources. The resources in the first group are described as *land*, those in the second group as *labour* and those in the third group as *capital*. A fourth factor, the *entrepreneur*, is usually added to the list although many economists, as we shall see later, do not distinguish a fourth type of resource.

Land

Land is taken to mean all the natural resources or free gifts of nature available to us. It includes, therefore, the area of land with its fertile soil, rivers, forests, the minerals beneath the soil and the riches in the seas. Until fairly recent times, in all societies, the vast majority of people worked on the land and early economists regarded land as by far the most important economic resource. They were much concerned with the fact that, unlike the other economic resources, it was strictly limited in supply.

The supply of land

It is true that the total surface area of land is fixed in supply, but the area of cultivable land can be varied. It can be reduced by erosion, overcropping and neglect and it can be increased by drainage, irrigation and reclamation. Most of the problems in economics are not concerned with the total supply of land, but with the supply of land for a particular use. In this sense the supply of land is not fixed, for a great deal of land can be transferred from one use to another. The supply of land for growing wheat can be increased by using less of it to grow barley; the supply of building land can be increased by reducing the supply of farmland.

But there are cases where the supply of land for a particular use is fixed. An important example is the supply of shop sites in the High Street; this is fixed and nothing can be done to increase the supply. The same feature is also apparent when the product depends upon certain soil and climatic conditions. Only certain areas can produce genuine Burgundy or Champagne and similarly there is only a limited number of Mediterranean beauty spots. It is also true that there is an upper limit to the amount of mineral resources in the earth's crust, a point dramatically illustrated by the present worries about the future supply of oil.

Another feature of land which is of great economic importance is that it has no costs of production; it is a free gift of nature. This is not true of the other factors of production and it raises important and interesting questions about the income from land.

Labour

The supply of labour

Labour is human effort of all types, manual and non-manual, skilled and un-skilled. The size and quality of a country's labour force is a most important determinant of that country's ability to produce goods and services. The term 'the supply of labour', however, cannot be measured simply by counting the number of workers available; it refers to the *hours of labour services* available per week (or per year). It depends upon (a) the number of workers and (b) the number of hours, on average, which each worker is prepared to work. Thus, a reduction in the average length of the working week would reduce the supply of labour even though the number of workers remained unchanged. An extension in the average length of annual holidays would also reduce the supply of labour.

In any particular country, the supply of labour depends upon:

a   the size of the population;

b   the proportion of the population which is available for work and willing to work;

c   the average number of hours worked by members of the working population. These are important features of an economy and they are discussed more fully in the chapter on population (Chapter 14).

The efficiency of labour

Although the *quantity* of labour is important in determining the amount of goods and services which a country can produce, the *quality* of the labour force is also of great importance. A worker-hour of labour supplied by the highly skilled technician, designer or chemist is quite different from the worker-hour supplied by unskilled labour because what each of them produces in one hour will have very different market values. In economics we are concerned with the value of what is produced as well as the volume. The efficiency of labour is generally referred to as the productivity of labour and this is measured in terms of the value of output produced per hour of work.

A country with a very efficient labour force clearly has, in effect, a greater supply of labour than a country with a similar number of workers but whose labour is less efficient. For this reason both firms and governments devote resources to improving the quality of labour. Governments provide education and training facilities, pass legislation aimed at improving working conditions and provide health services. Firms also undertake industrial and commercial training and many of them also provide workers with a variety of welfare and social facilities (e.g. works canteens, social and sporting facilities).

The efficiency of labour, however, also depends upon the quality of the resources with which labour has to work. Workers in firms which are well organized and managed and which make use of up-to-date technical equipment will obviously achieve higher levels of productivity than workers in firms which are badly managed and use out-of-date equipment.

Capital

Capital consists of such things as factories, machines, power stations, roads, and railways. In other words, it consists of all those things which people have made to aid them in production, that is, things which are produced not because they are wanted for their own sake, but because they help people to make the things which satisfy their wants. Goods which are wanted for their own sake because they provide immediate satisfaction are known as *consumer goods* (e.g. food, clothing, radios, books). Things which are produced in order to increase people's ability to produce consumer goods and services are known as *capital goods*. The bow and arrow, the axe and the spear are examples of the earliest forms of capital and people soon learned that a net would greatly increase their ability to catch fish.

Perhaps the most striking feature of modern methods of production is the enormous amounts of capital they use. In many modern industries this amounts to thousands of pounds worth of capital for each person employed. For example, in 1976 it was estimated that in UK manufacturing industry there was £7500 of capital equipment for each employee. In Japan the figure was £30 000 and for West Germany it was £23 000 per employee.

Types of capital

Businesses usually classify their capital as either fixed capital or working capital.

Fixed capital, as the name suggests, is long lasting. It consists of those things which do not change their form in the course of production and which wear out relatively slowly. A firm would describe its buildings and machinery as fixed capital.

Working capital is 'used up' in the course of production in the sense that it is changed into some other form. It consists mainly of raw materials or semi-processed materials used in production. The farmer's seeds, the shoe manufacturer's leather and the printer's stock of paper are examples of working capital. A firm will also include in its working capital the cash reserves it holds for purposes of meeting its day-to-day expenditures (e.g. the purchases of materials and the payment of wages).

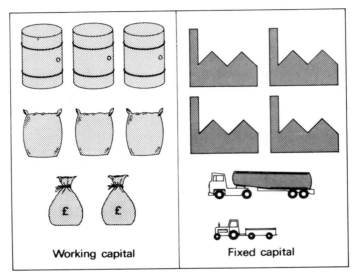

Working capital   Fixed capital

Fig. 2.1   Working capital and fixed capital

The supply of capital[1]

The economic resources which are used to make capital goods might have been used to produce consumer goods. The materials and labour used to make lorries might have increased the output of motor cars; the resources used to fit out a railway carriage could have produced more household furniture. All this means, of course, is that the opportunity cost of producing capital goods is the output of consumer goods which has to be foregone.

Society is usually prepared to make this sacrifice because the use of capital makes possible a much greater future output of consumer goods. By giving up a *relatively* small output of consumer goods this year (to make capital goods) there is the prospect of a relatively large increase in the output of consumer goods in a few years time.

In modern societies this sacrifice of current (i.e. present-day) consumption takes the form of saving. If we do not spend all our income, we are foregoing

[1] Capital is not the same thing as wealth. Capital is an important part of the national wealth, but wealth also includes stocks of goods (e.g. works of art) which are not capital items.

consumption. This decision to save, of course, might cause some unemployment in the industries making consumer goods. But if these savings are borrowed and used to finance the construction of capital goods, there will be increased employment opportunities in the capital goods industries. The act of saving, therefore, releases resources from employment in the making of consumer goods, but these resources will not find employment unless someone borrows the money and employs land, labour and capital in the making of capital goods.

Investment

In economics the word 'investment' does not mean buying shares on the Stock Exchange or putting money into a savings account. The word is used to describe *the creation of capital*. Investment takes place when factories are built, machines are manufactured, raw materials are produced and so on.

The total annual output of capital goods is described as *gross investment*. But capital is always wearing out and becoming obsolete so that the gross investment in any one year does not represent the amount by which the nation's stock of capital has increased. The extent to which the stock of capital 'runs down' each year is described as *depreciation*. Some part of the annual output of capital is required to make good the losses due to depreciation.

If gross investment exceeds depreciation, there is an increase in the national stock of capital. This increase is known as *net investment*. Thus,

Gross investment − Depreciation = Net investment

Net investment is a very important item. It tells us the rate at which the capital stock is increasing and *future* productivity depends very much upon the *present* rate of net investment.

The entrepreneur

Most of the factors of production we observe in the real world can be fairly easily identified and classified as land, labour or capital. Many economists, however, identify a fourth factor of production. They argue that, left to themselves, land, labour and capital will not produce anything; someone must organize and direct these factors of production. The person (or persons) who undertakes the responsibilities and risks of employing land, labour and capital and who decides how and where these resources should be used is described as *the entrepreneur*.

Entrepreneurs are the risk-bearers and the decision-takers. They are risk-bearers because they must purchase and employ the services of factors of production without any guarantee that their sales revenues will cover their costs. A great deal of production is undertaken *in the expectation* that profits will be

Fig. 2.2(a)   Land, labour and capital in the 1900s

Fig. 2.2(b)   Land, labour and capital in 1981

made, but there can be no certainty that this will be so and it is not possible to insure against losses in business enterprise.

Entrepreneurs must also take decisions on the location of the enterprise, the range of goods to be produced and the methods of production to be adopted. They must not only take these decisions, they must also see that they are carried out. Risk-bearing, organization and management are the functions of the entrepreneur, but they need not be carried out by the same person. In the one-person business all these functions are carried out by the owner, but in the large company the responsibilities are shared. The shareholders bear the risks and the directors are the decision-takers and managers.

The dispute over the fourth factor of production arises because some economists regard the tasks of the entrepreneur as no more than a specialized type of labour. They point out that the steeple-jack and the deep-sea diver take great risks and most labour runs the risk of being unemployed.

3 Economic systems

The economic problems facing all societies

All countries suffer from a relative scarcity of economic resources so that the basic economic problem facing all of them is the same – they must make choices between alternatives. Economists refer to this as the problem of *resource allocation*, because each society must decide how it should use (i.e. allocate) its land, labour and capital so as to produce the highest possible level of welfare for its citizens. There are three fundamental problems which have to be solved.

1 Which goods shall be produced and in what quantities?
2 What methods of production shall be employed?
   It is possible for most commodities to be produced by using different methods of production. Farm products may be produced by using large amounts of labour relative to the amounts of capital or by using large amounts of capital relative to the number of workers. Fig. 2.2 on page 12 illustrates these two different methods of producing cereal crops. Some manufactured goods may be produced by small firms using a lot of skilled labour or by large firms using mass-production methods.
3 How shall the goods and services produced be shared out?
   This is the problem of *distribution*. The ultimate aim of economic activity is the production of consumer goods and services. But even if the problems of production are solved there remains the problem of deciding the shares of the national output going to different individuals or groups of individuals.
   Should there be equal shares for all?
   Should those who produce more than others receive more than others?
   Should the output be shared out according to people's ability to pay the prices?
   Should the division be according to people's needs (as determined by the state)? There are different ways of solving these basic economic problems and it is useful to classify economic systems according to the ways in which they tackle these problems.

Traditional economies

These are communities with relatively low living standards where economic progress has been very slow and the way of life has remained unchanged for centuries. The African village and the Bedouin tribe are typical examples. The ways in which goods are produced, crops grown and the products distributed among the people have been decided long ago and the people simply carry on their customary ways of doing things. Sometimes the way of life is governed by religious beliefs and superstitions: certain omens may be looked for before crops are planted and harvested.

Such societies usually have a very rigid social structure. The people do not question the age-old customs which determine the way they live their lives and they tend to accept the fact that little will change during their lifetimes. What to produce and how to produce it are not really seen as economic problems; such things are governed by habit and custom. The same solution is applied to the problem of distribution because there will be some long-established way of sharing out what the community produces.

In the traditional society there will be relatively little exchange since families will tend to be largely self-sufficient, producing most of their needs for themselves.

Market economies

Any arrangement which enables buyers to do business with sellers is described as a market so that a market economy is one in which there is considerable freedom for people to buy what they want and to sell what they produce. Instead of producing goods and services for their own use, people produce 'for the market'. This does not mean that there is only one market; there are many thousands of separate markets. There are markets for agricultural commodities, for raw materials, for manufactured goods and for all kinds of personal services. In all these markets the goods and services have prices and can be freely bought and sold. Prices are free to move according to the quantities being offered for sale and the quantities being demanded. As we shall see later it is the movements in prices which play a crucial role in the market economy. How this type of economy works can best be understood by looking at its main features.

1 Private property

This is an important feature of a capitalist or market economy. It means that individuals have the right to own, control and dispose of land, buildings, machinery and other natural and manufactured means of production.

2 Freedom of choice

This means that individuals are free to set up in business for themselves, owners of land and capital may use these resources as they see fit, workers are free

15

to enter and leave occupations and consumers are free to spend their incomes in any way they wish. One must qualify these statements on the freedoms enjoyed by producers and consumers. The freedom to spend one's income as one wishes is not very meaningful for those who are living in poverty. The freedom to move into any occupation is not very meaningful if there is large-scale unemployment.

3 Self-interest

In a market or free enterprise economy, the pursuit of personal interests is given free expression. Everyone in the economy attempts to do what is best for themselves. Thus, we assume, each firm will attempt to earn maximum profits; owners of land and capital will hire them to the highest bidders; workers will always try to move to occupations offering higher rewards and consumers will spend their incomes so as to maximize their satisfactions.

4 The operation of the price mechanism

This is probably the most important aspect of the market economy, because this is the mechanism whereby the basic economic problems are solved. Very simply, the movements in prices cause producers and consumers to react in ways which lead to changes in production. This is best explained by means of a very simple example.

Suppose that consumers' tastes change and they display a growing preference for Commodity X and try to buy more of it. At the same time a similar competing good, Commodity Y, is becoming less popular. The increasing demand for X will raise its price and it will become more profitable to produce whereas the falling demand for Y will lower its price and make it less profitable to produce. These changes will cause a movement of land, labour and capital out of the industry making Commodity Y and more resources will tend to move into the industry making Commodity X.

Changes in demand cause changes in prices. These changes in prices cause changes in profits (or losses) and lead to a movement of resources from less profitable industries to more profitable activities. In theory, at any rate, the free choice of consumers determines *what* is produced.

Price movements also determine *for whom* the goods and services shall be produced. How much of the national output a person can obtain depends upon the size of his or her income. But these incomes are prices. The wage of a miner represents the price paid for mining labour, and, in a market economy, the income of a factor of production, like other prices, depends upon the quantities being supplied and demanded. Thus, when the demand for a product increases, the demands for the factors making that product also increase and so will their prices (i.e. incomes). Likewise, a falling demand for a product will lead to falling incomes in the industry making it.

5 Competition

The market system is a competitive system. The model of a market economy assumes that there is a large number of competing firms in each industry and a large number of individual buyers for each product. The firms in an industry compete on the basis of price. It is assumed that buyers faced with many competing sellers will always deal with the one charging the lowest price (all the producers in an industry are assumed to be supplying the same good). Under this system the successful firms will be those which can produce at the lowest cost, because they will be able to sell at the lowest prices and drive the less efficient firms out of business. Thus we see that the problem of *how* the goods shall be produced is decided by price competition.

6 A limited role for the government

The government has very few economic functions in a market economy. Its role is mainly one of maintaining law and order and defending the country against its enemies. Enforcing the law of contract will be an important job for the government because the world of business needs some means of making sure that people keep their promises to supply goods and services and to pay their debts.

Command economies

These economies are so named because all the important economic decisions are taken by a group of people who have the power to *command* the nation's economic resources. These powers to command will usually lie with the government which will have the authority to decide how the nation's resources of land, labour and capital will be used. The government will determine what shall be produced, how it shall be produced and how the incomes shall be distributed. The fact that the working of the economy is closely controlled by the government has led to this type of economy being described as a *centrally planned economy*. The main features of such an economy are as follows.

1 Public ownership

If the government is going to exercise full control over land and capital it will be necessary for it to own them. Thus, in a fully planned economy, it is usual to find that the land, factories, power stations, transport systems, mines, harbours, offices, shops and most houses are publicly owned (i.e. the property of the state). There will be some private ownership but it will tend to be limited to personal possessions although small businesses are often privately owned and sometimes farm workers are allowed to own small plots of land.

2   Planned production

Some kind of committee or other state organization will be required to draw up a detailed plan for the economy. This body will have to carry out a survey of the resources available, set production targets for different industries and then allocate the land, labour and capital to the different industries so that they can meet their targets.

Land and capital are not allocated by the movements of prices – they do not go to the highest bidders – they are directed to different uses by orders of the central government. Prices will play a relatively small part in the planning process and resources will not be distributed according to people's willingness and ability to buy them. They will be used in ways which the government thinks are desirable. But the price system will play some part because, while it is possible to direct land and capital to certain industries, it is difficult to direct labour. Workers will generally demand some degree of freedom of choice. Even in the fully planned society, it will generally only be possible to overcome a labour shortage in one industry and a labour surplus in another, by making wages more attractive where labour is in short supply.

3   Planned distribution

While it may not be impossible to plan fully the output of goods and services, it is difficult to see how the distribution of that output could be fully planned in a modern society. In theory, the goods and services could be shared out by some kind of physical rationing scheme; families might be given vouchers entitling them to so much of each good and service. This is not likely to be acceptable, however, because people will normally demand some freedom of choice in the way they spend their incomes.

If consumers are given freedom to spend as they wish, it is most unlikely that their spending plans will exactly match the outputs planned for the various industries. There will almost certainly be surpluses and shortages. These may be overcome, of course, by raising the prices of the goods in short supply and lowering the prices of the goods in surplus. Shortages can also be dealt with (but not overcome) by physical rationing schemes where each person is given a legal entitlement to a certain quantity of the good.

In this type of economy, the national economic plan is a very complex matter. The planned outputs of thousands of enterprises (mines, farms, power stations, transport systems, factories, shops, banks etc.) must all be fitted together. The planned output of a mine, for example, becomes part of the planned input for many other units of production. Once such plans are drawn up and put into operation it is very difficult to carry out any changes. National economic plans are normally drafted for periods of about five years and major changes cannot be introduced until a new plan is prepared. The complexity of the planning procedures and the task of supervising its operation calls for the employment of a large number of officials. Such a system is said to be bureaucratic.

Mixed economies

In the real world there is no completely planned economy. Even where there is a very large measure of centralized planning there is usually some degree of freedom of choice for consumers and workers and some use is made of the price mechanism. Similarly we find no example of an economy which relies completely on the price mechanism (such economies are often described as *laissez-faire* economies). In all of the so-called market economies in the real world, we find governments playing an important part in economic affairs. The communist world tends to lean strongly towards the fully planned economy while in the non-communist world far more reliance is placed on the price mechanism.

The UK and most of the developed countries in the non-communist world are described as mixed economies because there is a mixture of private and public ownership of industry and commerce and both state control and the price mechanism play important parts in the working of the economy.

Over the years the role of the state has tended to become more important because certain features of the market economy have become less acceptable. The features of a free market economy which have led to most criticism are set out below.

1 It leads to great inequalities of income and wealth. Private ownership of land and capital enables those who are most successful in the world of business to accumulate large amounts of wealth. Private ownership also enables people to acquire wealth by inheritance rather than by effort.

2 Competition gives rise to monopolies. The more successful firms will drive the less successful out of business. Eventually such competition will mean that an industry may come to be dominated by one or very few firms. Once competition has been eliminated (or greatly reduced) the surviving firm (or firms) will be able to exercise great market power. In other words they will be able to charge prices well above the costs of production.

3 The market system is unstable and subject to booms and slumps. The history of capitalist economies in Western Europe and North America shows that, left to itself, a free, or relatively free, economy is subject to recurring bouts of prosperity and depression. Most people find this state of affairs unacceptable, especially because of the uncertainty it creates with regard to employment.

4 In times of rapid economic and technical change, the burdens of change are 'unfairly' distributed. In a world of change, resources will have to be shifted

19

from industries which are declining to those which are expanding. In a market economy such shifts will take place, but it is the manner in which they take place which leads to dissatisfaction. The firms whose products are experiencing falls in demand will go bankrupt; workers will lose their jobs and shareholders will lose their capital. The unsuccessful (or unlucky) ones will bear the full costs of economic change. Many people believe that the costs of such change should be borne by the whole community. The state should tax those who gain in order to help those who lose.

5   The costs incurred by a firm take the form of the prices it pays for the resources it uses in production. The term 'costs of production' normally refers to this view of costs which the economist describes as *private costs*. But private costs may not be a measure of the full costs of production from the point of view of society as a whole; they only measure the costs incurred by the firm.

For example, a firm, in the course of production, may release waste matter which pollutes the atmosphere (or perhaps a river). This pollution is a cost borne by the community in the form of a nuisance, an inconvenience and, perhaps, as a danger to health. This particular cost does not appear in the firm's accounts. Similarly the private costs of constructing a major airport will not record the costs imposed on society in the form of increased noise and increased congestion on the roads leading to the airport.

The term *social costs* is used to describe all the costs associated with an economic activity, both those which are 'paid out' by producers and those which are not. Since, in a market economy, the price mechanism does not take account of these 'external' costs, it cannot be said to be an ideal system for deciding how economic resources should be used.

Test paper 1

Short-answer questions

1 'By devoting more of her resources to agriculture, the UK could produce more of her food at home.' What would be the opportunity cost of pursuing this policy?

2 Give some examples of the fixed capital used in the mining industry.

3 Under what circumstances would (a) a motor car and (b) a sewing machine, be classed as (i) capital goods and (ii) consumer goods?

4 Why, in economics, are goods and services which are provided by the state free of charge (e.g. hospital treatment and education in schools) *not* classed as free goods?

5 A colour television set costs £350, but it can be rented at £2 per week. A person decides to buy rather than rent and withdraws the money from her savings account (where it is earning interest at 8 per cent per annum). She pays £20 per annum insurance against repair costs. At the end of five years she declares that she has saved £70 by buying rather than renting. Would an economist agree with her?

6 In what sense are accountants, teachers, and lawyers 'productive' workers?

7 What is meant by the *real* exchange value of one hour's work?

8 Identify some of the characteristics of land which help to determine its value.

9 The population of a country is 10 million. The working age groups make up 60 per cent of the total. Why is the working population likely to be substantially less than 6 million?

10 The efficiency of labour refers to labour's productivity and this is usually measured in terms of output-per-worker-hour. Why is it not possible to obtain such a measurement for a large part of the UK labour force?

11 Which of the following industries are likely to employ large amounts of capital relative to labour?
  a motor car manufacture
  b chemicals
  c local government services
  d the high-fashion clothing industry

12 The national accounts of a country for one year showed that depreciation was £100 million and net investment was £250 million. What was the value of the total output of capital goods?

13 What is *mixed* in a mixed economy?

14 How does the operation of the price mechanism eliminate (a) a market shortage and (b) a market surplus of a commodity?

15 What is meant by the *profit motive* and in what type of economy does it have a powerful influence on production?

16 Who owns the land and capital in a socialist economy?

17 What is the meaning of the word *bureaucracy*? Which of the economic systems discussed in the text is most likely to be bureaucratic?

True or false?

18 **a** A Christmas or birthday present is an example of a free good because the person receiving it does not have to pay a price in order to get it.

b The opportunity cost of air is zero.

c Reading a novel for the pleasure it provides is described as consumption.

d Resources are scarce in poor countries but not in rich countries.

e We only have to make choices between alternatives because we do not have enough money.

f My deposit in the building society is part of my personal wealth but not part of the national wealth.

g The greater part of personal wealth in the UK consists of money.

h In order to build up a stock of capital we have to consume less than we produce.

i Undiscovered or inaccessible deposits of minerals are part of the total supply of economic resources.

j In a market economy the types and quantities of the goods produced are not influenced by consumers' preferences but are decided by the managers of firms.

Multiple-choice questions

19 Which of the following is not counted as land?
A fishing grounds
B mountain ranges
C forests
D motorways

20 The majority of the goods produced in the UK are bought by
A firms for investment purposes
B government
C consumers at home
D residents of overseas countries

21 Which of the following is *not* included in the study of economics?
A unlimited wants
B limited resources
C the problem of choice
D the price mechanism
E whether a particular good satisfies a good or bad purpose

22 The law of economic scarcity refers to the fact that
    A the more scarce the commodity, the more the people want it
    B no country can produce enough to satisfy all its people's wants
    C even in the richest country some people are very poor
    D in all societies shortages arise due to crop failures, strikes and
        technical breakdowns

Questions 23, 24 and 25 refer to the following terms.
    A consumption
    B income
    C exchange
    D capital
Match the statements below to the terms lettered A to D. Each letter may be
used once, more than once or not at all.
23 sitting at home playing records
24 the continuous flow of output from factories, farms, mines, shops and
    offices
25 the goods we produce which are intended to be used as factors of produc-
    tion

26 Which of the following is classed as *capital*?
    1 a firm's stock of raw materials
    2 the machinery used in a motor car industry
    3 an automatic washing machine installed in a launderette
    A 1, 2 and 3
    B 1 and 2 only
    C 2 and 3 only
    D 1 only
    E 3 only
27 Which of the following is/are value judgements?
    1 total world trade has been rising steadily
    2 the more efficient methods of production raise the quality of life
    3 the Chancellor of the Exchequer should increase the incentive to work
       by reducing income tax
    A 1, 2 and 3
    B 1 and 2 only
    C 2 and 3 only
    D 1 only
    E 3 only
28 In economics production is complete when the goods
    A are in a finished state
    B have reached the wholesaler
    C have reached the retailer
    D have reached the consumer

Data-response question

29 The figure shows a production possibility curve. It shows all the possible combinations of capital goods and consumer goods which a country *could* produce, with the existing techniques of production, when all its economic resources are employed. Under full employment conditions, therefore, this country could choose any position on this curve.

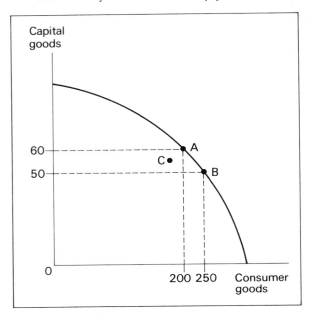

What are the missing words/numbers?

a   If this country chose to operate at position A it would produce _____ units of capital goods and _____ units of consumer goods.

b   If the country moved from position A to position B, the opportunity cost of the additional consumer goods would be _____ units of _____ goods.

c   If the country is operating at position C it means that some of its economic resources are _____ .

d   If the country moved from position C to position A, the opportunity cost of the additional output would be _____ .

e   If the country moved from position B to position A then it is likely that, in future, its production possibility curve would move _____ .

4 Production and productivity

Inputs and outputs

Although we frequently hear and see the words 'productivity' and 'production', it seems that the distinction between the two is not generally understood. The words do, in fact, have quite different meanings.

Production describes the processes of creating goods and services. It may also be used to describe the quantity of goods and services produced in a given time period. For example, a firm might announce that its total production last month was greater than it was in the previous month.

Productivity, however, is a measure of the efficiency with which production is carried on. It is a relationship between the quantity of goods and services produced and the amount of resources used to produce those goods and services.

For example, suppose that two firms are making similar footwear, one producing 100 000 pairs of shoes per month and the other firm producing 50 000 pairs per month. We know their total outputs (i.e. production) per month, but this information tells us nothing about the relative efficiencies of the two firms. In order to make a statement about efficiency or productivity we need information about *the outputs* (the amount of goods produced) and the *inputs* (the amount of resources used). If the firm producing 50 000 pairs of shoes per month is only using 40 per cent as much land, labour and capital as the firm producing 100 000 pairs per month, its productivity is much greater than that of the larger firm.

If there were only one factor of production, for example, labour, it would be relatively easy to measure productivity. We would simply divide the total output by the amount of labour used in production. If, for example, the larger firm mentioned above used 20 000 worker-hours of labour each month, productivity in that firm would be:

$$\frac{100\ 000 \text{ pairs of shoes}}{20\ 000 \text{ worker-hours}} = 5 \text{ pairs of shoes per worker-hour.}$$

This is, in fact, a very common way of measuring productivity, but it can be very misleading because labour is not the only input. This measurement of productivity takes no account of the amount of land and capital employed. Nowadays most increases in productivity are brought about by improvements in the quantity and quality of capital and in organization.

The division of labour (specialization)

Perhaps the most remarkable feature of modern production methods is the way in which work is specialized. The production of a good or service is broken down into a large number of separate and simple operations. Each worker is responsible for and spends the whole of his or her time carrying out one of these operations. Thus, in most industries, a finished product is the result of the combined efforts of many thousands of specialist workers. Each worker makes a very small (but important) contribution to the total production process.

This technique of breaking down production into a large number of specialist tasks is described as *the division of labour*. The most striking applications of this principle are provided by industries making such goods as motor cars, electrical appliances, radio and television sets. These industries (and many others) make use of assembly lines where each worker fits a single component as the product moves down the line.

The division of labour, however, is not a recent development. Very early in its history the human race realized the gains to be made by using the principle of specialization. People found that the total output of a group could be greatly increased (with no extra effort) when, instead of each person trying to provide for all their needs by their own efforts, each of them was made responsible for one of the activities (e.g. hunting, fishing, making clothes, building shelters, making weapons and so on).

The advantages of the division of labour

1 No two people have exactly the same abilities and aptitudes. The division of labour, by creating a very large number of different jobs, enables people to devote themselves to tasks for which they are best suited. It is true, however, that in the real world, ignorance, bad organization and lack of opportunity may prevent people from finding work which makes full use of their talents.

2 When workers concentrate on a single task which involves no more than a few simple movements, they are able to develop great speed and dexterity.

3 If workers are made responsible for several stages of production, they will have to move from one location to another, putting down one set of tools and picking up another (or move from one machine to another). In specialized production, it is the product which moves and no time is wasted by movements of workers.

4 When one worker carries out several operations, he or she must have a full set of tools for all the tasks required. For a large part of the time, therefore, much of that equipment will be lying idle (two jobs cannot be done simultaneously). When the work is specialized, however, each worker only needs one set of tools which can be put to continuous use.

5 A most important feature of the division of labour is that it has made possible the mechanization of production. When production is subdivided into many simple operations (there may be as many as one hundred operations in the making of a pair of shoes) the development of machinery

becomes a practical proposition. Even today it would be difficult to devise a machine which could convert a tree trunk into a sideboard, but when the principle of the division of labour is adopted, it becomes possible to use powered saws, planes, drills, lathes, polishers and so on.

There is no doubt that the continuous extension of the division of labour to the processes of production has brought about enormous increases in the productivity of labour. It has made it possible for millions of people to achieve standards of living which are extremely high by historical standards and, at the same time, to enjoy a much shorter working week. The use of machinery has also removed most of the back-breaking toil associated with human effort in earlier times.

Nevertheless, specialized production has not been an unmixed blessing and there are many features of mass-production methods which are the subject of much dissatisfaction.

The disadvantages of the division of labour

1 The lack of variety in the jobs on assembly lines is often a cause of boredom and frustration. Monotony and a lack of job satisfaction is the price a worker may have to pay for the higher income and the shorter working week which mass-production methods have made possible.

2 The role of many workers has been reduced to that of 'machine minders'; they have little scope for the use of skills, judgement and initiative. There has been a loss of the pride of performance which is associated with craft work. On the other hand we should take account of the fact that modern production techniques have created demands for a whole new range of skills in the design, construction and maintenance of complex machinery, in production planning, stock control, cost accountancy, the use of computers and so on.

3 In order to make extensive use of the division of labour the product must be standardized. Mass-production techniques are designed to produce vast quantities of identical articles. The general adoption of this method of production means that many thousands of people will be using identical motor cars, washing machines, television sets and so on. Our homes are full of standardized products. Critics of the system deplore the lack of variety which results from specialization. Against this viewpoint, however, it can be argued that, although the variety of any one product may have been reduced, the division of labour enables us to enjoy an enormous variety of different goods. Most of us can only afford to have a motor car *and* a washing machine *and* a television set *and* a refrigerator because they are standardized and hence low-cost products.

4 In a world where the demands for various goods and services are always changing and where new techniques of production and new materials are always being introduced, highly specialized workers are very vulnerable to

unemployment. The jobs they do are probably peculiar to the industry in which they are employed and, if they are made redundant, they may well find that their particular skill cannot be utilized in other industries. On the other hand, the relative simplicity of much of the work in mass-production industries means that such workers can be very quickly retrained for work in other industries.

5 Specialization makes us all very dependent on one another. All the things we use and consume each day (e.g. food, clothing, power, transport, buildings, machines, radios, books etc.) are produced by other people. We rely on others to buy the things which we help to produce and with our earnings we buy the things produced by other workers. In modern societies we cannot survive on the basis of our own efforts; we are not capable of producing for ourselves all the things we need each day. We depend upon the efforts of others and upon some efficient system of exchange so that we can obtain the goods and services which other workers produce. This dependence upon specialization and exchange means that what happens in one part of the economic system affects all the other parts. This fact is brought home to us most forcibly by strike action. We know that a strike by a relatively small group of specialists can bring an entire industry to a halt. The 1974 miners' strike put the whole economy on a three-day week.

The extent of the division of labour

The principle of specialization is not restricted to workers, it is applied to the whole of economic activity. There is specialization by industry and we have, for example, the chemical industry, the textile industry, the steel industry and so on. Within each industry, the firms specialize. In the textile industry there are firms which specialize in spinning, weaving, dyeing, printing and in many other stages in the production of textile fabrics. Within each firm the jobs themselves are specialized and the Census of Population lists more than 40 000 different occupations.

There is also a geographical aspect of the division of labour and in any one country there is usually a pattern of regional specialization. In the UK we have concentrations of certain industries in particular regions: cotton in Lancashire; pottery in North Staffordshire; footwear in Leicester and Northampton; cutlery in Sheffield and tinplate manufacture in South Wales. The principle is also applied on a world-wide scale and much of international trade is based on and has encouraged an international division of labour. Sometimes this specialization is due to features of climate or the uneven distribution of mineral deposits. Thus, we find that Brazil is a major supplier of coffee, Malaya of tin and rubber, South Africa of gold, the West Indies of sugar and the Middle East of oil. In other cases it is based on the national development of certain skills. Switzerland is famous for watches, Japan for motor cars, cameras and electronic equipment and Paris for fashion clothing.

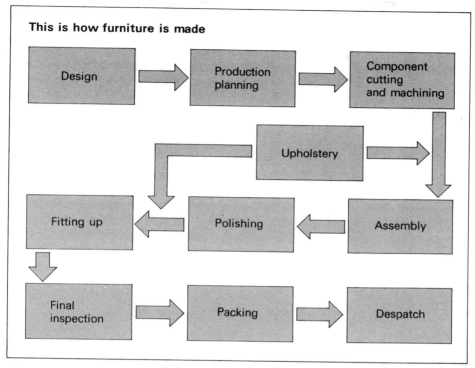

Fig. 4.1   *Specialization of processes*

Source: *Choice of Careers Booklet* 33, HMSO

Fig. 4.2   *Specialization of workers*

The division of labour and the extent of the market

While it is *technically* possible to apply the principle of the division of labour to the production of most goods, it is *economically* advantageous only where there is a large market for a standardized product. If we look at the industries where mass-production methods are most widely used, we find that they are industries which are able to sell thousands of identical products every week (e.g. cigarettes, detergents, cars, radios etc.). Where the size of the market is relatively small, a firm cannot apply the principle of the division of labour to any great extent. It would clearly be hopelessly uneconomic to set up an assembly line capable of making thousands of identical women's hats each week.

There are several reasons why the market for a particular product may be very restricted.

1 The public may demand variety. There are some goods and services where people prefer to have 'something different'. Women, in particular, usually demand some individuality in clothing, footwear and accessories such as handbags and jewellery. For products such as these, the market for any one design will be very small and there will be little scope for using the techniques of specialized production.

2 Repair work is another example of an economic activity which cannot be easily subdivided into a large number of separate operations. Each job tends to be different and in such trades as the repair of property, cars, shoes, watches etc., we find a large number of small firms where the division of labour is only used to a very limited extent.

3 Industries supplying personal services also tend to be made up of a large number of small firms. These personal services cannot be broken down into a large number of highly specialized tasks because people prefer to deal with one person. Thus, the family doctor, the local hairdresser, the family solicitor and small retail shops provide examples of services where the customer demands individual attention.

4 The number of potential customers may be small because the size of the market is limited by geographical factors. A small isolated community cannot support a number of specialist shops and in such communities one usually finds a general store catering for a variety of needs. Where transport costs are disproportionately high, production is usually confined to the local market and for this reason we find local bakeries and dairies. Improvements in transport, however, have tended to reduce the importance of this particular limitation on the size of the market.

5 There are small markets for very expensive products such as luxury yachts, expensive limousines and high quality sports cars. In these cases the size of market is limited by price.

How changes in output affect productivity

In the business world, market conditions are always changing and firms are obliged to vary their outputs to meet changes in demand. Suppose the demand for a product is increasing. A firm making this good will be encouraged to increase its output and the obvious way to do this is to employ more labour and buy more raw materials. In most cases firms will be able to carry out this sort of adjustment in a matter of days or weeks. It may happen, however, that the firm is already working at full capacity, that is, its buildings and machinery are being fully utilized. In this case, an increase in output is only possible if the firm extends its factory and installs more machinery. This may take many months. The two different situations described above are important in economic analysis and the economist describes them as short-run and long-run changes.

The short run and the long run

The factors of production are generally classified as variable factors and fixed factors.

Variable factors, as the name suggests, are those whose supply can be quickly and easily changed. They include most types of labour, raw materials, fuel and power, tools and some types of mobile machinery. By employing more or less of the variable factors, a firm is able to change its output in a matter of days or weeks.

Fixed factors are those which are durable, long-lasting and often take a long time to build, erect and install. Obvious examples of fixed factors of production are factory buildings and heavy machinery. The distinction between the short run and the long run is based on the time it takes for a firm to change the quantities of its fixed factors of production.

The short run is the period of time during which at least one of the factors of production is fixed. In this situation the firm can only change its weekly output by using more or less of the variable factors. For example, in the short run a firm engaged in the printing of textbooks may increase its output by taking on more labour (or working overtime), using more paper, more ink, more power and so on.

The long run is defined as the period of time the firm needs in order to change the amounts of all the factors it employs (i.e. both fixed and variable). For example, if the printing firm mentioned above found the demand for its goods steadily increasing, it might decide to extend its premises and install more printing presses. This would be a long-run change. Note that the term 'fixed' factors only applies to the short-run period because, in the long run, all the factors are variable.

It is not possible to specify the short run in terms of a given number of days or weeks; it all depends on the type of industry involved. In some industries, for example, those employing fairly simple equipment and unskilled or semi-skilled labour, the short run may be only a matter of months. In other industries such as steelmaking, oil refining or the generation of electricity, the short run will extend for several years, because it will take a long time for new plants to be built and brought into operation.

Average and marginal products

When a firm increases or decreases its output in the short run, the changes in output are not proportional to the changes in the quantities of variable factors employed. For example, each extra worker employed does not add exactly the same amount to total output. In order to explain the nature of short-run changes in output we can make use of a simple example in agriculture and assume that only two factors of production are employed, the fixed factor being land and the variable factor, labour.

Table 1 shows what happens when different amounts of labour are put to work on a fixed area of land, say 100 hectares, and the product we can assume, is wheat. It is also assumed that the techniques of production remain unchanged and that the workers are equally efficient.

Table 1 Total, average and marginal products (tonnes per annum)

No. of workers	Total product	Marginal product		Average product
0	0			0
1	20	20		20
2	80	60		40
3	165	85	Increasing returns	55
4	272	107		68
5	385	113		77
6	474	89		79
7	525	51	Diminishing returns	75
8	536	11		67

Table 1 shows that, as one would expect, the total product increases as the number of workers increases. It does not, however, increase at a uniform rate. The whole point of this table is to show the manner in which total output changes as the ratio between the fixed and variable factors changes. Looking at the different measures of output in turn we have,

1 *Total product*, which is quite simply the total amount produced by some given number of workers.

2 *Marginal product*, which is the change in total output brought about by increasing or decreasing the numbers employed by one person. Thus when the number employed is increased from five workers to six workers, we find that the marginal product of labour is 474 − 385 tonnes = 89 tonnes.

$$\text{marginal product of the 6th worker} = \text{total product of 6 workers} - \text{total product of 5 workers}$$

3 *Average product*, which is the output per worker employed and is calculated by dividing the total product by the number of workers.

$$\text{Average product} = \frac{\text{Total product}}{\text{Number of workers}}$$

Increasing and diminishing returns

In Table 1, as the number of workers rises from one to five, the increases in total product become progressively larger. Over this range of employment, the marginal product of labour is increasing and we have what are described as *increasing returns* to labour.

When the sixth worker is employed, however, the marginal product falls and continues to fall as more workers are employed. Thus over the range of employment, six workers to eight workers, the firm is experiencing *diminishing returns* to labour.

These changes in the marginal productivity of labour are not caused by differences in the efficiency of labour because we have assumed that all workers are equally efficient. The explanation lies in the changing proportions between the fixed and variable factors. At low levels of employment, the fixed factor (in this case, land) is being under-utilized; it is being inadequately tended. In simple terms 'the workers are too thin on the ground'. At higher levels of employment (when six or more workers are employed), there is insufficient land to keep them working at full capacity and the employment of extra workers adds progressively smaller amounts to total output.

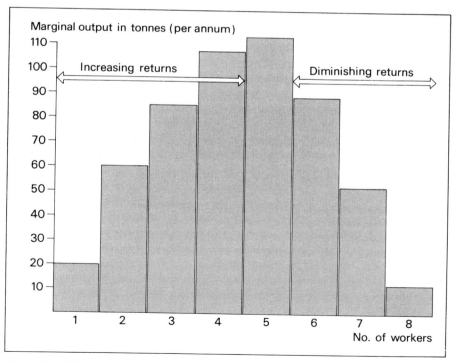

Fig. 4.3   The marginal product of labour

Fig. 4.3 is based on Table 1 and illustrates both increasing and diminishing returns to the variable factor (i.e. labour). The main purpose of the diagram is to draw attention to a most important 'law'.

The law of diminishing returns

This law states that, 'whenever successive equal amounts of a variable factor are put to work with a fixed amount of other factors, there will come a point where the additions to total output become progressively smaller.'

The Law of Diminishing Returns has many important applications. Our simple example refers to the operation of the law when increasing amounts of labour are applied to a fixed amount of land. But the law is just as applicable when increasing amounts of labour are combined with a fixed amount of capital, as when a firm with fixed amounts of factory space and machinery is trying to get more output from this fixed capacity. There is also clear evidence of the operation of the Law of Diminishing Returns when capital is the variable factor and land is the fixed factor. Increasing applications of fertilizer to a given area of land will, at first, yield increasing returns, but there must come a point where the increases in output begin to diminish. The same features are revealed when cows are subject to scientific feeding. At first the milk yields may rise at an increasing rate, but eventually there will be diminishing returns to the variable factor (i.e. cattle food).

We must note that the Law of Diminishing Returns applies when:
a   the units of the variable factor are equally efficient;
b   the techniques of production remain unchanged.
Improvements in the quality of capital, the efficiency of labour and in the organization of production will offset the effects of the law, for a time at any rate.

A glance at Table 1 will reveal that the average product of labour behaves in the same way as the marginal product; it rises at first and then begins to fall. Fig. 4.4 is another and perhaps 'more realistic' view of what happens when the proportions between the fixed and variable factors change.

What happens when a firm changes the amounts of *all* the factors it employs is discussed later in the book (Chapter 6). These long-run changes are described as changes in the *scale* of production.

The main divisions of production

Production is undertaken by firms and the ways in which these firms are owned and organized is described in Chapter 8. At this point, however, it would be useful to look at the three main activities into which production is traditionally divided.

1   The primary industries
These industries are often referred to as the extractive industries because they

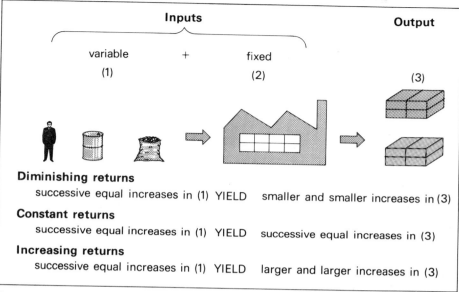

Fig. 4.4

are concerned with the extraction of basic materials – they extract the gifts of nature.
Examples: agriculture, mining, quarrying, fishing.

2 The secondary industries

These industries are engaged in processing or manufacturing the basic materials into finished or semi-finished products.
Examples: manufacturing, construction, gas, electricity, water.

3 The tertiary industries

These industries comprise all those firms which provide services for the primary and secondary industries and directly for the consumer.
Examples: transport, communications and other services.

The importance of the different sectors

The proportions of the labour force engaged in these different sectors vary very much from country to country depending on the level of economic development. In developed countries over the past fifty years there has been a dramatic fall in the proportion of the labour force engaged in the primary sector and, in more recent years the proportion working in manufacturing has also begun to decline.

The drop in the percentages of the working population in the primary and secondary sectors does not necessarily indicate any falling off in the outputs of these sectors. The changes in employment are due in part to technical changes such as automation in manufacturing and the shift to new techniques and new products which are much more capital-intensive (e.g. the movement from coal to oil and from natural to synthetic materials).

The distribution of the labour force between these different sectors of the economy provides a reasonably good indicator of a country's level of economic development. As productivity in the primary and secondary industries increases and real incomes also increase, we find more and more people employed in the tertiary industries, providing services of all kinds. A developed country will employ large numbers of people in education and health services and in public administration. There will also be growing employment in professions such as banking, insurance, accountancy, marketing and scientific services. As a community's standard of living rises there will also be a growth of employment in services catering for all kinds of social activities (e.g. motoring, holidays, meals outside the home and all types of entertainment). In the UK more than half the working population is engaged in the tertiary sector.

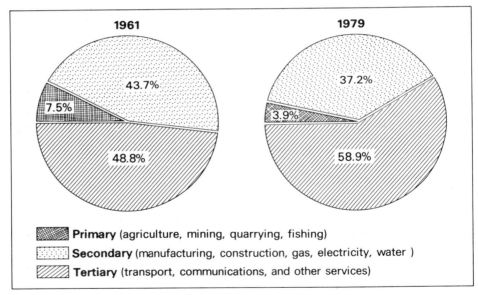

Fig. 4.5   Employment in the UK

Source: *Economic Trends*, HMSO, November 1980.

5 The costs of production

'Cost', like 'productivity' and 'production', is another example of a word which is carelessly used in everyday discussions but which must have a precise meaning when used in economics. At first glance, the expression 'a firm must cover its costs' seems a sensible enough statement, but it is, in fact, not very meaningful, because it does not say *which* costs are being referred to. As we shall see later, there are many different types of cost and in making statements about a firm's costs of production we must be careful to specify which particular cost is being referred to.

Variable and fixed costs

The distinction between these two types of cost will be easy to grasp because it is based on the difference between variable and fixed factors which has been discussed earlier.

Variable costs

These are the costs of the variable factors. They are often referred to as direct costs because they vary directly as output varies. Variable costs include the wages of direct labour (those workers who may be engaged or dismissed as the firm's output changes) and the costs of raw materials, fuel, power, packaging and transport. All these costs will increase as output increases and decrease as output falls.

Fixed costs

These are the costs of the fixed factors. They do not vary as output varies. Fixed costs include such expenses as rent, rates, insurance, interest on loans, depreciation and, most probably, the salaries of some management staff. All these costs are fixed for fairly long periods of time and have no direct connection with the level of production in the short run. For example, once an assembly line is installed, the capital costs of the equipment will be the same whether it is being worked at full capacity or being run at only half its capacity. Fixed costs are sometimes referred to as indirect or overhead costs.

A note on depreciation

One important fixed cost which is often overlooked in general discussion because it is not 'paid out' in the same way as other costs, is depreciation. Rent, rates, insurance and interest on loans are cost payments made at regular intervals to persons or firms supplying the various services. Depreciation represents the loss in value of the firm's capital due to wear and tear and obsolescence. It is treated as a fixed cost because plant and machinery is assumed to lose value over time regardless of the use made of it.[1] When a firm purchases a new machine it will make some estimate of its useful life and 'write down' its value over this time period.

For example, if a firm buys a new machine for £100 000 and estimates its effective life as ten years, it may depreciate it by the straight line method which means that it reduces the machine's value by £10 000 per annum. It will treat this £10 000 as a fixed cost of production and place this sum of money in a depreciation fund to cover the eventual cost of replacement.

Total cost (TC)

When variable costs are added to fixed costs we obtain the total cost of production.

Variable costs + Fixed costs = Total cost

Average cost (AC)

This measures the cost per unit of output. It is obtained when total cost is divided by total output.

$$\text{Average cost} = \frac{\text{Total cost}}{\text{Number of units produced}}$$

Sometimes it is important to measure the average variable cost and in this case, total variable costs are divided by the total output.

Marginal cost (MC)

This is a measure of the amount by which total cost changes when output is changed by one unit. For example,

$$\frac{\text{marginal cost}}{\text{of the 10th unit}} = \text{total cost of 10 units} - \text{total cost of 9 units}$$

How changes in marginal and average products affect costs

It is fairly obvious that total costs will vary directly as output varies. As more

---

[1] This is true of motor cars as a glance at any book listing second-hand car values will demonstrate.

goods are produced, more labour, more materials, and more fuel and power will be used so that total costs must increase. But total costs and total output will not change to the same extent. It total output is increased by 20 per cent, it does not follow that total costs will increase by 20 per cent.

If we concentrate on short-run changes, the explanation of increasing and diminishing returns in the previous section should help us to understand the way in which costs of production change as output changes.

If the firm increases its output by employing more workers, using more materials and other variable factors, it will at first experience increasing returns. Each successive increase in the amount of variable factors employed will lead to larger and larger increases in output. To put it more simply, each increase in the firm's *inputs* will lead to larger and larger increases in *output*. Since marginal and average products will be increasing, average and marginal costs will be falling. For example, if the wage rate remains constant and the average and marginal products of labour are increasing, the labour costs per unit of output must be falling.

At some point, however, the firm will experience diminishing returns and each increase in the firm's inputs will lead to progressively smaller increases in output. Under these conditions average and marginal costs will be rising. These relationships can be made clearer by using a simple arithmetical example.

Assume an individual firm with a fixed amount of land, buildings and machinery is increasing its output by employing more of the variable factors. Table 2 shows how its costs might be affected.

Table 2   A firm's costs of production (£s)

Units of output (per week)	Fixed costs	Variable costs	Total cost	Marginal cost	Average cost
0	1000	—	1000		infinity
1	1000	350	1350	350	1350
2	1000	560	1560	210	780
3	1000	740	1740	180	580
4	1000	1000	2000	260	500
5	1000	1400	2400	400	480
6	1000	2000	3000	600	500
7	1000	2850	3850	850	550
8	1000	3960	4960	1110	620

Table 2 takes account of all the different costs of production discussed in this chapter. The fixed costs relate to such things as rent, rates, insurance, depreciation and interest on loans. Variable costs are made up of wages and the costs of materials, power, packaging, transport and so on. An examination of the last two columns reveals that, as explained earlier, average and marginal costs at first decline (due to increasing returns) and then begin to rise (due to diminishing returns).

The firm's cost curves

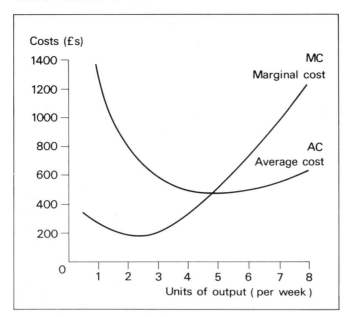

Fig. 5.1
The firm's cost curves

Fig. 5.1 is based on the information in Table 2 and shows the average cost curve (AC) and the marginal cost curve (MC). Both curves are U-shaped and the MC curve always cuts the AC curve when AC is at a minimum. The reason for this is the fact that when MC is below AC it will be pulling average cost downwards; when MC is above AC it will be pulling average cost upwards.[1] It must, therefore, pass through the minimum value of AC.

There is one further point to note in Fig. 5.1. The points which make up the MC curve have been plotted on the mid-points on the horizontal axis, that is between 1 and 2 units of output, between 2 and 3 units of output and so on. This is because marginal cost refers to the *changes in* total cost as output changes by one unit.

The output at which AC is a minimum is described as the optimum output of the firm. In a sense it is the *technically* best output.

There is a further important reason why average cost tends to fall as output increases. The fixed costs remain the same whether the firm produces 1 unit, 10 units or 100 units per week. The greater the number of units produced, the smaller is the amount of fixed cost which each unit of output has 'to carry'. This point is clearly illustrated in the example concerning the introduction of a new technical product described on page 41.

The MC and AC curves turn upwards as the firm increases its output and the

---

[1] This fact may be illustrated by using the example of a batting average in cricket. If my existing batting average is 20 runs and I score 40 runs in my next innings then clearly my average score will increase (marginal score greater than average score, hence average increases). If I only score 10 runs my average will fall (marginal score less than average score, hence average falls).

fixed factors become overloaded. But there are other reasons why these costs will tend to rise. It may be necessary for the firm to introduce overtime working at higher wage rates; less efficient labour may have to be recruited; less efficient stand-by machines may be pressed into use and the increasing demand for materials may raise their prices.

Production costs in the real world – some examples

Industries which make use of large amounts of very expensive fixed capital, such as the steel, chemicals, oil and motor car industries, have very high fixed costs and relatively low variable costs. In these industries high-volume production leads to a great reduction in average costs as the fixed costs are spread over large outputs. The following quotation from an article in the *Sunday Times* (18 June 1978) makes this point very clearly. It concerns the recent rapid development of micro-electronic circuits.

> Despite being one of the most complex industrial processes known to man, the technology can produce very complex devices at very low prices, if, and only if, they are made in very high volume. A ten-fold increase in production can, in some circumstances, result in an 80 per cent decrease in the manufacturing cost of each unit. When made in tens of millions of units a year, even highly complex devices can be made at a cost of only a few pounds. As an example, the price of portable calculators fell from about £100 to about £5 in the space of six years.

Introducing a new model or design

The remarkable way in which increasing output reduces average cost in industries which are capital-intensive may be illustrated by a simple arithmetic example. It concerns a firm producing technical products and it illustrates the problem of trying to fix a price for a new range of models or designs. The firm, as we shall see, *does not know* its average costs of production when it launches its new model. Its average cost depends upon the quantity produced and this in turn depends upon how successful the firm is in selling the product. The price, however, will have to be decided before the firm has any definite information on the demand for its new model.

Fixed costs

Research and development	£20 million
Setting up factory (i.e. re-tooling, purchase of machines etc.)	£20 million
Total fixed costs	£40 million

Estimated life of project 8 years, hence fixed cost per annum = £5 million

Variable costs
Labour, materials, and other variable factors = £1 per unit

1   Low volume output
If production is at the rate of 100 000 units per annum,

Fixed costs	£5 000 000
Total variable costs	£100 000
Total costs	£5 100 000 Average cost (cost per unit) = £51.00

2   High volume output
If production is at the rate of 10 million units per annum,

Fixed costs	£5 000 000
Total variable costs	£10 000 000
Total costs	£15 000 000 Average cost (cost per unit) = £1.50

We can now see why the question, 'How much does it cost to produce this article?' is not a very sensible question. It would be a perfectly legitimate question if some particular quantity were specified.

Costs in printing and publishing

An excellent example of high fixed costs and very low marginal costs is provided by the publishing industry. An understanding of the costs of production in this industry helps to explain why some books with many pages are often very much cheaper than other books with far fewer pages.

Most of the costs of producing a book are fixed costs. The costs of editing the manuscript and redrafting it in a form suitable for the printer; the preparation of the artwork (diagrams and illustrations); the setting up of the type; the preliminary advertising and any advance payments to the author are all fixed costs. They will remain the same whether the book sells 100 or 100 000 copies. Once this work is completed, the marginal cost of the book will be relatively small; it will amount to the costs of the paper, printing, binding and royalties to the author. As in the previous example, with heavy fixed costs and low marginal costs, the average cost of a book falls very sharply as output increases.

Costs, revenue and profits

Firms will only continue to produce, in the long run, if they are making profits. In economic theory it is assumed that firms will always try to earn maximum profits. It should be fairly obvious that a firm will be making profits where,
a   total revenue exceeds total costs, or, what is the same thing, where
b   price (i.e. average revenue) exceeds average cost.
A simple calculation of profits can be made by using the total cost figures in

Table 2 and assuming that the firm is selling its product at a price of £550.

Table 3

Units of output per week	Total cost(£)	Total revenue(£)	Total profit(£)
0	1000	0	−1000
1	1350	550	−800
2	1560	1100	−460
3	1740	1650	−90
4	2000	2200	+200
5	2400	2750	+350
6	3000	3300	+300
7	3850	3850	0
8	4960	4400	−560

Table 3 reveals that the most profitable output is 5 units per week. The relationships between total revenue and total cost can be seen more clearly in Fig. 5.2 which is based on the figures in Table 3.

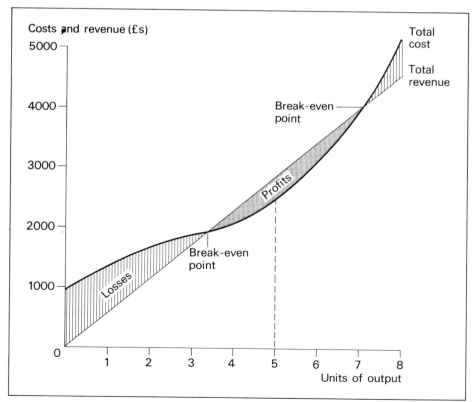

Fig. 5.2   Profits and losses

The total cost curve does not start at the origin because there are fixed costs of £1000 when output is zero. The total revenue curve is a straight line because the price does not change as more units are sold. There is a range of output from 3.25 units to 7 units per week where the firm is making profits. At an output of 5 units, the vertical distance between the total revenue and total cost curves is at a maximum; this is the most profitable output. The break-even points show the outputs where the firm's total revenue is just covering its total costs.

6 Economies of scale

Output changes in the long run

Chapter 5 dealt with changes in output in the short run. We now look at some of the economic effects of long-run changes in the firm's output. The long run is the period of time a firm needs to change the amounts of all the factors it employs. For example, the long run is the time it takes for (a) a firm to expand the size of its factory or (b) a mining company to open up a new mine, or (c) a producer of natural rubber to bring new trees into production.

These kinds of changes are described as changes in the *scale of production*. It is a feature of production that a change in scale does not usually lead to a pro-portionate change in output. If a firm doubles its size, output does not usually double; it may increase by more or less than 100 per cent. Table 4 illustrates what might happen when a firm changes its scale of production.

Table 4   Changes in the scale of production

Size of firm (units of factors employed)			Annual output (tonnes)	Changes in annual output	Changes in scale of production	
Land	*Labour*	*Capital*				
5	2	4	100 ⎫			
10	4	8	300 ⎬	200%	100%	increasing returns
15	6	12	500 ⎬	66⅔%	50%	to scale
20	8	16	625 ⎬	25%	33⅓%	decreasing returns
25	10	20	725 ⎭	16%	25%	to scale

In Table 4 it can be seen that, as the firm begins to increase its scale of production, output increases more than proportionately. For example, when the size of the firm increases by 100 per cent, annual output increases by 200 per cent. If the firm continues to grow, total output will continue to increase, but there comes a point where the increase in the scale of production is accompanied by a less than proportionate increase in output. When the percentage increase in output is greater than the percentage increase in the size of the firm, we say that the firm is experiencing *economies of scale*. If, when the size of the firm increases, output increases less than proportionately, the firm is experiencing *diseconomies of scale*. Table 4 shows that the firm experiences economies of scale until its output reaches 500 tonnes per annum, but further growth brings diseconomies of scale.

Economies of scale and average costs

If we assume that the prices of the factors of production remain unchanged then economies of scale will result in lower average costs of production. If, by using twice as much land, labour and capital, a firm increases total output by 150 per cent then average cost must have fallen (if factor prices do not change).

In most industries, increases in the scale of production will, for a time, lead to economies of scale (i.e. falling average costs), but there appears to be some limit to the size of the firm beyond which inefficiency tends to creep in and average costs begin to rise. In other words, as a firm continues to grow, there will come a point where it will begin to experience diseconomies of scale. There will be some scale of production where the firm is at its most efficient size and average cost is at a minimum; this is known as *the optimum size* of the firm. The optimum size of the firm will vary enormously from industry to industry. As we shall see later, it depends very much on a firm's ability to use mass-production methods and whether it can make effective use of efficient but very expensive large units of capital. In the manufacture of low-priced motor cars, for example, the optimum size of the firm is very large indeed, but in industries like the footwear industry, the optimum size is still quite small.

The advantages of large-scale production

In looking for the advantages of large-scale production we must look for those features which lead to lower average costs. The total costs of the larger firm will obviously be greater than those of the smaller firm; we want to know why its average cost might be lower. The supermarket's total costs are much higher than those of 'the shop on the corner'. Its rent, rates, heating and lighting expenses are very much greater; it employs far more workers; it spends far more on advertising; it uses far more expensive equipment and so on. But its *average costs* (i.e. cost per unit sold) are very much lower than the average costs of the small shop. The value of its sales per employee and per square metre of selling space are very much greater than that of the small shop.

The various features of larger-scale production which bring about reductions in the average costs of the firm are set out below.

Technical economies

1 The larger the firm, the greater its ability to make use of the principle of the division of labour. In the larger firm, production can be broken down into many more specialized operations than is possible in the smaller firm.

2 A large firm can make much more effective use of large units of capital which, in the small firm, would be grossly under-utilized and hence costly to use. Capital equipment such as the large overhead cranes on building sites, giant presses in car production and combine harvesters in farming are extremely efficient and can be operated at low average cost when they are

used to their full capacity. Where output is small, however, such equipment would be lying idle for much of the time and the fixed cost per unit would be very high.

3   A most important technical economy of scale is related to the volume of containers and units of transport. If the dimensions of a container are doubled, its surface area increases by four times and its volume by eight times. This simple arithmetical fact accounts for the development of the Jumbo jet, mammoth oil tankers and 'juggernaut' lorries. The costs of producing these things, the power required to move them, and the labour required to operate them do not increase proportionately with their size (see Fig. 6.1). Similar economies of increased dimensions apply to blast-furnaces, oil refineries and chemical plants.

4   In manufacturing where a series of specialized machines each carry out one part of the process of production, a problem arises in balancing the outputs from different machines. Machine A might produce 50 units per hour while Machine B (carrying out the next stage in production) might be capable of handling 125 units per hour. A firm with a small output, say 50 units per hour, will only be working Machine B at 40 per cent of its capacity. A large firm will be able to employ numbers of each machine in the ratio of 5 of A to 2 of B and so keep all the machines working to full capacity.

5   A large firm can maintain a research and development department to help improve the quality of its product and its methods of production. Such a department may be considered an economy of scale if the results of its work enable the firm to increase its efficiency and lower its average costs of production.

Marketing economies

The larger firm can buy its materials in bulk and obtain them at lower prices. It can also obtain preferential treatment on quality and delivery. By placing large orders it enables its suppliers to take advantage of mass-production methods. Just as the large firm can make full use of highly specialized equipment, so it can fully employ highly specialized staff. The employment of specialist salespeople may lead to increases in sales, and the employment of specialized buyers to economies in purchasing which more than offset the costs of employing such people.

Further marketing economies are obtained because the administration, handling and packaging costs of dealing with large orders do not increase proportionately with the size of the order. For example, the cost of typing an invoice for 1000 articles is no more than the cost of typing one for 10 articles. Furthermore, as explained earlier, the costs of containers and transport required to deal with a larger order will be *proportionately* less than the costs of dealing with a small order.

A large firm's advertising costs will be much greater than those of the small firm, but its advertising costs *per unit sold* are likely to be much smaller.

47

Financial economies

All firms borrow money for purposes of investment and to finance their activities during periods when their income is less than their expenditure. Larger firms have considerable advantages in the financial markets. The fact that they are larger, have more valuable assets and are well known, means that, in general, they offer better security to the lenders of money. They can, therefore, borrow at lower rates of interest than the small firm and they also have more sources of finance available to them (see Chapter 9).

Carrying capacity and mileage[1]		Payload as a percentage of weight total	Total operating costs per mile	Index of operating costs per tonne–mile[2]
1.5 tonne (30 cwt) VAN 300 miles per week		50	61.03p	100
4 tonne LORRY 400 miles per week		61.5	71.62p	44
10 tonne LORRY 600 miles per week	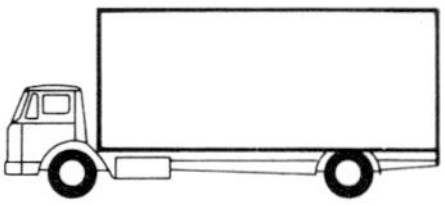	64.5	76.12p	18.7
20 tonne LORRY 1000 miles per week	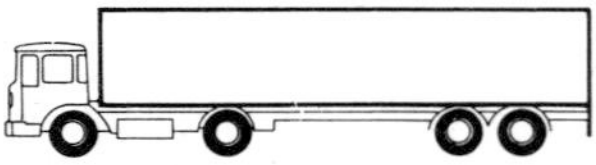	71.4	79.17p	9.7

Fig. 6.1 Economies of scale (transport)

[1] In general the larger the vehicle the greater the mileage.
[2] i.e. the costs per tonne-mile for a 4-tonne lorry are only 44 per cent of those for a 1.5 tonne van.

Source: Based on *Commercial Motor's* Tables of Operating Costs, 1980.

Risk-bearing economies

The large firm has far more opportunities than the small firm for 'spreading the risks' of trading. The small firm is most likely to be producing one particular product and/or to be selling in one particular market. In other words 'all its eggs are in one basket'. A big firm may produce a variety of products and changes in the demands for these products are likely to offset each other. A fall in the demand for one good may be balanced by an increase in the demand for another. The *total* demand, therefore, is likely to be much more stable than the demand for any one product. The small firm may be limited to the local or national market, but the large firm may sell in both the home and overseas markets. An example of a multi-product firm selling in different product markets is provided by Unilever which produces margarine, frozen foods, soft drinks, tinned food, cosmetics, soaps, detergents, toothpaste and other products. It also has very large home and overseas markets.

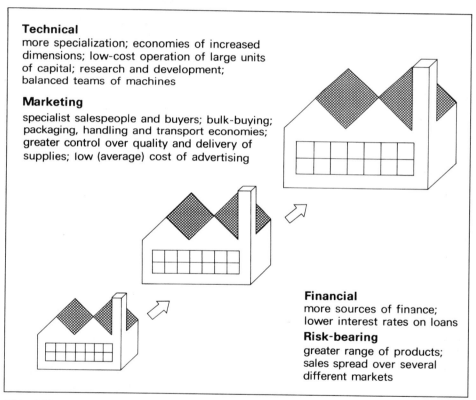

Technical
more specialization; economies of increased dimensions; low-cost operation of large units of capital; research and development; balanced teams of machines

Marketing
specialist salespeople and buyers; bulk-buying; packaging, handling and transport economies; greater control over quality and delivery of supplies; low (average) cost of advertising

Financial
more sources of finance; lower interest rates on loans

Risk-bearing
greater range of products; sales spread over several different markets

Fig. 6.2   Internal economies of scale

Diseconomies of scale

The list of advantages of larger-scale production is very impressive, but growth in the size of the firm can also create problems. We have already noted that there seems to be an optimum scale of production for each particular industry and that growth beyond this optimum size seems to lead to diseconomies of scale. The main causes of these diseconomies appear to be associated with the increasing complexity of the management problems as firms grow larger. The task of creating a smoothly running organization becomes progressively more difficult as the size of the firm increases.

Large organizations are subdivided into several specialist departments such as production, sales, stores, accounting, buying, personnel and so on. It is not an easy task to coordinate the activities of many large departments. Management must not only take the decisions; it must see that these decisions are carried out. There is, therefore, a problem of communications in the larger firm. Keeping everyone informed of what is required of him or her and, at the same time, maintaining accurate and up-to-date information on what is happening in every section of the enterprise are responsibilities of management which become increasingly difficult to carry out as the firm grows larger.

It is becoming more and more apparent that the major challenge facing the management of the large enterprise is the maintenance of high morale in the labour force. This is a matter of industrial relations. Individual workers in a labour force of many thousands find it difficult to identify themselves with the objectives of the firm. Too often, it seems, they feel that they are not known to the management, they play little or no part in the decisions which affect their job and they see themselves as little more than numbers on the wage sheets. In situations like this it is very difficult to get the full cooperation of the workers, whose apathy can easily turn into resentment or outright hostility. This is not, of course, an inevitable consequence of large-scale production and many large firms have very good industrial relations between management and workers. It does, however, indicate that under certain circumstances technical and other economies of scale may be offset by management diseconomies.

External economies of scale

All economies of scale arise from growth in the scale of production, but it is usual to classify them into two main types, internal and external. *Internal* economies arise from growth in the size of *the firm*. The economies dealt with up to this point have all been internal economies.

External economies of scale arise from growth in the size of *the industry* and are especially important where the industry happens to be heavily localized. All firms belonging to a large and heavily localized industry, whatever their size, benefit from external economies. These economies, sometimes described as economies of concentration, are of several types.

1 Ancillary trades

When an industry becomes established in a particular location and reaches a certain size, it attracts firms whose business is to supply the main industry with a variety of goods and services specially designed to meet the needs of that industry. Thus in the Leicester/Northampton region we find firms which specialize in the production of shoe machinery and in the servicing and repair of that type of machinery, other firms specialize in the production of lasts, toe-stiffeners, buckles, shoe-linings and other accessories for the footwear industry. In the Birmingham/Coventry area there are specialized engineering enterprises supplying machinery, tools and components to meet the needs of the motor car industry. The presence of these ancillary trades enables the main industry to satisfy its specialist needs more easily and more cheaply. It is quite obvious that a firm supplying soles for many footwear manufacturers can produce them at a lower cost than any individual manufacturer of footwear. But the specialized production of machinery, parts and components for a particular industry only becomes an attractive economic proposition when *the industry* has grown to a size where it provides a large market for these things.

2 Specialized services

Heavily localized industries also attract firms which specialize in providing services for the industry. These firms offer services such as wholesaling, specialized transport facilities, the collection and processing of waste products and technical advice. The banks and insurance companies in the area will become familiar with the particular needs of that industry. It will become relatively easy for firms in the industry to form a trade association to represent the interests of the entire industry (in dealings with trade unions and government), to organize meetings for the exchange of information, to arrange trade exhibitions and to publish a journal of particular interest to the trade. Local colleges will find it worthwhile to organize courses for the industry's apprentices and management personnel. When a large number of firms engaged in similar activities are located in the same region they may be encouraged to combine together and form a jointly-owned research establishment serving the needs of all the firms in the industry.

3 Labour

An important external economy arises from the fact that labour, in the area where the industry is localized, becomes skilled in the trades and adapted to the working conditions in that industry. Thus a new firm setting up in the area, or an existing firm wishing to expand would have little difficulty in obtaining labour with the necessary skills.

7 The mobility of the factors of production

Mobility and specialization

Many times in this book we make reference to the fact that we live in a world of change. A nation's rate of economic progress depends very much on its ability to adjust to changes in technology, in people's spending habits, in the patterns of world trade and so on. New machines and new methods of production provide opportunities for increases in productivity. New materials, new products and improvements in transport and communications bring opportunities for the development of new markets. But changes such as these present problems as well as opportunities. A smooth and rapid adjustment from one kind of technology to another is only possible when the factors of production can be easily switched from one activity to another.

As production becomes more specialized, this kind of movement becomes more and more difficult. People who undertake long periods of training to become highly skilled (e.g. architects, surgeons, physicists) become experts in their own fields, but are very immobile in the sense that they cannot easily move into another occupation. Similarly, a piece of capital equipment which has been specially designed for one purpose (e.g. a petrol tanker, a blast-furnace or an oil rig) is extremely efficient in one use, but it is not capable of performing any other function; in other words it is immobile.

Types of mobility

There are two kinds of mobility:
1 *Geographical mobility* refers to the movement of a factor of production from one location to another. This is clearly a matter of great importance when a government is trying to persuade capital and labour to move to some under-developed region, or when it is trying to relieve congestion in great cities.
2 *Occupational mobility* describes the movement of a factor of production from one occupation to another. Again it is a matter of great concern to a government which is trying to maintain full employment. In a world where the demands for different products are always changing, factors can only remain fully employed if they are able to move easily from industries with declining demands to those experiencing increases in demand.

The mobility of land

Land has no mobility in the geographical sense. A shortage of land in a particular area cannot be overcome by 'bringing in' more land. This obvious fact is the main explanation for the very high land values in cities and for the 'high rise' developments which have occurred in urban areas in recent years.

A great deal of land, however, is occupationally mobile because it could be used as agricultural land, or for playing fields and parks, or as a site for houses, shops, schools or offices, or for the building of roads or airports and so on.

The mobility of capital

A great deal of the capital in use is both geographically and occupationally mobile. For example, machine tools, electric motors, power tools, transport and communication equipment, and raw materials can be moved from one location to another and can be used in many different industries.

Some capital, such as factory buildings, railway networks, steelworks and dock installations, cannot be said to be mobile geographically because the costs of dismantling would be too great to make the movement worthwhile, Likewise, as mentioned earlier, highly specialized capital equipment has no occupational mobility. Many buildings however, are occupationally mobile since they can be adapted and put to different uses.

The mobility of labour

1 Geographical mobility

One would expect labour to be the most mobile of the factors of production and, indeed, history does provide some striking examples of large-scale movements of labour from one region to another. During the late nineteenth century there was a massive movement of Europeans to America and thousands of American settlers crossed the continent from East to West in search of land and work. In more recent times many immigrants have entered Britain from Commonwealth countries and there has also been a large-scale movement of workers from Southern Europe to the more prosperous countries of the EEC.

Most of the major migrations, however, took place over fairly long periods of time and were often the result of severe political, economic and social pressures. There are, in fact, very real barriers to the geographical mobility of labour. Some evidence of this is provided by the fact that different regions within the same country often experience, over long periods of time, very different unemployment rates. If labour were really mobile, workers would tend to move from areas of high unemployment to areas of low unemployment and differences in regional unemployment rates would be greatly reduced. The geographical mobility of labour is restricted in a number of ways.

a   The international movement of labour is seriously limited by immigration controls and by barriers of language and custom.

b Many people may not be able to meet the costs of moving a family from one part of the country to another (or from one country to another).

c A desire and willingness to move to a job in another area may be frustrated by a housing shortage. This is a particularly difficult problem when the person wishing to move is looking for rented accommodation, but even owner-occupiers may find it difficult to move when there are large regional differences in house prices.

d The desire to maintain local family and social ties makes many people reluctant to move away from the area in which they live.

e Lack of knowledge of job opportunities in other towns and cities may also be a barrier to geographical mobility.

2 Occupational mobility

In the UK more than 3 million people change their jobs every year. This seems to point to a high degree of labour mobility. In fact, of course, much of this movement represents changes of job *within* an occupation (a movement from one firm to another). Economic change also calls for the movement of workers from one occupation to another and there are many barriers to this kind of movement.

a Natural ability. Many occupations require natural abilities which are only possessed by a relatively small percentage of the population (e.g. mathematicians, surgeons, athletes and entertainers of international standard etc.)

b Education and training. If people lose their jobs they cannot move immediately into another job which requires a long period of specialized education and training. They may also be debarred from entering a particular trade because they have not served the required apprenticeship.

c Institutional barriers. Entry into an occupation may be restricted by the regulations of trade unions or professional associations. These bodies sometimes have the power to determine the number of employees recruited into the trade or profession.

d Finance. If people desire to be self-employed and to set up in business for themselves, a certain amount of capital is required to purchase the necessary stock and equipment. This means that those without financial resources have little chance of becoming entrepreneurs (although borrowing the funds is a possibility).

e Ignorance. The movement of people from one occupation to another may be restricted by inadequate information on job opportunities.

3 Improving the mobility of labour

In most developed countries governments give a high priority to policies which increase the mobility of labour. In the UK the major emphasis has been placed on measures to increase occupational rather than geographical mobility, although financial help is offered to those seeking work in another part of the country. The principal aids to occupational mobility are as follows.

a   Information services. Employment exchanges and the newer more attractive Job Centres provide the means whereby those seeking jobs are brought into contact with those seeking workers.

b   Retraining. The government has established many retraining centres where people can learn new skills on highly concentrated courses. Workers attending these courses receive financial help while undergoing training.

c   Redundancy payments. The movement of workers from declining to expanding industries and from low-productivity to high-productivity occupations is not a smooth and painless process. It means that some workers in declining industries lose their jobs and we must expect some resistance to redundancies. In order to cushion the effects of redundancy and to encourage a willingness to accept the need to change jobs, the government operates a scheme of redundancy payments. Dismissed workers receive a cash payment the size of which depends on their length of service and current wage. There is also a scheme whereby unemployed workers received, for a period of up to six months, unemployment pay which is higher than the standard rate.[1] The aim of these schemes is to reduce the financial hardship associated with unemployment and to provide an adequate income for redundant workers seeking alternative employment.

The mobility of the entrepreneur

Most labour is trained for some specialized task, but the basic skills of management are common to all industries. Managers are expected to be able to organize and control and to exhibit qualities of leadership and initiative.

Managers can employ people to advise them on the various aspects of the business. They will consider the recommendations of their staff on technical, financial, personnel, sales and other problems and then it it their task to take the necessary decisions. This is not an easy task because departmental heads will tend to see things from their own point of view. The design which the engineer would like to make is most probably not the design the sales person would like to sell. Decision-taking is the essence of management and this function is common to all industries. The entrepeneur, therefore, is probably the most mobile, both occupationally and geographically, of all the factors of production.

---

[1] This is because it is related to previous earnings. There are plans to phase out this scheme in 1982.

Test paper 2

Short-answer questions

1 A firm reorganizes its methods of production, but employs the same amount of land, labour and capital. The working week is reduced from 40 hours to 38 hours while the productivity of labour increases by 10 per cent. What happens to total output?

2 If two firms are making identical products, one may be considered more efficient than the other if the ratio of its ____ to its ____ is greater than that for the other firm. What are the missing words?

3 'Specialization makes people more productive, but it also makes them more interdependent.' Explain.

4 'The principle of the division of labour can only be extensively applied to industrial production if the products are standardized.' Explain.

5 Why does the application of the principle of the division of labour increase the opportunities for the use of machinery?

6 The Law of Diminishing Returns states that, 'as successive equal amounts of the ____ factor are combined with the ____ factors, there will come a point where the ____ product starts to diminish'. What are the missing words?

7 If a firm is working under conditions of increasing returns, total output is ____ at a/an ____ rate.
Which of the following are the missing words, (i) increasing, (ii) decreasing, (iii) constant?

8 The figure opposite shows the changes in total output in two firms (A and B) as they increase the number of workers employed with fixed amounts of capital and land. Which firm is experiencing diminishing returns to labour? Explain your answer.

9 In a printing firm, which of the following items would be classified as
   a   fixed costs; and
   b   variable costs?
   i   interest payments on loans
   ii   purchases of paper
   iii depreciation of machinery
   iv   operatives' wages
   v   packaging and transport costs

10 A firm employs ten workers at a weekly wage of £100. In order to recruit more labour it has to offer higher wages. It takes on one extra worker but has to raise wages to £105 per week. What is the marginal cost of the eleventh worker?

11 In the manufacture of motor cars, aeroplanes, television sets and other complex technical products, average costs fall sharply as output increases. What is the main reason for this sharp fall in average costs?

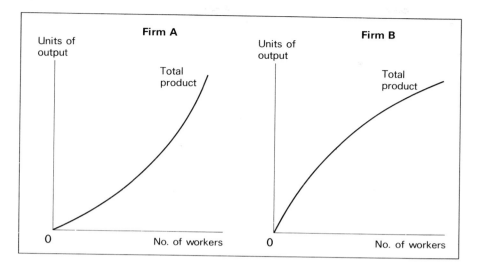

12 An increase in the prices of the factors of production (e.g. wages) does not necessarily mean that costs of production will increase. Why not?

13 A firm uses three machines to carry out successive operations in the manufacture of its product. The output of Machine A is 20 units per hour, of Machine B 30 units per hour and of Machine C 50 units per hour. What is the minimum hourly output necessary to maintain full capacity working of these machines and how many of each machine will be required?

14 A newspaper article described a massive new container ship as a good example of economies of scale. It is twice the size of its predecessors (in terms of length, breadth and depth) but it cost three times as much to construct and its operating costs are three times as great. Is the writer of the article correct? Explain your answer.

15 'In general, larger firms are *more credit-worthy borrowers* than small firms.' Explain the term in italics and its significance with respect to costs of production.

16 What barriers might prevent the easy and rapid movement of redundant steel workers into skilled work in electronic engineering?

17 Why is a person living in a rented house likely to be more immobile geographically than someone living in an owner-occupied house?

18 Which of its payments for labour is a firm likely to treat as fixed costs of production?

True or false?

19 a Diminishing returns set in when total product begins to fall.
b An increase in production means that productivity must have increased.

c If all the workers in an industry are equally efficient, the marginal productivity of labour will be constant.

d Highly specialized labour and capital tend to be occupationally immobile factors.

e An increase in fixed costs will not affect marginal costs.

f Capital-intensive industries have a high ratio of fixed costs to variable costs

g Diseconomies of scale often arise because the skills of management do not increase proportionately with the size of the firm.

h The fixed factors of production are those whose quantities cannot be varied in the long run.

i If technical progress speeds up the rate at which the machines in an industry become obsolete, the firms in that industry will experience an increase in fixed costs.

j Government measures to increase the mobility of labour are part of its policy for the maintenance of full employment.

Multiple-choice questions

Questions 20 to 22 are based on the following table which shows the total outputs produced by different combinations of capital and labour.

Units of output

Units	4	18	30	45(e)	60
of	3	15(c)	25	38	50
capital	2	10	18(b)	30	40
	1	5(a)	10	20(d)	28
		1	2	3	4

Units of labour

The questions refer to the following changes in the combinations of capital and labour.

A (a) to (b)
B (a) to (c)
C (a) to (d)
D (d) to (e)

Which of the above illustrates,

20 diminishing returns?

21 economies of scale?

22 constant returns?

23 Which of the following is/are most likely to lead to an increase in the productivity of labour?

1 an increase in the labour force
2 an extension of the working day
3 modernization of the equipment used in the industry

A 1, 2 and 3
B 1 and 2 only
C 2 and 3 only
D 1 only
E 3 only

24 The Law of Diminishing Returns refers to a situation where, as more variable factors are combined with the fixed factors,

1 total revenue falls
2 marginal cost falls
3 marginal product falls.

A 1, 2 and 3
B 1 and 2 only
C 2 and 3 only
D 1 only
E 3 only

25 The question is based on the following table.

Units of variable factor employed	Marginal product (tonnes)
1	10
2	15
3	20
4	18
5	10

What is the average product when 3 units of the variable factor are employed?

A 6⅔ tonnes
B 15 tonnes
C 20 tonnes
D 45 tonnes

26 In the production of which of the following commodities are we likely to find the division of labour extensively applied?

1 expensive jewellery
2 ball-point pens
3 frozen food
4 high-fashion clothing

A 1 and 3 only
B 1 and 4 only
C 2 and 3 only
D 2 and 4 only

27 Marginal cost is always equal to

A   average variable cost

B   total cost – total fixed cost

C   the change in total variable cost as output changes by one unit

D   the average cost of the last unit produced

28 A firm enjoys the following advantages.

1   It is able to place large orders for its raw materials and obtains them on preferential terms.

2   The locality in which it is situated has an abundant supply of labour skilled in the types of work carried out by the firm.

3   The transportation of its raw materials and finished products is undertaken by firms which specialize in meeting the transport needs of the industry to which the firm belongs.

Which of the above is/are external economies of scale?

A   1, 2 and 3

B   1 and 2 only

C   2 and 3 only

D   1 only

E   3 only

Data-response questions

29 The table below gives details of the costs of production of a small firm operating in a very competitive market. It cannot fix the price of its product because many other firms are making identical products. The price is determined by market forces (supply and demand) which are beyond the control of the individual firm.

Output (units per week)	Fixed costs (£s)	Marginal cost (£s)
0	100	—
1	100	100
2	100	80
3	100	50
4	100	90
5	100	150
6	100	170

a   Copy out the table and add further columns to record total costs and average costs.

b   What is the total variable cost when output is 4 units?

c   *i*   What output would maximize the firm's profits when market price is £160?

   ii   What is the firm's total profit at this output?

d   When the price falls below _____ , the firm makes losses at all outputs. What is the missing figure?

30 A firm producing Commodity X has the following costs.

Fixed (indirect) costs per annum		Direct costs per unit of X	
Depreciation	£8000	Labour	£3
Rent and rates	£6000	Materials	£3
Interest on loans	£4000	Fuel and power	£1
Insurance	£4000	Packaging and transport	£1
Other overheads	£2000		

The market price of X is £12 per unit.

a On a piece of graph paper plot the graphs of total revenue and total cost (horizontal scale up to 15 000 units).

b Shade in the areas representing (i) losses and (ii) profits.

c What volume of sales must the firm achieve in order to break even?

d What are the profits/losses when sales are 9000 units per annum?

8 The organization and ownership of firms

Some important terms

A study of the way in which production is controlled and organized requires an understanding of the terms used to describe the different types of industrial and commercial organizations.

The firm

A firm is a unit of management. It is an organization which trades under a particular name, controls the use of land, labour and capital, and makes decisions on methods of production, product design, marketing techniques and so on. It may vary in size from the employment of one or two people to many thousands. In many cases, especially where it is small, the firm is also the unit of ownership, but increasingly this is not the case, because a number of firms may be subject to unified control.

An enterprise

If one company holds more than 50 per cent of the voting shares in another company, the former controls the latter. Thus we have parent companies and subsidiary companies and, in many cases, these subsidiary companies retain a separate identity. Since they trade under their own names and have their own separate managements, they are classified as firms, but the ownership of such firms lies with the parent company. The unit of ownership and control is defined as an *enterprise*; it may be a single firm, or a parent company owning and controlling several subsidiary firms. These latter enterprises are often described as *holding companies* (see page 68).

A factory

A factory is a unit of production. It may also be described as a *plant* or an *establishment*. Clearly a small firm will have one establishment while a large firm may control many establishments located in different parts of the country and, quite often, in different parts of the world.

For example, Thorn Electrical Industries Ltd is an enterprise owning and controlling a large number of subsidiary companies and some eighty major factories located in the UK and overseas. Among the familiar names which make up this enterprise are Kenwood, Mazda, Bendix, HMV, Ferguson, Ultra, Marconiphone, Tricity, Main, Moffat and Parkinson Cowan.

An industry

One of the most difficult terms to define is an industry. In the simplest terms an industry is a group of firms making identical products, but this definition is of little use in helping us to understand the real world. Rolls Royce cars are very different from Reliant cars, but both firms are part of the motor car industry. Knitted pullovers are very different products to men's socks, but firms making these products are regarded as belonging to the hosiery industry.

Nevertheless, the most widely used definition of an industry is that of a group of firms making products which are similar and which are close substitutes for one another. This definition helps us to identify firms belonging to many of the major industries (e.g. furniture, pottery, radio and television, footwear, textiles, motor cars and so on). A problem arises, of course, with multi-product firms such as Dunlop which cannot be placed in any one industry.

Industries may also be usefully defined in terms of the basic materials or by the kind of technology used in the industry. Thus, firms in the rubber industry make a wide variety of products but they all use the same basic materials. Firms in the hosiery industry also make a wide range of products but they all use the same technical process, that is, knitting.

Types of business organization

1 The one-person business

This is the oldest form of business organization and there are more one-person businesses or sole proprietors than any other form of enterprise. It is very easy to establish this type of firm; there are no complicated legal formalities to be undertaken and it often requires very little capital to start such a business. Many hundreds of such firms are set up every day, but, unfortunately, a very large number close down every day. Lack of experience by people starting up in business for the first time and a lack of resources to carry them through 'a bad patch' are the main reasons for the high mortality rate among small firms.

The one-person business is extremely common in agriculture, retailing, personal services (e.g. hairdressing) and many types of repair work. Probably the main advantage of this form of business organization is its ability to adjust very quickly to changes in the customers' requirements. It is a very flexible organization because decisions about what should be done and how it should be done do not have to wait upon consultations with partners or meetings with directors. There is also a very strong incentive for the sole proprietor to increase the efficiency of the firm, because he or she will personally reap all the rewards if the business prospers and equally will have to bear any losses which result from a poor performance.

A major drawback to this form of enterprise is the fact that the entrepreneur's liability for his or her business debts is unlimited. This means that personal property (e.g. house and car) may have to be sold to meet the claims of creditors should the business fail. The one-person business is not able to issue shares and, because it has few valuable assets, or is not well known, it may find it difficult to borrow from banks and other financial institutions. The main sources of funds are likely to be the proprietor's own savings and such loans as can be obtained from relatives and friends.

2 Partnerships

According to the Partnership Act of 1890, a partnership is a voluntary association of from two to twenty people which is formed with a view to carrying on business for profit. However, subsequent changes in the law have created certain exceptions to these conditions and unlimited membership is available to partnerships in some professions (e.g. law, accountancy, stockbrokerage).

Partnerships can obviously raise more capital than a sole proprietor and management can be carried out in a more specialized manner. Each partner can be made responsible for managing a particular aspect of the business (e.g. production, sales, administration). Indeed, partnerships are often formed in order to bring some particular skill into the business.

The disadvantage of unlimited liability, as with one-person businesses, also applies to partnerships and, in an ordinary partnership, each partner is fully liable for the activities of the other partners. It is possible, however, to form a limited partnership where a partner's liability for the debts of the firm are limited to the amount of capital that partner has invested in the business. Even in a limited partnership, however, there must be at least one partner whose liability is unlimited. A limited partner can take no part in the management of the firm.

Partnerships are easy to form but they are also easy to dissolve. By giving notice to the others, a partner can dissolve the partnership at any time. Thus, a successful partnership depends upon goodwill between the members and continuous harmonious working relationships. With the ever-present possibility of disputes between the members, especially in more risky trading enterprises, partnerships tend to be rather unstable. This form of organization is very common in professions such as law, medicine, accountancy and surveying.

3 The joint stock company

Companies are firms incorporated under the Companies Acts (1948–80). The stock (or capital) of the company is divided into small units (e.g. shares) and this enables many people to contribute varying amounts to its total capital. Profits are divided between the shareholders in proportion to the number and types of shares they own. Companies are 'legal persons' quite distinct from their owners. They can do all the legal things an ordinary person can do: own land and property, employ people, sue and be sued in the courts and so on.

Limited liability

Over 99 per cent of the companies in the UK are limited companies, which means that the owners have limited liability for the company's debts. This is a most important feature of companies. The shareholders' responsibilities for the debts of the company are strictly limited to the value of the shares they have agreed to buy. Once shareholders have fully paid for their shares they have no further liability for the company's debts.

Public and private companies

Companies can be public or private. There are about 600 000 companies registered in the UK of which some 15 000 are public companies. Private companies tend to be small and are often family firms, while public companies are generally larger firms. Although there are far fewer public companies, they are much more important than private companies in terms of numbers employed, value of assets owned and value of output.

Companies, both private and public, must have at least two members. Private companies cannot invite the public at large to subscribe to their share capital, but public companies may issue invitations to the general public to buy their shares. A public company must have a minimum share capital of £50 000.

The formation of companies

Limited companies must be registered with the Registrar of Joint Stock Companies and must submit to the Registrar certain documents for approval.

1 The Memorandum of Association

This document sets out the manner in which the company will conduct its affairs with the outside world. The following list of items indicates the kind of information contained in the Memorandum.

a   The company's name. In the case of a limited company the name must contain the word 'limited'; in the case of a public company the name must include the words 'public limited company'.
b   The address of the company's registered office.
c   The objects of the company. A registered company can only carry on business in those activities which are set out in the Memorandum.
d   A statement that the liability of the members is limited.
e   The amount of capital the company wishes to raise by issuing shares and the types of shares to be issued.
f   The agreement of the founder members to form a company and their promises to purchase the stated number of shares.

2   The Articles of Association

This document sets out the manner in which the company will be organized and controlled. It will deal with such matters as,

a   the procedure for calling a general meeting,
b   the rights and duties of the directors,
c   the manner in which the directors will be elected,
d   the borrowing powers of the company.

3   A Statutory Declaration

This document states that the promoters of the company have complied with the requirements of the Companies Acts.

If the Registrar is satisfied that the provisions of the Companies Acts have been met a *Certificate of Incorporation* will be issued which establishes the firm as a legal entity. A private company may now commence business.

In the case of a public company, there are certain other legal formalities to be completed before the Registrar issues a *Certificate of Trading* which enables the public company to begin operations.

Registered companies are subject to a considerable degree of state control under the Companies Acts. The main purpose of this legislation is to protect investors against fraud and to safeguard the interests of shareholders. The law obliges companies to publish details of their operations, their financial and management structures and their annual incomes and expenditures. Much of this information appears in the annual reports of companies, but a great deal of other information is available for public inspection at the Office of the Registrar of Companies.

The importance of the joint stock company

There are several reasons why the joint stock company is by far the most important form of business organization in the private sector of the economy.

1   Limited liability

The introduction of the principle of limited liability greatly reduced the risks associated with investment in business enterprise and encouraged large numbers of people to subscribe to the capital stock of companies. The limitation of a shareholder's liability has made it possible to raise the vast sums of money required to finance the large-scale organizations in modern industrial societies.

2   Continuity of existence

Many industrial enterprises require heavy investment in fixed capital which has a long life and which will have to yield profits for many years if it is 'to pay for itself'. Investors will only subscribe capital for this type of project if they are assured that the firm will have a continuous existence over many years. The joint stock company has the advantage of perpetual life; it exists independently of the life of its members. If shareholders die or sell their shares it has no effect on the life of the company. The limited company can, therefore, take a much longer view than the one-person business or the partnership.

3 Transferability of shares

An important feature of the joint stock company is the fact that its shares are freely transferable. A company needs to have permanent use of the capital which its members provide, but few people, if any, would be prepared to make a permanent loan to a company. The transferability of shares neatly solves this problem. The company has the permanent use of the share capital while shareholders, by selling their shares, can, at any time, convert their shareholdings into some other form of asset. Since the market prices of shares fluctuate, they might, of course, make a loss.

4 Combining resources

The joint stock company provides a means whereby economic resources, which might otherwise lie idle, can be put to work. Many people who have accumulated savings (or acquired funds in other ways) have little desire or ability to use them directly in setting up and running a business. On the other hand there will be people with considerable organizing ability and technical expertise who are anxious to put these abilities to work but who do not have the financial resources for this purpose. The formation of a company enables sums of money and management skills provided by different groups to be brought together in one organization.

5 Separation of ownership and control

The previous point indicates the possibility of a separation of ownership and control which is an important feature of the larger companies. There is no single entrepreneur in such companies and the functions of risk-bearing and control are exercised by different groups. The shareholders bear the risks while the responsibilities of management are borne by the Board of Directors (elected by the shareholders). In the large company, the shareholders will be very numerous and widely dispersed; they will almost certainly lack the knowledge and skills to play any effective part in running the company. If the directors have the same objectives as the shareholders (e.g. to maximize profits at all times, or to earn satisfactory profits over the longer period), this separation of ownership and control will present no problems. Management, however, may decide to aim for maximum sales rather than maximum profits (since their salaries and prestige are closely linked to the size of the firm), or they may pursue policies which minimize risks (e.g. extend the range of products). In other words it is possible for shareholders and managers to have conflicting interests.

Although shareholders in the larger companies can play no real part in the day-to-day management of the company, they can show their approval or disapproval by using their votes at the annual general meeting when directors come up for re-election. In fact, such rights seem to be rarely exercised. A recent survey of forty-eight major companies showed that attendance at these meetings rarely exceeded 1 per cent of voting capital and the average annual general meeting lasted about 20 minutes. Among the smaller companies, however, ownership and control is usually in the same hands.

6 Take-overs and holding companies

The company structure lends itself to take-overs and the formation of holding companies. A company as a legal person can acquire the ownership of another company. Thus, Company A may make a formal offer for the voting shares in Company B. This offer may be in cash or in the form of a share exchange. For example, one share in Company A may be offered as the price of one share in Company B. Quite often the offer takes the form of cash, plus shares in the company making the offer.

Sometimes a company is formed for the express purpose of acquiring controlling interests in two or more firms. Such a company is known as a holding company. This is a legitimate method by which the size of an enterprise may be increased in order to take advantage of economies of scale, to obtain greater security by increasing the range of products or to become more competitive in foreign markets. But the ease with which such mergers and take-overs can take place has led to some concern about the dangers of concentrating economic power in relatively few hands. Some takeovers may be motivated by the desire to reduce competition rather than to increase efficiency.

The capital structure of companies

On its formation the company is given the power to raise some given amount of capital. This is known as its *authorized capital*.

In the early stages of its development a company is not likely to raise the full amount of its authorized capital. The amount which it actually raises is known as its *issued capital*.

A company may not ask the people who subscribe for its shares to pay for them in full when they are issued. When issuing £1 shares, for example, it may ask for 40p per share to be paid on application and a further 40p per share to be paid when the shares are allotted. The remaining 20p per share can be called up at some time in the future. The amount of money actually paid by the shareholders is known as the *paid-up capital*.

For example Company X may have an authorized capital of £100 million. Its issued capital may consist of 50 million £1 shares on which 50p per share has been called up. Its paid-up capital, therefore, is £25 million. It may, of course, call up the unpaid amounts at any time.

1 Preference shares

The holders of these shares, as the name implies, are permitted to share in the profits of the company before other shareholders. Preference shares generally carry a fixed rate of interest although there is a *participating* preference share which gives the holders rights to a further share in the profits after the ordinary shareholders have received some minimum rate of return. There is also a *cumulative* preference share which carries a right to the payment of any arrears of interest which may have accumulated during years when profits were insufficient to pay the fixed rate of interest. Preference shares do not usually carry voting rights although holders of them may be entitled to vote at the annual general meeting in years when their fixed interest claims have not been met.

2 Ordinary shares

The holders of ordinary shares bear most of the risks because they have no guaranteed income and they are 'at the end of the queue' for a share in the profits. On the other hand they rank for dividend without limit after all the other claims on profits have been satisfied. The dividends on ordinary shares, therefore, fluctuate far more than the return on other types of shares and in bad years the ordinary shareholders may receive no dividends at all. Ordinary shares normally carry voting rights and it is the purchase of these shares which is important in take-over bids.

3 Debentures

A company may obtain capital additional to that raised by the sale of its shares by issuing debentures. A debenture is not a share; it is a document acknowledging a loan to the company. Unlike a shareholder, a debenture-holder is not an owner of the company. Debenture-holders' claims rank before those of shareholders and they are often given added security in the form of some legal claim on the assets of the company. When this is the case, the debentures are described as *secured* debentures. The fixed rate of interest on debentures must be paid whether the company makes a profit or not and, in the event of the company defaulting in its payments, the assets of the company may be seized and sold in order to meet the claims of secured debentures.

The following details (Table 5) might serve as an aid to the understanding of the capital structure of companies. It is an extract from the annual report and accounts of a major British company (Unilever Ltd.).

Table 5   Capital structure (£ million)

	Authorized	Issued and fully paid
Preference share capital		
5% first cumulative preference	0.2	0.2
7% first cumulative preference	3.5	3.5
8% second cumulative preference	1.2	1.2
20% third cumulative preferred ordinary	0.2	0.2
	5.1	5.1
Ordinary share capital		
Ordinary (in 25p shares)	136.2	45.8
Total share capital	141.3	50.9

Loan capital		
6¾% secured debenture stock	1985/88	11.0
5½% unsecured loan stock	1991/2006	2.2
7¾% unsecured loan stock	1991/2006	54.7
Bank loans	1982/87	50.0
Total loan capital		117.9

Notes on Table 5:

a   The debenture stock is secured by a floating charge on the company's assets (i.e. all the assets of the company are offered as a security).

b   Preferred ordinary shares rank after preference shares but before ordinary shares in the distribution of profits.

c   The dates attached to the items under Loan Capital refer to the periods during which the company must repay the various loans.

d   Both preference and ordinary shares carry voting rights.

4   Cooperative societies

There are two main types of cooperatives, worker cooperatives and consumer cooperatives. It is the latter which are most widely known and every region in the UK has its cooperative retail society. Some of the earliest and most interesting attempts to apply the cooperative principle to production, however, were in manufacturing rather than in retailing.

Worker cooperatives

The idea of worker cooperatives has a long history, although most of the early experiments did not meet with a great deal of success. The main principle behind worker cooperatives is that the enterprise should be owned and controlled by the workers engaged in it. The workers provide the capital, take all the management decisions (either collectively or by electing managers from their own ranks) and they share out the profits on some agreed basis.

There are strong idealistic motives behind the formation of a worker cooperative, but many of the earlier experiments probably failed for one or more of the following reasons:

a   a lack of management experience among the workers;

b   inadequate funds for plant and machinery;

c   a lack of the financial resources required to keep the business going until its products had established themselves in the market;

d   a desire to distribute profits rather than plough them back into the firm;

e   the election of popular rather than effective managers.

At the beginning of the twentieth century there were about 200 worker cooperatives in the UK and they were strongly supported by the retail cooperative societies which purchased much of their output. By the early 1960s, however, the number of worker cooperatives had fallen to about 30, most of them in printing, clothing and footwear. In the past decade there has been a great revival of interest in this form of enterprise and in 1980 it was reported that about 300 worker cooperatives were operating in a wide variety of industries. In 1978 the government established a special agency to help worker cooperatives with technical advice and expertise. Worker cooperatives have proved to be very successful enterprises in France and Spain.

Consumer cooperatives

In the UK the cooperative principle has been applied far more successfully to consumer control rather than worker control. In the cooperative wholesale and retail societies the owners are the consumers, that is, those who purchase the goods and services rather than those who make them.

The first cooperative retail society was formed in Rochdale in 1844 by some poor weavers. From this humble beginning the movement has grown to become the largest single retailing organization in the UK with more than 10 million members and more than 10 000 shops.

The basic principles of cooperative enterprise have remained largely unchanged since the days of the Rochdale pioneers.

a   Open membership. There is no maximum to the number of members and these may join and leave at any time.

b   Democratic control. The minimum shareholding is £1 and the maximum £5000, but the rule is 'one member one vote' (unlike the joint stock company where voting rights are related to the number of shares held).

c   Distribution of the surplus in proportion to the value of purchases. Members (i.e. the owners) do not receive a dividend related to their investments in the society. A dividend is paid which is proportional to the value of a member's purchases from the society. Nowadays, however, all customers receive dividend stamps whether they are members of the society or not, although members are normally given some kind of bonus on their stamps.

d   Payment of interest on capital. Members receive a fixed rate of interest on their share capital.

The management of a cooperative retail society is the responsibility of a committee (usually part-timers) elected by the members. The day-to-day operations of the business are controlled by full-time managers appointed by the committee.

Traditionally the cooperative societies have always pursued social and political objectives. They finance and organize educational programmes and actively support political movements which seek to extend the idea of worker and consumer control of industry. The cooperative societies started as working-class movements and their objectives were (and are) to help the working classes, not only financially, but socially and politically.

In the UK, the retail societies have been substantially reorganized in recent years. A large number of the smaller societies have disappeared as mergers have taken place. The aim has been to form larger units in order to take advantage of economies of scale. Fierce competition from the larger retail companies has forced the cooperative societies to adopt similar marketing techniques to those used by their rivals, for example, the single Co-op brand, large-scale advertising and the opening of superstores. This has often meant that the original idea of local ownership and control has been lost and local loyalties weakened. The cooperative societies account for about 7 per cent of the national retail trade, about 15 per cent of the grocery trade, and supply about one-third of the country's fresh milk.

The retail societies own and control the Cooperative Wholesale Society (the CWS) which supplies a large proportion of the goods sold by the retail societies. The CWS is a large-scale importer and manufacturer; it is also Britain's largest farmer. The cooperative movement in the UK is also an important supplier of services and operates large-scale banking and insurance businesses. It should be noted that the industrial enterprises owned by the CWS are not run as worker cooperatives; the workers are employees of the CWS.

5 The public corporation

In the UK and many other non-communist countries several industries have been taken into public ownership (i.e. nationalized). The fact that these industries produce and sell goods and services led, at the time of nationalization, to a great deal of discussion and argument on the best form of organization for publicly-owned *trading* enterprises. It seemed to be generally accepted that a government department staffed by civil servants, such as those responsible for education, health and foreign affairs, was not a suitable form of organization for running a business which produced and sold goods and services. Government departments are subject to very close control and supervision by ministers and by Parliament. It was felt that the managers of a trading enterprise should not be restricted in this way, otherwise they would be inhibited from taking the kind of risks which have to be taken in running any successful trading business.

The public corporation was the form of business organization adopted for the control and management of the British nationalized industries. Like the company, the public corporation is a legal entity, but ownership is vested in the state and there are no shareholders. In effect, a nationalized industry belongs to the people. The management structure of a public corporation is very similar to that of a joint stock company. There is a Board of managers who have similar responsibilities and powers to those of directors, but a major difference lies in the manner of their selection. The members of a nationalized industry Board are *appointed* by the Minister of the Crown who is responsible for the overall performance of the industry; the directors of a company are elected by the shareholders. The Board of a nationalized industry has to manage and organize the day-to-day running of the industry but it is responsible to the government and not to a body of shareholders.

As is the case with a company, a public corporation must prepare and make public an annual report and statement of accounts. This annual report is subject to review by Parliament. Since there are no shareholders, a public corporation cannot raise funds by an issue of shares. In the UK, public corporations obtain long-term loans directly from the government and most of their short-term borrowing is from the banks. In more recent years, however, nationalized industries have borrowed substantial amounts from overseas (the Treasury normally guarantees these loans).

Whereas a joint stock company is formed primarily for the purpose of making profits, public corporations are charged with the task of 'operating in the public interest'. This is a rather vague term (see page 119), but generally speaking, public corporations are expected to take account of the national interest as well as the particular interests of their own industry. They are not permitted to aim at maximizing their profits, but they are expected to pay their way over the longer period. Most of the public corporations in the UK have been given financial targets which represent some agreed percentage rate of return on the capital employed. A particular public corporation, for example, might be told that it should aim to earn a surplus equal to 5 per cent of the capital employed. These targets are not the same for each industry and the general idea is that they should provide an incentive for management to achieve some desired level of efficiency. Any surplus earned by a public corporation must be used for the purposes of lowering prices, raising wages or for investment in new capital.

9   Business finance

Why firms need to borrow

Many independent businesses are started with the original owner's savings and perhaps with the help of family and friends. If the business is successful its growth will bring about the need for more financial resources and inevitably this means some kind of borrowing. All firms, those which are long-established and those in their early stages of development need to borrow money. The main purposes for which firms require borrowed funds are:

a   to purchase fixed assets (land, factories, machines etc);
b   to purchase raw materials;
c   to cover the cost of holding stocks of finished goods;
d   to pay wages and other expenses until such time as income is received from the sale of the firm's products;
e   to deal with situations such as a temporary fall in demand;
f   to purchase other companies (i.e. take-overs);
g   to finance investment abroad.

Even when a company uses 'its own money' for these purposes it is still 'borrowing'. When companies retain profits within the firm and use this money for purposes such as those outlined above, they are, in fact, borrowing from their shareholders. For this reason we find that the item *retained profits* appears on the liabilities side of the company's balance sheet; it represents a loan *from* the shareholders *to* the company.

Short-term and long-term loans

A firm's demand for loans can be divided into a demand for long-term capital and a demand for short-term capital. It will tend to seek short-term loans to cover variable costs such as payments for raw materials, wages and the costs of holding stocks. It will borrow on a long-term basis to finance its fixed capital requirements.

A unit of fixed capital will earn income over many years. It will 'pay for itself' over perhaps ten or fifteen years (referred to as its *pay-back period*) so that it is sensible to finance it with a loan which is repayable over a similar period of time, or by means of a permanent loan such as that provided by ordinary shareholders.

On the other hand a short-term loan is appropriate for the purchase of raw materials because, in most cases, the means of repaying the loan is generated in a matter of a few weeks or months. A furniture manufacturer who borrows money to purchase timber will have converted this material into chairs, tables, or kitchen cabinets in a matter of weeks and the sale of these goods will provide the means of repaying the loan.

How firms are financed

Table 6   Sources of funds for industrial and commercial companies, UK

	Percentage of total		
	1976	1978	1980
Internal funds (retained profits)	73.2	76.5	61.6
Issues of ordinary shares	5.4	4.9	3.4
Issues of preference shares, debentures and other loans and mortgages	4.8	1.8	10.0
Bank borrowing	16.6	16.8	25.0
	100.0	100.0	100.0

Sources: *British Business*, 15 February 1980; *Financial Statistics*, February 1982.

1   Internal funds

All successful firms, whatever their size, may 'finance themselves' by retaining some of their profits within the firm and using this money to pay for programmes of modernization or expansion. As Table 6 indicates, this is by far the most important source of finance for companies in the UK.

It is sometimes said that a firm, by using its own money, is benefiting because it does not have to pay interest charges as it would if it borrowed the money. This is not strictly correct because there is an opportunity cost involved in using retained profits to finance investment. This cost is equal to the *interest foregone*, that is, the interest the funds might have earned had they been used to buy a riskless asset such as government securities.

2   Issuing shares and debentures

A smaller private company might raise capital by an issue of shares but it would have to approach the potential buyers privately; it could not make a public appeal. A public company can offer its shares to the general public and for this purpose it will make use of one of the specialist firms known as *issuing houses*. Most of these issuing houses are well-known merchant bankers who deal in all aspects of company finance.

The issuing house will be responsible for advising the company on the type of share to be issued and on the price at which the shares are to be offered. It will carry out all the administrative work involved in preparing and launching the issue. It will produce and publish the *prospectus* which, under the Companies Acts, must contain a full account of the company's history, prospects and intentions, together with details of its financial position and recent trading performance. The prospectus also contains an application form on which members of the public can apply for the shares or debentures.

The issuing house will arrange for the share issue to be *underwritten*. For the payment of a premium, underwriters will insure the share issue against failure by guaranteeing to take up any unsold shares. An issue of shares can be carried out in various ways.

a *Public issue by prospectus*. This is the method outlined above.

b *Placing*. This method tends to be used when the issue is a relatively small one. The issuing house arranges for fairly large blocks of the shares to be 'placed' with (i.e. bought by) institutions such as insurance companies, pension funds, and stockbrokers.

c *Offer for sale*. In this case the entire share issue is bought outright by the issuing house itself. It then acts as a principal rather than an agent by selling the shares on its own behalf.

d *A rights issue*. This procedure is quite different from the methods outlined above. The offer of new shares is made directly to the company's existing shareholders in proportion to the number of shares they already hold. For example, a company might offer, 'one new share for each four shares already held'. Normally shares issued in this way are offered at prices substantially below the market price of the company's existing shares. The 'rights', therefore, are valuable and any shareholders not wishing to take up the offer can sell their rights on the open market. A rights issue is one of the cheaper ways of issuing shares; no prospectus is needed and advertising costs are minimal.

e *Issues by tender*. In this case the public is invited to submit bids for the new shares (as in an auction) and the shares are sold to the highest bidders.

3 Bank loans

Bank lending to industry and commerce has traditionally been of a short-term nature and the banks have tended to specialize in providing money for what has been described earlier as working capital. The interest rate on bank loans tends to be variable (i.e. it changes according to market conditions). Short-term loans are often renewable by agreement with the bank and so may run for quite long periods of time. In recent years, the banks have increasingly engaged in medium-term lending to industry (i.e. for periods of up to seven or ten years). Table 6 shows that bank loans now provide a substantial proportion of the loans which companies obtain from external sources. Through their specialist subsidiary companies the banks are also important suppliers of hire-purchase and leasing facilities (explained later).

4 Specialist institutions

Over the years, and especially since the Second World War, a number of financial institutions have been set up to meet particular needs of companies requiring finance.

The Finance Corporation for Industry (FCI) provides long-term loan facilities for larger companies. Amounts from £1 million to £25 million are provided at both fixed and variable rates of interest.

The Industrial and Commercial Finance Corporation (ICFC) provides funds for the small to medium-sized company including long-term loans for periods of up to twenty years. It is prepared to supply amounts ranging from £5000 to £2 million and will, if necessary, purchase new or existing shares in a business.

Technical Development Capital Ltd. is a subsidiary of the ICFC and provides finance for high-risk ventures to help people who are trying to produce and market new technical products. Loans are usually provided at a fixed rate of interest.

There are several other financial institutions specializing in providing funds for industry. One of the most important of these is the *National Enterprise Board* (the NEB). This is a public corporation which can provide funds in the form of long-term loans or by the purchase of shares. The NEB is described in more detail on page 115.

5 Other important financial institutions

The major part of the money required for investment by industry and commerce does not come from the savings of a relatively few rich people but from the relatively small individual savings of millions of people. There are a number of important institutions which exist for the purposes of collecting and investing these personal savings.

1 Pension funds and insurance companies

The rise in real incomes since the Second World War, and the fact that payments to these institutions receive preferential tax treatment, has led to an enormous growth in the annual premiums collected by pension funds and insurance companies. Together they account for about 45 per cent of personal savings in the UK.

Although these institutions will be meeting large demands for current payments in the form of various insurance claims and from existing pensioners, their current income greatly exceeds their outgoings and they have large surpluses available for investment purposes. The income which these companies receive in the form of dividends and interest from their investments enables them to offer pensions and other benefits (e.g. endowments) which greatly exceed the total money value of a member's contributions to the funds.

In 1978 a press advertisement by the British Insurance Companies stated that they had some £7 million per day available for investment. They had a total of £28 000 million invested in Britain, distributed as follows:

34% in stocks and shares in companies;
26% in government and local authority securities;
16% in factories, warehouses, shops and offices;
13% in mortgages and loans;
11% in cash and other liquid assets.

The picture for pension funds both in respect of the amounts available for investment and the way in which the money is invested is very similar to that for insurance companies. Fig. 9.3 on page 85 illustrates the growing importance of these institutions as providers of finance for companies.

2 Investment trusts

These are limited companies, but the money they raise from the sale of their shares is not used to buy real capital; it is used to purchase shares in other companies. The managers of investment trusts are experts in financial investment and they use their shareholders' funds to buy shares in what they believe will be profitable companies. People buying shares in an investment trust are spreading their risks because each share in the trust represents a very small investment in a large number of other companies. The dividends paid out by the investment trust are derived from the dividends on the shares held in other companies.

3 Unit trusts

These operate in a similar manner to investment trusts, that is, the money subscribed by members is reinvested in the shares of a wide range of industrial and commercial companies. There are, however, important differences.

a   Unlike the investment trust, which is a joint stock company, unit trusts are trusts in the legal sense. The stocks and shares bought by the managers of the trust are held by trustees (e.g. well-known banks).

b   Unit trusts are more attractive to the small investor. The units are in small denominations (25p) and the smallest initial amount required from an investor is usually between £25 and £100.

c   Units, unlike shares, cannot be sold on the open market. Any holder of units, however, can sell them back to the trust at any time. The prices of existing units will vary from day to day according to the profitability of the companies in which the trust holds shares. Each day, unit trusts publish two prices, the lower price is the one at which they are prepared to repurchase units and the higher price is the one at which they are prepared to sell units.

4 Building societies

These are very specialized institutions in the sense that the savings which they collect are channelled almost exclusively towards the purchase of property. Building societies make loans to house purchasers in the form of mortgages, whereby the society takes possession of the deeds of the property as a security for the loan. The rate of interest they charge on their loans is determined by the rate they have to offer savers in order to attract the necessary funds.

6 Hire-purchase and leasing

One way in which a firm may 'borrow' is to acquire its capital assets on hire-purchase terms. It receives the equipment (e.g. machines, lorries, office equip-

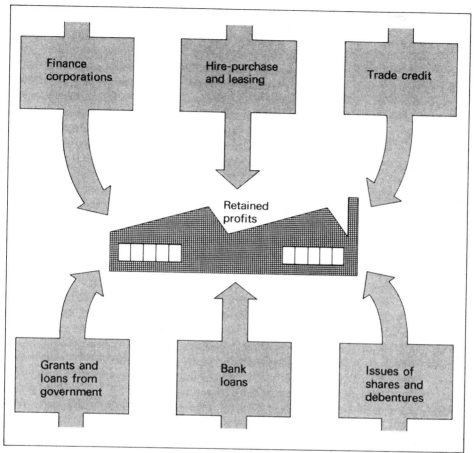

Fig. 9.1   Company finance

ment) on the payment of an initial deposit and then pays the outstanding amounts by instalments over a period of years. The firm is, in effect, receiving a loan equal to the value of the goods (less the deposit). Most of this instalment credit, as it is called, is supplied by *finance houses*. These institutions accept deposits from customers (as does a bank) or borrow from banks and other financial institutions and then use these funds to pay the seller the cost of the goods being purchased (less the deposit). The finance house then collects the instalments from the purchaser, charging a higher rate of interest than that which it pays on its own borrowings. This form of instalment buying is also very important in the markets for consumer durable goods.

In recent years there has been a great expansion in the *leasing* of capital equipment. Whereas under hire-purchase schemes, the user of the equipment eventually becomes the owner (when all the instalments have been paid), under leasing this is not usually the case. The operators of leasing schemes, normally banks and finance houses, purchase the capital goods and then offer them on what are, in effect, rental terms. The customer makes regular payments to the leasing company to cover the costs involved (interest charges, wear and tear, depreciation etc.). The scheme is simply another way of providing finance to firms since the alternative would be for the firm to obtain a loan and buy the equipment.

7 Trade credit

If a firm obtains supplies of materials or equipment from other firms and is given a period of time, say three months, in which to pay for the goods, then, assuming that it pays three months after delivery, it is receiving a three month loan. This is the system of trade credit under which suppliers of goods help to finance their customers. The total amount of trade credit outstanding at any time is very large indeed. The customers receiving trade credit, of course, pay interest on their loan because they lose the discount they would have received had the goods been paid for immediately upon delivery.

8 The government

In the UK, and in most other countries, the government is a very important source of finance for industry. This particular role of government is discussed in Chapter 13.

The Stock Exchange

The Stock Exchange is a market place for the buying and selling of shares, debentures and government securities. It is primarily a market in second-hand or existing securities rather than in new issues, although new issues can be placed with dealers on the Stock Exchange.

It is a most important part of the capital market (i.e. the market in long-term loans), because, if such an institution did not exist, it would be much more difficult for firms to raise money by selling shares and for governments to borrow by selling securities. Many shares are permanent loans and many debentures and government securities are not repayable for many years after the date of issue. Most people would not be prepared to lend money on these terms. Although they wish to earn income on their savings and accumulations of wealth, they also want their investments to have some degree of *liquidity*. This means that they want to be in a position where they can turn their investments quickly and easily into cash whenever their plans and circumstances change and put them in a situation where they need cash. It is true that transferable shares and securities could be sold without the services of a Stock Exchange, but if each shareholder had to organize the sale individually, it could be a difficult, inconvenient and time-consuming process (the shares would have to be advertized in the press and/or friends contacted). The Stock Exchange removes these difficulties by providing a market where, at some price, shares can always be bought and sold.

Activities in the Stock Exchange

The main Stock Exchange is in London although there are provincial exchanges in Glasgow, Liverpool, Manchester, Birmingham, Edinburgh and other large cities. The operations in the Stock Exchange are carried out by two kinds of dealers; brokers and jobbers.

Members of the public cannot transact business in the Stock Exchange. Anyone wishing to buy or sell shares must employ a *stockbroker* who will charge a commission for the service. *Jobbers* work within the exchange and do not deal directly with the public. All their business is transacted with brokers (or other jobbers) and they act as principals rather than agents. This means that they buy and sell shares on their account and their profits depend on the success of their trading. They hope to judge the market trends so that they sell shares at higher prices than those which they paid for them. There is a traditional way of doing business in the Stock Exchange.

A broker who has received instructions from a client to buy or sell shares in, say, ICI, will approach a jobber and ask 'What is ICI?'. The jobber who does not know whether the broker wishes to buy or sell, might reply, '398p to 400p'. This indicates that the jobber is prepared to buy at 398p and to sell at 400p. The broker will now approach other jobbers and ask for similar quotations. He will finally deal with the one who offers the best price for his client.

There is, therefore, competition between the jobbers who must adjust their prices according to changes in supply and demand. If they pitch their buying prices too high, they will find themselves buying huge quantities of shares which they might have to dispose of at a loss. If they fix their prices too low, they will find themselves taking large orders for shares which they do not possess. They must, however, honour their contracts and they will have to buy the shares which they have agreed to supply to the brokers. It could happen that they will find themselves paying higher prices than those at which they have agreed to sell.

Jobbers tend to specialize in the shares of companies in particular industries such as shipping, mines, oil, land, property and so on. The largest single market in the Stock Exchange, however, is that in government securities.

About 9000 securities are listed on the Stock Exchange and dealings are permitted in any other security listed on any other recognized Stock Exchange in the world. It must be noted that not all shares are transferable on the Stock Exchange. Only those public companies which have satisfied conditions laid down by the Stock Exchange Council may have their shares dealt in on the

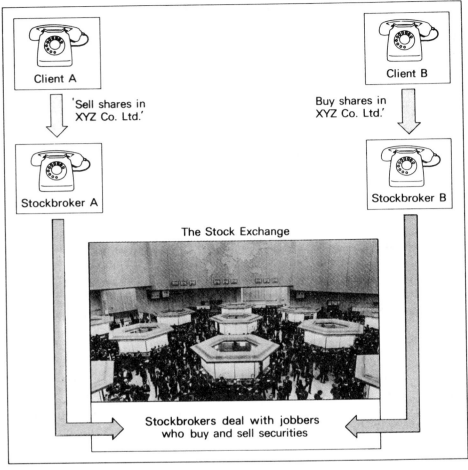

Fig. 9.2   The Stock Exchange

Stock Exchange. Such shares are referred to as *quoted shares*, indicating that the company has received a Stock Exchange quotation. Less than one-half of the public companies in the UK have their shares quoted on the Stock Exchange. The stock officially listed on the Exchange include the following.

a   Gilt-edged: These are securities issued by the UK government. The government borrows by selling these securities to the general public and to financial institutions.

b   Bonds issued by local authorities and other public bodies: these are similar to gilt-edged securities.

c   Debentures.

d   Preference shares.

e   Ordinary shares.

Share prices, dividends and yields

Most shares have a *nominal* or face value; this is the value printed on the share. Of more interest to the prospective purchaser or seller is the *market* value of the share and, since this is determined by supply and demand, it can vary from day to day. If the market price is higher than the nominal price, the share is said to be *at a premium*; if the market price is equal to the nominal value, the share is said to be *at par*; if it is lower, the share is selling *at a discount*.

The dividend on a share is expressed as a percentage of the nominal value. If a dividend of 20 per cent is declared on a share which has a nominal value of £2, the holder will receive a dividend of 40p.

The yield on shares is calculated by expressing the money value of the dividend as a percentage of the market price. The example below should make this clear.

nominal value of share = £5   market value of share = £8
dividend declared   = 10%   value of dividend per share = 50p
yield on this share $= \dfrac{50p}{£8} \times \dfrac{100}{1} = 6.25\%$

There are many factors influencing the supply of, and demand for, particular shares. Among the more important of these are:

a   the recent performance of the company and especially the level of profits it has been distributing to shareholders;

b   forecasts of the future prospects made by company chairmen in their annual reports and by financial journalists in the national newspapers;

c   recent and expected future changes in government policy (e.g. changes in taxation);

d   reports of inventions and innovations (e.g. micro-processors and their applications);

e   expected future changes in costs due, for example, to rises in the prices of imported materials or the current level of wage demands.

Speculation

The Stock Exchange is a relatively free market where prices change from day to day according to the shifts in the demand for, and supply of, the different shares. In this kind of market we invariably find speculators at work. Speculators do not buy shares for the income they yield; they buy them because they hope to make a gain (known as a *capital gain*) from a change in their prices.

A *bull* is the peculiar term used to describe a speculator who believes that the market price of a particular share is about to rise and hopes to make a profit by buying those shares now and selling them at a higher price in the immediate future.

A *bear* is a speculator who believes that the price of shares is about to fall and who hopes to make a gain by selling shares now and then buying them back later at lower prices.

Speculators hope to make gains by correctly anticipating *future* price movements. Thus they will tend to buy when prices are low and falling because they anticipate that the next change will be a rise in prices. They will tend to sell when prices are high and rising in order to make profits on the shares they bought at lower prices. It is said that this kind of speculation by well-informed professionals helps to keep share prices more stable, because speculators will be increasing the demand when prices are low and increasing the supply when prices are high. But even professional speculators might guess wrongly about future trends in share prices and, if they do, their activities will lead to even greater swings in prices.

In a market like the Stock Exchange moods of optimism and pessimism tend to be infectious and amateur speculators often 'jump on the bandwagon'. In a falling market they will rush to sell and in a rising market they will rush to buy. Speculation of this type can cause share prices to move to totally unrealistic levels so that they provide a most unreliable guide to the performance and prospects of different companies. We must remember, however, that a large proportion of shares are held by institutions such as insurance companies and pension funds which tend to hold them for income rather than for speculative purposes.

The functions of the Stock Exchange – a summary

1 By increasing the marketability of shares and bonds it facilitates the raising of new funds for industry and government.

2 Movements in share prices act as indicators to investors and help to direct the flow of savings to those industries which have the best prospects for profits and growth. This particular view of the Stock Exchange is based on the assumption that share prices accurately indicate different companies' performances and prospects; they may not always do so (see comment above about speculation).

3 It helps to ensure that the existing assets of a firm are profitably managed. If a firm is doing badly, the market price of its shares will be relatively low. This means that the company can be bought cheaply and it will be a target for take-over bids. Critics of this view point out that there is evidence to show that many take-overs have not led to any significant improvements in efficiency.

4 The Stock Exchange provides a means of valuing assets held in the form of shares and bonds. This is important for assessing taxes on capital and wealth and for the valuation of assets being taken over by the state (e.g. nationalization).

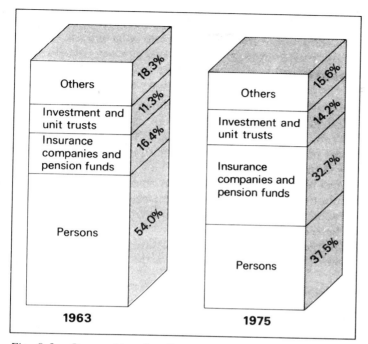

Fig. 9.3   Ownership of ordinary shares, UK

Source: *Economic Trends*, HMSO, September 1977. (The 1975 survey results were the most recent ones available in September 1981.)

Test paper 3

Short-answer questions

1   'At the beginning of the eighteenth century about 92 per cent of the labour force worked in *the primary sector* of the economy; today only about 4 per cent do so.' Explain the term in italics. What sectors employ the other 96 per cent of the labour force and what percentages (approximately) are employed in each of them?

2   What is the difference between an enterprise and an establishment?

3   How do we decide on the industry to which a firm belongs?

4   The proprietors of some firms are said to have *unlimited liability*.
    a   What is meant by the term in italics?
    b   In what types of organization do we find this state of affairs?

5   'One great advantage of the joint stock company is the continuity of its existence.' Explain.

6   a   ordinary shareholders
    b   preference shareholders
    c   debenture holders
    i   Rank the above in order of priority for payments of income.
    ii   Which of the above are owners of the company?
    iii   Which group is likely to have the most variable income?

7   What is 'public' about a public company?

8   If a company (or issuing house) making a public issue of shares, finds that the total applied for greatly exceeds the number of shares being offered, how does it deal with the situation?

9   What are the main differences between a joint stock company and a public corporation in respect of,
    a   ownership of the enterprise?
    b   the aims of the enterprise?
    c   appointments to the boards of management?

10   The ABC Co. Ltd, has the following issued and paid-up share capital:

    10 000   £1   7½% preference shares
    20 000   £1   ordinary shares

    The company has £2750 profits available for distribution to its shareholders.
    a   What dividend will it declare on its ordinary shares?
    b   If the market price of the ordinary shares is £2, what is the current yield on these shares?

11   Who owns the CWS?

True or false?

12 **a** Jobbers deal directly with the public but brokers only deal with job-bers.

b There are more sole proprietors than any other form of business orga-nization.

c It is not possible to transfer the ownership of shares in a private com-pany.

d A registered limited liability company has a legal identity quite separate from that of its owners.

e The complete control of a company lies in the hands of those who own 51 per cent or more of the total capital of the company.

f All shareholders and debenture holders have the right to vote at the company's annual general meeting.

g The funds raised by an issue of ordinary shares is described as loan capital.

h The ICFC and the FCI are financial institutions formed primarily to rescue firms facing bankruptcy.

Multiple-choice questions

13 *Limited liability* means that

A whatever the size of their shareholdings, all shareholders are responsi-ble for equal shares of the company's debts

B companies are only allowed to incur debts up to some legal maximum

C shareholders cannot suffer a loss greater than the value of the shares they have agreed to purchase

D shareholders' responsibilities for the debts of the company are limited to the market value of the shares they hold

Questions 14 to 18 refer to the following organizations.

A a partnership
B a cooperative society
C a private joint stock company
D a public joint stock company
E a public corporation

Which of the above,

14 limits voting rights to 'one member one vote'?
15 has the Exchequer as the main source of funds for capital investment?
16 can apply for its shares to be quoted on the Stock Exchange?
17 is, of the five types of business organization mentioned, the easiest to set up?
18 has its managers appointed rather than elected?

Questions 19 and 20 are based on the following items.
    1   retained profits
    2   a public issue of shares
    3   bank loans
    4   loans from the FCI
    5   trade credit
19 Which of the above would be likely sources of *working capital*?
    A   1 and 2 only
    B   1, 2 and 4 only
    C   1, 3 and 5 only
    D   2 and 3 only
    E   3, 4 and 5 only
20 Which of the above are likely sources of *long-term capital*?
    A   1 and 2 only
    B   1, 2 and 4 only
    C   1, 3 and 5 only
    D   2 and 3 only
    E   3, 4 and 5 only

21 A public company's ordinary shares (nominal value £1) are being quoted on the Stock Exchange at 80p. If the company pays the expected dividend of 10% what will be the yield on these shares?
    A   8%
    B   10%
    C   12½%
    D   20%
22 Limited partners
    1   do not run any risk of losing the funds they have invested in the firm
    2   may not take any part in the management of the firm
    3   are entitled to a share in the profits
    Which of the above statements is/are correct?
    A   1, 2 and 3
    B   1 and 2 only
    C   2 and 3 only
    D   1 only
    E   3 only
23 Which of the following is *not* a public corporation?
    A   NCB
    B   BBC
    C   NFC
    D   ICI
    E   CEGB

Data-response questions

24 The question is based on the following data.

The XYZ Company Limited – Balance Sheet as at 31 December 1980

Liabilities		**Assets**		
Ordinary share capital	£15 000	*Fixed assets*		
Retained profits	£5 000	Freehold factory	£11 000	
Mortgage loans	£10 000	*less* depreciation	£1 000	£10 000
	£30 000	Plant and Machinery	£20 000	
		less depreciation	£2 000	£18 000
Current liabilities		*Current assets*		
Creditors	£10 000	Stocks of finished goods		£7 000
Bank overdraft	£8 000	Stocks of unfinished goods		£2 000
		Debtors		£8 000
		Cash balance		£3 000
	£48 000			£48 000

   a Why are share capital and retained profits shown as liabilities?
   b What is meant by the item 'creditors'?
   c Why is depreciation deducted from the value of fixed assets?
   d What is meant by the term 'current assets'?
   e Why is the term 'debtors' shown as an asset?
   f What is the total *stake* which the owners have in this firm?
   g What is a mortgage loan?

25 The following statements are examples of the kind of items one finds in the financial pages of our national newspapers.
   1 'Brokers are sitting on the sidelines trying to figure out what happened to cause the disastrous bear market that roared in last October and savaged a full $100 000 million from Wall Street's shares.'
   2 'In the Stock Exchange, a stock shortage due to the absence of willing sellers led to widespread gains which belied the string of adverse announcements of short-time working, redundancies and reduced profit margins in the second quarter of the year.'
   3 'Companies faced with financial pressures on this scale have a limited number of options.
     a They can cut spending on fixed capital.
     b They can cut working capital; figures just released show that manufacturers and retailers had reduced their inventories by 2% in the first quarter of the year.
     c They can cut overhead costs by closing factories.'
Write brief explanations of the terms, events and situations referred to in these quotations.

10   The structure of industry

The survival of the small firm

Although the general trend is towards larger plants and firms, there is a very large number of successful small firms in the UK. In 1980 it was estimated that there were about 80 000 small firms in manufacturing while in retailing there were about 250 000. Table 7 (page 91) gives details of the numbers of small firms in different industries in 1976.

In some cases a firm remains small, because, although it may be successful and have the potential for further growth, the proprietor may not want to incur the additional worries and responsibilities of running a large enterprise. Some other important reasons for the ability of small firms to survive and prosper are set out below.

1   The size of the market

The various reasons why the size of the market for a particular good or service may be restricted were explained in Chapter 4. A demand for variety, a demand for personal service and heavy transport costs were seen as some of the major reasons why economies of large-scale production might not be achieved. Small firms are able to operate successfully where the market for the product is relatively small.

2   Cooperation between small firms

It is possible for small firms to enjoy certain economies of scale through schemes of cooperation. A number of small manufacturing firms may operate jointly-owned research laboratories (e.g. as in the footwear and pottery industries). Many small grocery shops have formed links with wholesaling organizations (e.g. Mace, VG, and Spar) so that they can obtain the economies of scale associated with the marketing of national brand names and bulk buying. Farmers may form a jointly-owned buying agency so that they can obtain the advantages of bulk purchases of seeds, fertilizers and animal feedstuffs. Similarly large units of capital such as combine harvesters may be collectively owned by a number of farmers so that greater use reduces the average costs of running such equipment.

3   Specialist suppliers to large firms

In many manufacturing industries a process of *disintegration* has taken place. The finished product (e.g. a motor car) is made up of a large number of standardized parts and these are put together in large assembly plants. Many of these parts and components are made by quite small firms. For some components, the output of a relatively small firm is large enough to meet the needs of a very large assembly plant.

4 Technical factors

In some industries where the units of capital are still relatively small, for example, sewing machines and knitting machines, it is not possible to achieve great technical economies of scale. In industries using such equipment, the small firm suffers no great technical disadvantages. In some cases, technical progress has worked to the advantage of the small firm. Recent developments in electronic engineering have made available calculating and control equipment in relatively small and inexpensive forms. Only a few years ago, it would have required large and expensive units of capital to provide similar services.

The advent of micro-processors has brought with it a host of new and relatively inexpensive machines. These are easy to set up and operate, can sit comfortably on a desk top and can handle a range of common business tasks such as payrolls, stock control and word processing. (*Financial Times*, 3 March 1980.)

5 Flexibility

The small firm, as mentioned on page 63 is usually a flexible organization which can adapt itself fairly quickly to changes in customers' requirements.

Table 7   Small firms in the UK, 1976

Sector	No. of small firms (000s)	Employment Small firms (000s)	% of total in industry
Agriculture	150	420	60
Manufacturing	100	1575	23
Construction	290	715	43
Transport	60	245	38
Wholesaling	75	315	37
Retailing	235	990	40
Finance	20	35	5
Property	35	40	44
Professional services	50	275	47
Catering	100	580	64
Motor trades	50	190	40
Other services	105	550	58
All others	35	280	60
	1305	6210	

Source: *Financial Times*, 4 June 1980.

The small firms referred to in Table 7 are defined as those having an annual turnover of less than £150 000 (for wholesaling less than £600 000 and for motor trades less than £300 000). In manufacturing small firms are those with less than 200 employees and, in construction, less than 25 employees.

The size structure of firms

In the UK, industrial enterprises vary from giant organizations such as the General Electric Company (GEC) and Imperial Chemical Industries (ICI), each of which have more than 100 000 employees, to many thousands of small firms, many with less than 25 employees. The 1978 Census of Production showed that, in manufacturing industry, about 80 per cent of the factories in the UK had less than 50 workers, but these plants only accounted for about 13 per cent of total employment in manufacturing. Larger units (those with more than 500 employees) accounted for about 2.5 per cent of the number of factories, but for more than 50 per cent of total employment (see Fig. 10.1).

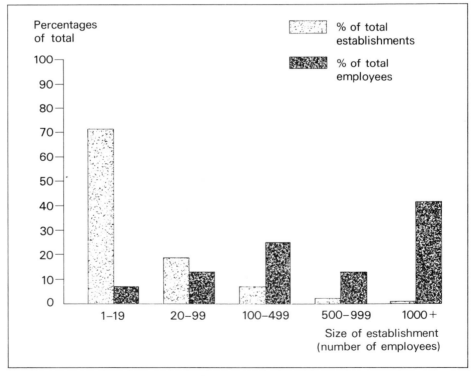

Fig. 10.1   UK manufacturing industry, 1978

Source: *Business Monitor*, PA 1002, HMSO.

92

These statistics deal with establishments (i.e. factories or plants), but we get a similar picture when we look at the statistics on the sizes of enterprises or firms. About 90 per cent of the firms in manufacturing have fewer than 100 workers, but they only account for about 20 per cent of total employment. In contrast the 100 largest firms (about 0.1 per cent of the total) account for about 37 per cent of total employment in manufacturing.

The statistics used in Fig. 10.1 measure the size of factories in terms of the numbers of employees, but this measure tends to exaggerate the importance of labour-intensive industries (e.g. leather and clothing industries) and underestimates the importance of firms in capital-intensive industries (e.g. oil and chemicals). For this reason economists also measure the size of the firm by using statistics which show the *value of the capital employed* by firms, or the *value of output*.

Why firms grow

There are many reasons why firms try to increase their size and some of these have already been discussed in detail in Chapter 6.

1 The costs motive

There is no doubt that the desire to reduce average costs of production by increasing the scale of production is a very important reason why firms try to increase their size. The cost advantages of large-scale production were explained in Chapter 6.

2 The market motive

The larger the firm, the larger its share of the market and the desire to exercise greater control over the market is another important reason for growth in the size of the firm. In general, a firm which has, say, 70 per cent of the total market for a product will have far more market power (i.e. face much weaker competition) than a firm which has only 10 per cent of the market.

3 The security motive

Larger firms with their greater resources are much better equipped to deal with the problems of fluctuations in demand. This motive is most clearly seen at work in the development of multiproduct firms. By producing a variety of products (as is the case nowadays with most large firms) there is likely to be a much more stable total demand (see page 49).

4 The power and prestige motive

An important reason why some of the firms in the non-communist world have reached such a huge size appears to have been the desire of their founders to create a vast industrial empire rather than the pusuit of personal wealth. Henry Ford, William Lever and William Morris (Lord Nuffield) are examples of entrepreneurs who seemed to have had this kind of personal ambition.

How firms grow

Firms grow in two ways, by extending the market for their existing product, or by extending their range of products. They might increase their outputs by finding new applications for their basic technology. Dunlops, for example, used their expertise in rubber technology to create markets in sports goods, footwear, upholstery, floor coverings and so on. Hoover used their experience with small electric motors to move into the markets for floor polishers, spin-dryers and washing machines.

In more recent times the size of the firm has tended to increase by the processes of *amalgamation* and *merger*. Where amalgamated firms are engaged in making similar products, the principal aim will be to achieve economies of scale and greater market power. Where the firms are making very different products the motives for amalgamation will be greater financial strength and greater security. The joining together of two or more firms is described as integration. It can take two main forms, vertical integration and horizontal integration.

Vertical integration

This term describes the joining together of firms operating at different stages of the production process. When a firm takes over its suppliers, as for example when a chocolate manufacturer takes over a cocoa plantation, or a car manufacturer acquires a body building plant, it is described as vertical integration backwards. Forward vertical integration occurs when a firm takes over one or more of its market outlets, as for example, when a manufacturer takes over a chain of retail stores or an oil company takes over a number of petrol stations.

A firm is likely to integrate backwards because it wishes to have a greater control over its supplies both with regard to the quality of the materials and the regularity of their delivery. Forward integration is often carried out to improve the quality of the market outlets. The major breweries have taken over a large number of public houses and invested heavily in improving the facilities and accommodation in these premises. The major oil companies have acquired most of the petrol stations and spend large sums on modernization. Since manufacturers generally incur the major costs of advertising their products, they regard the quality of the shop, garage or public house in which their goods are bought as an important feature of their marketing efforts. An expensive advertising campaign will yield poor results if the 'point of sale' (i.e. the market outlet) is a squalid inefficient enterprise. The take-over of market outlets might also be a defensive measure by a firm which is worried about losing its market share because rival producers are acquiring retail outlets which previously distributed this firm's products.

Vertically integrated firms may encounter increased management problems. When firms are merged, different management teams must be combined (or some of them eliminated) and the newly formed board of directors may have the task of managing widely separated enterprises each engaged in a different type of activity. It should be possible, however, for the integrated firm to achieve economies by centralizing certain services for the whole group (e.g. finance, purchasing, administration, transport and so on).

Horizontal integration

This term describes the joining together of firms engaged in producing similar goods or service. Thus, a merger of two or more mining companies or the merger of firms owning chains of clothing shops would be described as horizontal integration. The important incentive for horizontal integration is the prospect of achieving economies of scale from greater outputs, bulk buying, the ability to make effective use of large units of capital equipment, more specialized marketing techniques and so on. This type of integration also increases market power because a merger of firms making similar things obviously reduces the number of competitors.

Firms also merge horizontally in order to *rationalize* the use of their combined assets. For example, suppose that three firms, each with a large factory producing three different electrical appliances decide to amalgamate. Rationalization would probably mean that each factory would tend to specialize in one of the products. This greater specialization should lead to a lowering of average costs. Alternatively each of the independent firms might have been working below full capacity (i.e. with relatively high average costs). In this case the merger might lead to a closing down of the less efficient plant so that the two remaining plants could work at full capacity.

Conglomerates

Sometimes amalgamations take place between firms which are not related in any way. The goods produced by the separate firms are not similar (as is the case with horizontal integration) and the firms do not form part of the same total production process (as is the case with vertical integration). This type of integration is described as a conglomerate merger and the motives for it are usually financial. The idea is that the separate enterprises would benefit from centralized and expert financial management.

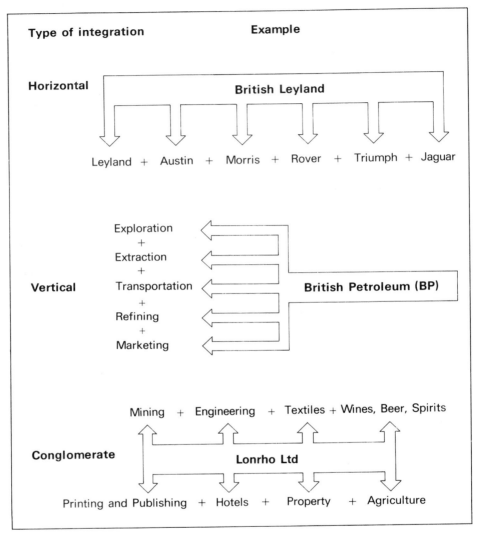

Fig. 10.2   Integration

Multi-national companies

A multi-national enterprise is one which owns and controls firms in several different countries. Many of the larger firms in the UK belong to multi-national companies. Ford, Hoover, Kodak, General Motors, ICI, and BP, are good examples of multi-national enterprises. Some of these multi-national firms are very large indeed; they have annual outputs greater in value than the national incomes of many countries. Multi-nationals account for 60 per cent of the trade in manufactures in the developed world and most of them are based in the USA, but Britain, France, West Germany and Japan are also important bases for multi-national enterprise.

These powerful organizations have a great influence on the economies of the countries in which they operate. Decisions to invest in Country A rather than Country B, or to close down the factory in Country C and expand the factory in Country D are obvious examples of the way in which the plans of multi-nationals can affect output and employment in different countries. They can, of course, carry out specialization on an international scale. A motor car company may decide to mass produce engines in one country and gear boxes in another and to assemble its cars in several countries. Investment decisions by multi-national companies are often influenced by trade barriers. If a country has a high tariff on imported electrical appliances an international company making these goods may decide to set up an assembly plant within that country in order to avoid the high costs of importing its products.

In most countries in which they operate, multi-national companies are usually important exporters. This is because their products have world-famous names and the enterprises have well-established world-wide networks of factories, agencies, distribution channels, servicing organizations and so on.

11   Distribution

The process of production does not end until the product is in the hands of the consumer. Most of the subjects we have discussed up to this point have been concerned with problems of 'making' or creating goods and services. There is, however, a large sector of the economy, employing nearly 3 million people, which is concerned with bringing the products to the consumer. This particular economic activity is usually described as *distribution*.

The pattern of distribution

Goods are moved from producer to consumer by a variety of routes.

1   The traditional method is for manufacturers to supply their goods in bulk to wholesalers who then 'break bulk' by distributing relatively small quantities of each type to individual retailers.
2   Recent developments in the structure of the retail trade have led to changes in the pattern of distribution. There are now many very large retail firms each with many retail shops. These organizations are large enough to place bulk orders and deal directly with manufacturers. They have by-passed the independent wholesaler but they have not eliminated the wholesale function because they operate their own warehouses and transport networks.
3   In some cases, the manufacturing, wholesale and retail stages are integrated within a single firm. As noted earlier, many breweries sell through their own public houses and oil companies both manufacture and distribute petrol.
4   One chain of distribution by-passes the traditional retail outlet. Mail order firms deal directly with households and use large expensively produced catalogues as their means of contacting customers and displaying their wares. Local agents working on a part-time basis obtain orders and payments are made through them.

The wholesale trade

The wholesale stage, whether it is carried out by an independent wholesaler or contained within the large integrated firm, is a most important link in the total production process. The wholesaler helps to solve the basic problem of distribution which arises from the fact that producers wish to supply on a large scale and to dispose of their goods as quickly as possible. Consumers, on the other hand, wish to buy small quantities of a variety of goods as and when they need them. Wholesalers provide a number of services which help the producers to sell in bulk and enable the retailers to meet the consumers' demands for (a) small quantities and (b) a variety of goods from which to choose.

1 Breaking bulk

Wholesalers buy large quantities and divide these into smaller quantities for distribution to retailers. A single delivery from the wholesaler can supply the retailer with a variety of goods made by different manufacturers. The existence of a wholesale stage leads to a great saving in transport costs. This is demonstrated in Fig. 11.1 which shows (a) distribution with no wholesale stage and (b) distribution with a wholesale stage.

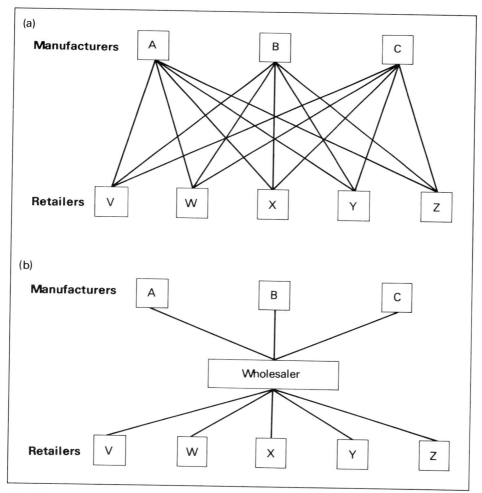

Fig. 11.1

2 Holding stocks

Consumers normally expect to obtain a commodity just when they require it and in order to provide this service someone must hold stocks. Retailers, with limited space and limited financial resources cannot hold sufficient stocks to meet all possible demands. Wholesalers, by carrying large stocks, enable the retailers to meet unexpected and exceptional demands often within a matter of hours. The holding of stocks is a capital-intensive activity, because large sums of money are 'tied up' in the stocks held by wholesalers.

3 Information and advice

The wholesaler's warehouse is often an important display and advice centre. Retailers visit these warehouses to inspect new products and to obtain information and advice on the range of goods available. They do not have to visit a large number of different manufacturers for these purposes. These contacts also enable the wholesaler to feed back useful information to the manufacturers.

4 Bearing risks

The holding of large stocks brings with it the risks that the goods held may fall in price, go out of fashion or, perhaps, deteriorate. On the other hand the stocks may increase in value and so increase the wholesaler's profits. Wholesalers also carry the risk of default by retailers since they normally supply goods on credit and many retailers are very small and vulnerable firms.

The retail trade

The retail stage is the last link in the chain of production. Retailers provide consumers with the important service of making a variety of goods and services available locally. They provide producers with convenient outlets to the buying public. They also perform an important marketing function for producers by displaying their goods and offering advice on them. Where products are bulky and heavy, retailers normally offer a delivery service and where the products are of a technical nature they provide after-sales services.

Types of retail outlet

In its widest sense retailing embraces all the activities which provide goods and services directly to the general public. Apart from shops it includes public houses, garages, launderettes, street markets and so on. In this section we shall confine ourselves to the various types of retail shops and mail order houses.

1   Independent retailers

Numerically these are the most important form of retail outlet and although their share of the market has been declining (see Fig. 11.2) they still account for a substantial share of the total value of retail sales. Independents are usually sole traders or 'one-shop' firms. They offer the consumer the convenience of the near-by shop and the service is often based on the shopkeepers' personal knowledge of their customers. The small local shops often remain open for much longer hours than the larger city-centre stores.

2   Voluntary groups

Serious competition from larger firms has forced many independent retailers to join one of the voluntary groups (or chains) such as Mace, Spar or Wavy Line. A voluntary association of small retailers acting as a single buyer is able to purchase goods in bulk and obtain discounts similar to those obtained by the large retail organizations. These groups carry out the wholesale function, market many of their own brands and often undertake national advertising.

3   Multiple shops (chain stores)

These are organizations with a fairly large number of shops. Each organization usually has its own particular style of shop front and interior layout so that they are easily identifiable in all the larger towns. Some of them such as Burtons (the tailors), Halfords and W.H. Smith tend to specialize in a particular range of goods while others such as Woolworths, Marks and Spencer, Boots and Littlewoods market a much wider range of commodities. Fig. 11.2 demonstrates the success of the multiples in increasing their share of the total retail market in recent years. This success has been based largely on the ability of these firms to achieve economies of scale. They buy in large quantities; carry out their own wholesaling; employ specialist buyers and marketing experts; establish nationally-known brand names; operate centralized administrative and financial control and they are able to raise funds on the security of their valuable city-centre properties.

4   Department stores

Most larger towns have one or more department stores. In effect a department store comprises several specialist shops under one roof. Harrods, Lewis's, Selfridges and Debenhams are well-known names in this field. Most of the larger cooperative retail societies also have department stores. These shops carry a wide range of goods which are sold in large specialized departments (e.g. furniture, carpets, clothing, electrical goods and bedding departments). They also offer many services within the store such as catering, banking, hire-purchase, hairdressing, theatre and holiday booking agencies and so on. The variety of goods and services available within the one store offers consumers the attractive prospect of doing all or most of their shopping in one building. Although department stores sell a variety of goods, most of them belong to one or other of a number of very large organizations which are able to make bulk purchases of the different lines stocked by the stores.

5 Supermarkets

A supermarket is generally defined as a self-service food store with a sales area in excess of 2000 square feet (190 m^2). The use of the techniques of self-service and self-selection has enabled retailers to obtain impressive gains in productivity by substituting capital and land for labour. The number of supermarkets increased rapidly during the 1960s and 1970s and the average size of supermarkets has been steadily increasing. Many of the larger ones are controlled by multiple firms such as Sainsburys, Tesco and Fine Fare.

Supermarkets, however, are now much more than grocery shops because they have diversified into wines and spirits, electrical goods, clothing, DIY materials and a wide range of household utensils and equipment. This process has led to the development of the *superstore* which is defined as a supermarket with a sales area in excess of 25 000 square feet (2300 m^2) and in which food might occupy less than one-half of the selling space.

Supermarkets concentrate on commodities which have a rapid turnover, that is, they aim to 'turn over' their stocks as quickly as possible. In this context,

$$\text{Turnover} = \frac{\text{Value of sales per annum}}{\text{Average value of stocks held}}$$

Thus, if a store achieves annual sales valued at £1 000 000 and the average value of stocks held in the store is £100 000, the rate of turnover is 10. Supermarkets buy in bulk, carry out their own wholesaling and packaging, advertise nationally and market many of their own brands. A further development of the supermarket is the *hypermarket*, defined as a single-storey retail outlet with at least 50 000 square feet (4650 m^2) of selling area. These very large self-service stores are usually established on the outskirts of towns on sites which enable them to offer extensive car-parking facilities.

6 Discount stores

Discount stores are large 'retail warehouses' in the sense that they usually occupy large single-storey premises away from city centres and sell on a cash and carry basis. They deal in consumer durables and several of them specialize in domestic electrical appliances. By providing minimal services they operate with low labour costs and their premises are relatively cheap to build and maintain compared with the large city-centre stores.

7 Mail order houses

Mail order firms sell a range of goods similar to those found in a department store. All transactions with customers are conducted by post. Local agents working on a commission basis use colourful and attractive catalogues to obtain orders for goods which can normally be purchased in instalments. Customers are offered the convenience of 'shopping in their own home'. Although postal distribution is relatively expensive, mail order firms obtain economies of scale by bulk buying and usually occupy out-of-town premises with low overheads (i.e. rent, rates, maintenance and depreciation).

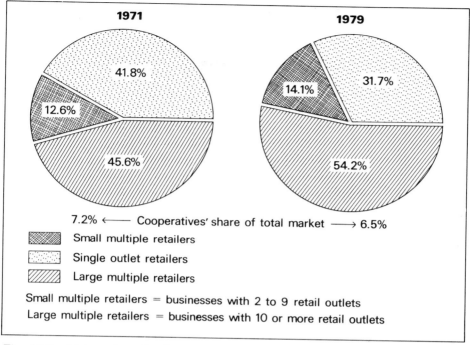

Fig. 11.2   *Value of retail sales*

Sources: *British Business*, 29 May 1981; *Annual Abstract of Statistics*, HMSO, 1981.

The changing structure of retailing

Over the past two decades there has been something of a revolution in the structure of the distributive trades. The main feature has been the very marked trand towards the large-scale self-service enterprises. There are several factors which account for this development.

1   The abolition of Resale Price Maintenance (RPM)

The Resale Prices Act of 1964 led to the virtual abandonment of RPM and this opened the way for keen price competition among retail shops. For many years before the 1964 Act, manufacturers had been able to fix the retail prices for their products so that there was little or no price competition at the retail stage. The same good was sold at the same price in all retail outlets. The more efficient retailers could not demonstrate their superiority by charging lower prices. Once the practice of RPM was abandoned, however, the scope for economies of scale in retailing was quickly revealed by the growth of the multiples and supermarkets. These organizations, operating with lower average costs, were able to charge lower prices.

2 Improved marketing techniques

The introduction of cheap, lightweight, plastic wrapping materials made it possible to standardize and pre-pack a whole range of goods and especially foodstuffs. Large-scale advertising created mass markets for these products. The familiarity of brand names and the pre-packing and labelling of all kinds of goods made possible the great expansion of self-service retailing. The introduction of frozen foods also gave advantages to the larger firm, which could undertake the heavy capital investment in the specialized equipment needed to store, transport and retail these goods. The multiples and supermarkets, because of their ability to place large orders, are able to exercise considerable power over their suppliers; they can demand preferential treatment in matters such as quality, price and delivery.

3 Social factors

Bulk buying has become a common feature of household shopping. Two developments have been particularly important in bringing about the changes in shopping habits. There has been a steady increase in the number of married women who go out to work. In 1961 about 30 per cent of married women had jobs outside the home, but in 1980 this percentage was rather more than 50 per cent. For many of these working wives, a weekly visit to the supermarket is more convenient than the older custom of daily shopping for small quantities in a number of different local shops. The second important development has been the increasing extent of car ownership. Rather more than 60 per cent of households in the UK has the use of a car. One shopping expedition to the supermarket using the car as a means of transport is sufficient for the family to satisfy its demands for grocery and household goods for a week or even longer, especially where the family is equipped with a deep freeze.

The wider ownership of cars is, of course, due to rising real incomes and this feature is also responsible for the fact that a greater proportion of consumer expenditure is being devoted to consumer durables. This has also helped to increase the sales of the multiples, discount stores and mail order houses. The survival of so many independents, however, indicates that the services they provide are still in great demand.

12 The location of industry

Industrial location and production costs

One of the important decisions to be taken when an entrepreneur is starting in business or thinking about expansion, is where to locate the firm (or the new branch of the firm). Although social and political factors play a part in such decisions (e.g. the management might prefer to live in a particular part of the country), there are some very important economic considerations which influence the choice of the site. These will be mainly concerned with the effects of different locations on the costs of production. We assume that the firm will be attracted to that location which minimizes its costs of production.

1 Transport costs

The two principal ways in which transport costs affect the location of an industry are in the movement of its raw materials and in the movement of its finished product. In other words, it is faced with the choice of a site near to its suppliers or a site near to its markets. The strength of the attractions of these alternative sites depends very much on the nature of the process carried out by the industry.

If the raw materials are bulky, heavy and costly to transport while the finished product is light, compact and relatively cheap to transport, the industry will be pulled towards the sources of its raw materials. This factor largely explains the location of industry on the coalfields in the early days of industrialization. Coal was the main source of energy and it is relatively costly to transport.

When the process carried out greatly reduces the weight and bulk of the materials used in production, the quantity to be transported will be much less when the industry is located near the source of the raw materials. This is the case in the production of sugar from sugar beet, the processing of iron ore and in the burning of coal as a source of energy. We can also see why industries which use bulky and heavy imported materials will be attracted to ports in order to minimize transport costs.

Where the transport costs of finished goods are much higher than those for the basic materials there will be a strong attraction to locations near to the market. This will be the case where the manufacturing process increases bulk as it does in industries producing furniture and domestic appliances such as freezers and washing machines, and in the baking of bread. Transport costs will also be relatively high where the product is fragile or perishable. These features partly explain the attraction of London as a location for the furniture trade, the radio and television manufacturers and for the great wholesale markets in fresh foodstuffs.

In more recent years, however, the relative importance of transport costs has declined for two main reasons. Firstly, there has been a steady improvement in transport facilities: in the means of carriage (lorries, ships, planes); in the techniques of handling (e.g. fork-lifts, containers); and in the transport networks (motorways, sea ferries). Secondly, the industrial structure has been changing; the heavy industries have become relatively less important and the newer industries produce goods for which transport costs are less significant. The substitution of electricity, gas and oil for coal has removed the attraction of coalfield locations.

2   The price and availability of labour

Supplies of capital and land are not usually important determinants of location as far as manufacturing and commercial activities are concerned; these factors are normally available in a number of alternative locations. Labour, however, as we have seen earlier (page 53) is relatively immobile in the short run. This immobility may mean that labour is in surplus in some regions but in short supply in other areas. Although trade unions usually negotiate national wage rates, labour costs might be higher in areas of labour shortage as firms are obliged to pay bonuses of various kinds in order to obtain and hold on to their supplies of labour. If there are regional differences in the availability and costs of labour these will clearly influence a firm's decision on the location of its plant.

The availability of labour with particular skills is also important to firms in industries such as pottery, metal working trades, engineering and some sections of the textile and clothing industries. This is a major reason why new firms tend to be drawn to the established centres of particular industries. Centres of heavy industry will tend to have a surplus of female labour and this will attract industries which use predominantly female labour such as textiles and the assembly of light electrical equipment.

3   Acquired advantages

In the past, industries may well have been attracted to a particular location by the natural advantages of a site such as the availability of raw materials or access to sources of energy (coal or water) or because of favourable climatic conditions. But even when these natural advantages have disappeared (e.g. the exhaustion of some mineral deposit) or have become unimportant (e.g. proximity to coal supplies), the concentration of an industry in a particular region yields important benefits of its own. These advantages are not natural, they are acquired and develop as the industry grows larger. They have already been explained in Chapter 6 under the heading 'External economies of scale'.

Industrial location and government policy

In the UK and in most other developed countries, the geographical distribution of industry is not decided entirely by market forces; the managers of a firm are not free to decide the location of new factories. The government exercises a considerable degree of control over industrial location and has a variety of

Fig. 12.1   Regional unemployment, UK, May 1981

Source: *Dept. of Employment Gazette*, HMSO, June 1981.

107

ways of influencing the siting of a new enterprise. There are several reasons why governments have decided to control the geographical distribution of industry.

1 Between the two world wars, different regions in the UK experienced very different unemployment rates. There were times when the unemployment rate in some towns exceeded 50 per cent while in others it was less than 10 per cent. Regional differences in unemployment rates have persisted since the Second World War although the actual levels of unemployment have been smaller (see Fig. 12.1). The relatively higher rates of unemployment are found mainly in those regions which, in the nineteenth century, were dominated by the older staple industries (e.g. coal, cotton, steel and shipbuilding). Employment in these industries began to decline after the First World War because (a) they had lost important overseas markets (e.g. cotton and coal) or (b) technical progress had produced new and superior substitutes (e.g. oil for coal) or (c) new techniques led to a massive replacement of labour by capital (e.g. mining and steel). The situation was made even more serious because the newer industries (e.g. electrical goods, motor cars, food processing) tended to choose locations in the Midlands[1] and the South East whereas the older industries had been concentrated in Northern England, South Wales and Central Scotland.

2 A firm setting up a new factory does not incur all the costs of establishing the enterprise. Some of the costs fall on the community. A new factory (or factories) might lead to increased congestion which in turn leads to increased expenditure on roads and perhaps on the provision of more houses and schools.

3 A heavy localization of industry also leads to the growth of sprawling conurbations such as we now have in London, Glasgow, Birmingham and Manchester.

4 The concentration of a major industry in one region means that the prosperity of that region is heavily dependent upon the fortunes of that one industry.

The regional problem

These factors and others have given rise to what is known as the regional problem. Prosperous areas tend to become more attractive as industrial locations while declining areas become less and less attractive. An expanding industrial centre will develop a skilled labour force, good transport links, a network of suppliers and the high level of incomes in that area will attract a variety of service industries. On the other hand declining regions with falling incomes will tend to lose the young and qualified people on whom the future development of the region depends.

[1] The recent and severe decline in the demand for British motor cars has had a serious effect on employment in the West Midlands (see Fig. 12.1).

Geographical immobility of labour, however, may well lead to a situation where there is unemployment in some areas and labour shortages in others; this represents a waste of valuable resources. If there is a serious drift of population to the more prosperous areas, it will give rise to congestion and shortages of accommodation in these areas. There will be demands for more houses, schools, hospitals, libraries and so on in the high employment areas while these forms of social capital may not be fully utilized in the declining areas. To some extent this problem is revealed by the great differences in the prices of land and houses in the South East of England when compared with those in Northern England.

Regional policy

Government regional policy is aimed primarily at improving the employment situation in the less prosperous areas. By increasing the variety of industrial and commercial activities in each region, it also hopes to reduce the dependence of any one region on one particular industry. Regional policy is also concerned with reducing the overcrowding and congestion in the great conurbations. In the post-war period a number of New Towns have been established in order to draw people and industry away from the great cities. There are two main ways of dealing with regional differences in unemployment rates.

1 'Taking workers to the work'. The government might by various means such as the payment of removal expenses and assistance with housing, encourage a movement of workers from the depressed regions to the prosperous areas. While such assistance is provided in the UK, there are great problems in implementing such a policy. As already noted (page 53) there are serious barriers to the geographical mobility of labour, not least of which is the shortage of rented accommodation. Such a movement of labour would also hasten the decline of the less prosperous regions.

2 'Taking work to the workers'. Most of the government's measures to deal with the regional problem tend to concentrate on persuading new industry to move into the areas with relatively high unemployment rates. These measures are outlined below.

Assisted areas

For purposes of regional policy, certain parts of the country have been identified as in special need of government aid. These are the assisted areas, of which there are three categories.

1 Development areas
These are mainly the older industrial areas where major industries have been declining for many years. They cover large areas of Scotland, Wales, Northern

England and some parts of Devon and Cornwall. Northern Ireland is also a development area.

2   Special development areas

These are much smaller regions, usually within the development areas, where there are particularly acute problems caused by such things as closures of collieries, steelworks or shipbuilding yards. These areas are found in the Scottish and Northern regions, in Merseyside and North and South Wales. Some parts of Devon and Cornwall are also classed as special development areas.

3   Intermediate areas

These regions lie on the fringes of the development areas and have similar but not such severe problems. Before they were brought into the scheme, they suffered because they did not qualify for the assistance available in the development areas but they could not offer the advantages of locations in the more prosperous areas.

In 1979 some 40 per cent of the employed population lived in assisted areas, but policy changes announced in that year aimed to reduce the areas qualifying for assistance and, when implemented, the new measures will reduce the proportion of the labour force in assisted areas to about 25 per cent.

Forms of aid

In order to encourage firms to move into the assisted areas, the government uses a variety of financial incentives.

1   The Department of Industry has powers to erect new factories in the assisted areas and then rent or sell them on very favourable terms. In some cases these factories may be offered rent-free for a limited time.
2   Government grants are available to help meet the cost of training local labour for new jobs and to cover the costs of moving key workers, stocks and essential machinery into the assisted areas.
3   Service industries moving to assisted areas also qualify for government aid in the form of rent subsidies and removal grants and grants in respect of each new job created.
4   In the placing of government contracts, preferential treatment may be given to firms in assisted areas.
5   The most important financial inducement takes the form of regional development grants on new plant and equipment and on new buildings. In 1981 these grants were payable as follows.

Regional development grants (% of total cost)

	Special development areas	Development areas	Intermediate areas
Buildings	22	15	nil
Machinery and equipment	22	15	nil

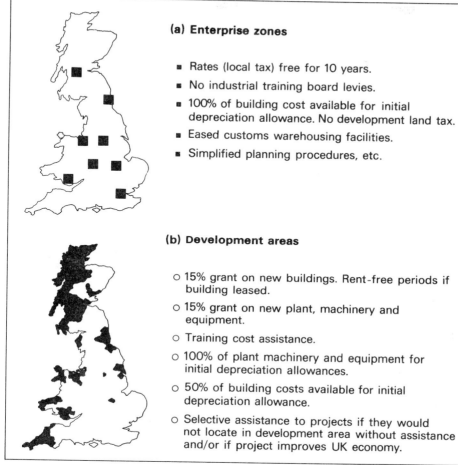

(a) Enterprise zones

- Rates (local tax) free for 10 years.
- No industrial training board levies.
- 100% of building cost available for initial depreciation allowance. No development land tax.
- Eased customs warehousing facilities.
- Simplified planning procedures, etc.

(b) Development areas

○ 15% grant on new buildings. Rent-free periods if building leased.
○ 15% grant on new plant, machinery and equipment.
○ Training cost assistance.
○ 100% of plant machinery and equipment for initial depreciation allowances.
○ 50% of building costs available for initial depreciation allowance.
○ Selective assistance to projects if they would not locate in development area without assistance and/or if project improves UK economy.

Fig. 12.2

Source: Fig. 12.2 is based on an advertisement by the Corby Industrial Development Centre.

6 As a result of membership of the European Economic Community, the assisted areas in the UK qualify for aid from the Community. Grants and loans have been received from the European Regional Fund, the European Investment Bank, the European Social Fund and the European Coal and Steel Community (see pages 284–5).

Planning controls

The measures outlined above take the form of inducements. The Town and Country Planning Acts give the government powers to influence industrial

111

location in a more negative manner. Industrial development in the UK can only be carried out if the local authority grants planning permission and this permission can only be granted if the Department of Industry has approved the project and issued an Industrial Development Certificate (IDC). IDCs are not required for projects in any of the assisted areas but they are required in all the non-assisted areas for premises above 50 000 square feet (4650 m^2). The idea of this scheme is that by making it difficult for a firm to obtain planning permission for new developments in areas with high levels of employment, it might be persuaded to go to an assisted area.

Enterprise zones

In 1980 the government announced plans to deal with the serious problems of decline and decay in the centres of many large industrial cities. Demolition of slums and older industrial and commercial properties had not been followed up by redevelopment and many large cities had central areas which were becoming less and less attractive to new enterprises. The government proposed to set up 'enterprise zones' in a number of cities and to provide various inducements for firms to move back into city centres. Such firms are promised exemption from rates, very favourable tax treatment of capital expenditures, exemption from the requirement to obtain IDCs, speedy planning approvals and exemption from any training levy by Industrial Training Boards.

Effects of regional policy

Some critics of regional policy argue that the pressures and inducements which persuade firms to choose locations in assisted areas rather than in the well-established centres of the industry (e.g. a car firm building a factory in Scotland rather than Coventry) have led to an increase in the average costs of production. The basis of this argument, of course, is that these plants are not able to obtain the external economies of scale which are available in the areas where most of the industry is concentrated. The fact that the government has to offer such large and varied financial inducements seems to indicate that the firms themselves are, in general, reluctant to move to the assisted areas. Regional policy will mainly affect the established large firms who wish to expand their existing plant. If this is in a non-assisted area they are likely to be refused an IDC, but they will be offered a great deal of government help if they choose to build a branch factory in an assisted area. The branch factory operating many miles from the parent factory, however, may be a higher cost alternative to an extension of the main plant. This argument, of course, does not take account of the social benefits of increased employment in the development areas or the social costs of allowing the parent plant to be extended in a prosperous area. It may also be true that if a sufficient number of new enterprises can be established in a particular location, then that area might well begin to generate its own advantages (i.e. external economies of scale).

Another major criticism of regional policy is that the system of capital grants has been particularly attractive to those firms which use a lot of capital relative to labour. The policy, therefore, has attracted some firms to assisted areas which have received large government grants but which have created relatively few jobs (e.g. chemical plants and the installations of oil companies). It has also been argued that the refusal to grant an IDC may lead to a firm cancelling its plans for expansion or perhaps it may consider the alternative form of expansion and take over another firm in its own locality.

As against these arguments, studies have shown that firms in many industries are 'mobile' in the sense that different locations do not have any great effects on their costs of production so that a movement to an assisted area would not be cost-increasing. We must also bear in mind the fact that the true cost of the government measures to attract firms to assisted areas is very much less than the total amount spent on grants and other forms of financial assistance. The creation of jobs brings about a fall in government spending on unemployment pay and other social security benefits. Although the differences in regional unemployment rates remain, there seems little doubt that government policies have had a considerable impact. In the 1960s, for example, it is estimated that the various measures were responsible for the creation of about 220 000 jobs in the assisted areas.

13 Government and industry

The UK, like most Western industrialized countries, has a mixed economy. Some firms (e.g. the public corporations) are publicly owned, many firms are privately owned and some (e.g. British Petroleum) are both privately and publicly owned (i.e. the state holds a substantial proportion of the shares).

The public sector comprises central government, local government and the public corporations. In 1980, out of a total employed labour force of 25 million, the public sector employed about 7.3 million distributed as follows:

a   some 2 million in the public corporations;
b   about 2.3 million in central government;
c   approximately 3 million in local government.

But even in the private sector of industry there is a great deal of government activity in the form of various controls, financial incentives and other forms of assistance. The fact that the government has accepted responsibility for the overall performance of the economy (and especially for the level of unemployment) has tended to lead to an increasing role[1] for the government in influencing the structure and efficiency of British industry.

The government's industrial policies

1 Public ownership

Since the Second World War a relatively large sector of the British economy has been taken into public ownership. The subject of nationalization is discussed in some detail later in this chapter.

2 Industrial location

A large part of the government aid to industry is devoted to reviving industrial activity in the assisted areas (see Table 8). The government's regional policy is also aimed at reducing congestion in the great conurbations, the redevelopment of inner city areas and at providing a more balanced industrial structure in the various regions. These topics were discussed in Chapter 12.

3 Restructuring industry

The government has provided substantial financial assistance to industries in decline and to those badly hit by foreign competition (e.g. shipbuilding, motor cars and aircraft) in order to help them with restructuring and modernization

[1] The conservative government elected in 1979 was pledged to reduce the size of the public sector.

programmes. The government also attempts to increase industrial efficiency by providing finance for research and development. In the UK, about one-half of all expenditure on research and development (whether carried out in the private or public sectors) is financed by the government. Public money is also used to enable firms to launch new products, for example, large sums were provided in order to develop Concorde and, more recently, the government has supplied funds to establish facilities for the production of micro-chips.

An important institution with responsibilities for improving the efficiency and structure of industry is the *National Enterprise Board* (*NEB*). This public corporation was set up by the government in 1975 with funds (potentially £1000 million) for investment in industry. Its aims are to provide finance to assist promising firms, to promote mergers where it believes they will improve performance and to encourage the development of new technology. It buys shares in the companies it assists and may also play a part in the management of such firms. The NEB may also take a company completely into public ownership. Its main aim is to promote the reorganization of industry with a view to greater efficiency. It also has the task of holding and managing the government's investments in private industry. The NEB is expected to earn a reasonable rate of profit on its investments, but where it is called upon to help an ailing firm it receives compensation from the government. The Conservative government elected in 1979 proposed to reduce the powers of the NEB to intervene in private industry and aimed to restrict its role to that of a holding company.

4 Selective financial assistance

The 1972 Industry Act gives the government wide powers to offer selective financial assistance to firms in both the assisted and non-assisted areas. Each case is judged on its merits. The aim is to encourage investment that otherwise would not have taken place and to persuade firms to bring forward their investment plans. Assistance under this Act has been given to large firms in financial difficulties (e.g. British Leyland). There is also a scheme to provide help to individual industries where they are undertaking modernization programmes. Selective assistance is available in the assisted areas for projects which create additional employment or which help to maintain existing employment.

Table 8 Department of Industry aid (£ million)

	1980–81
Regional development grants	337
Provision for land and buildings	21
Selective assistance to industry in assisted areas	24
Selective assistance to individual industries and firms	79
Funds for the NEB	278
Scientific and technological assistance	142
Support for aerospace, shipbuilding and steel	191
	1072

Source: *Financial Times*, 1 August 1980.

5 Industrial training

The government recognizes the need for a mobile and skilled labour force and in recent years there has been a great expansion of government-financed and government-sponsored training schemes. These cover both the training of apprentices and the retraining of redundant workers (see page 327).

6 Planning, consultation and advisory services

The relationships between government and industry are not entirely formal – they do not consist solely of controls and regulations. In the UK, the government's industrial policies rely a great deal on consultations and voluntary agreements between the three parties most concerned, namely, employers, trade unions and the government. Employers are represented by the Confederation of British Industry (the CBI) and labour by the Trades Union Congress (the TUC).

These three groups are represented on the *National Economic Development Council* (NEDC). This is an important body which undertakes studies of national economic problems (e.g. the rate of economic growth) and the problems of particular industries or particular aspects of the economy (e.g. rising imports or low productivity). It publishes details of its analysis and makes recommendations on the nature of the changes it would like to see carried out. The NEDC is an important part of the British planning mechanism. It does not have the powers to enforce its recommendations; it merely *indicates* the targets which it thinks are desirable and attainable. The government will frame its policies so as to facilitate the achievement of these targets and attempts, through the NEDC and by other forms of consultation and persuasion, to get both sides of industry to cooperate in meeting these targets (e.g. a higher level of exports or a faster rate of economic growth).

The work of the NEDC is supplemented by a number of Economic Development Committees (EDCs) and, more recently, by Sector Working Parties (SWPs). These committees have members drawn from trade unions and management and each of them concentrates on the problems of a particular industry or sector of an industry. They consider such matters as export performance, import trends, potential future markets, labour and training requirements, investment, the effects of taxation policy and so on. They recommend appropriate government policies and by means of consultation with the management and workers of the firms concerned try to bring about improvements in industrial performance.

These planning bodies are increasingly concerned with trying to get government and industry to work together on long-term plans. In the recent past, frequent changes in government economic policy have made it difficult for industry to plan ahead with any great degree of confidence.

The government is also active in operating or supporting a large number of agencies which provide assistance to industry in the form of training, advice, publicity and so on in respect of such matters as industrial relations, exporting, marketing, problems of the small firm and the recruitment of labour.

Nationalization

In the UK, the nationalized industries employ about 7 per cent of the nation's labour force and account for about 15 per cent of total fixed investment. The four largest employers in the country (after central government) are nationalized industries. These industries supply basic goods and services to industry and essentials of life to individual consumers. They produce about 10 per cent of the total output of the UK economy. The nationalized industries account for about one-third of all the plant and equipment bought by British industry and for several sectors of industry they are the sole domestic customer (e.g. coal-cutting equipment, heavy electrical cables, specialized telephone equipment). They dominate four important sectors of the economy.
1 Energy: coal, gas, electricity and a part of North Sea oil.
2 Public transport: railways, airlines, bus services, waterways, docks, air-ports, and a part of road haulage.
3 Communications: postal and telephone services.
4 Iron and steel.
In addition to these, the aerospace and shipbuilding industries are publicly owned. Public ownership of the 'basic industries' is a common feature of most industrialized countries in Europe (see Fig. 13.1).

Arguments for nationalization

Most of the UK nationalized industries were formerly under private ownership and the majority of them have been purchased by the state in the years since the Second World War. A variety of arguments have been used to support the transfer of industries from private to public ownership.

1 'Natural' monopolies
The industries which supply gas, water, electricity and telephone services are capital-intensive. They need a vast network of cables or pipes in order to supply their customers. In addition, such things as power stations, reservoirs and telephone exchanges also require a heavy investment in capital equipment. This means that these industries can only achieve a relatively low average cost if this capital is used to the fullest possible extent. Competition in such industries would lead to a duplication of costly installations and hence a wasteful use of economic resources.

This is, of course, an argument for monopoly (i.e. a sole supplier) rather than an argument for nationalization. The argument for public ownership rests on the fact that monopoly control over the supply of such things as electricity,

117

Privately owned : ◯ all or nearly all

Publicly owned : ◔ 25% ◑ 50% ◕ 75% ● all or nearly all

	Postal services	Telecommunications	Electricity	Gas	Railways	Coal	Airlines	Motor industry	Steel	Shipbuilding
Austria	●	●	●	●	●	●	●	●	◕	N/A
Belgium	●	●	◔	◔	●	◯	●	◯	◯	◯
United Kingdom	●	●	●	●	●	●	◕	◑	◕	●
France	●	●	●	●	●	●	◕	◑	◯	◯
W. Germany	●	●	◔	◑	●	◑	●	◔	◔	◔
Netherlands	●	●	◕	◕	●	N/A	◕	◯	◔	◯
Italy	●	●	◕	●	●	N/A	●	◑	◑	◕
Spain	●	◔	◯	◑	●	◑	●	◯	◕	◕
Sweden	●	●	◑	●	●	N/A	◑	◯	◕	◕
Switzerland	●	●	●	●	●	N/A	◯	◯	◯	N/A

Fig. 13.1   *Ownership of the basic industries*

Source: *The Economist*, 4 March 1978.

gas, water and communications gives the suppliers the power to exploit consumers by charging prices well above the costs of production. Those who support nationalization argue that the only effective way of preventing such exploitation is to have publicly-owned monopolies in industries such as those mentioned above. It is also argued that industries supplying products or services which are essential to the operations of other industries, as well as being necessities to householders, should be run in the national interest rather than for private profit.

2   Modernization and restructuring of industry

When a major industry has been experiencing a steady decline in demand, it may, after several years of low profits (or losses) find it difficult to attract funds to finance modernization and reorganization (e.g. integration into fewer and larger units). The government might think, however, that the industry is important to the future development of the economy and, with the necessary injection of capital, it might have a successful future. The government might then decide that the only way in which the necessary money can be provided and the reorganization carried out is by transferring the whole industry to public ownership. Arguments such as this were used to support the nationalization of coal, railways, shipbuilding and, to some extent, steel.

3   To help manage the economy

A further argument for having a number of large and important industries under public ownership is that it provides the government with a most direct means of influencing the performance of the whole economy. The government has powers to modify the investment plans, the location decisions, the purchasing plans, and the prices and employment policies of the nationalized industries. Since these industries are so large, their activities affect all the other sectors of the economy.

4   Social costs and benefits

The Acts of Parliament which established the nationalized industries direct that they should be run 'in the public interest'. Many people understand this to mean that the managements of these industries should not aim solely at *economic* efficiency. They should not aim to operate at the lowest possible cost or to earn the maximum rate of profit. Nationalized industries are expected to take more account of the *social* effects of their activities than would be the case with a privately owned enterprise. Thus, a nationalized industry would be expected to recognize the social benefits as well as the private benefits of its operations. It might make a loss on a new underground line, but the social benefits of reduced congestion in the city streets may be considered to be of greater value than the operating losses. Similarly loss-making pits may be kept open because the social costs of closures may be thought to be greater than the private benefits of closing the mines.

5   Political arguments

For a large number of people, the main arguments for nationalization are political rather than economic. Taking industry into public ownership is seen by socialists and others as an important part of a policy for reducing the inequalities of income and wealth. It is also seen as an essential feature of a democratic society because, it is believed by many people, the means of production (land and capital) should be owned and controlled by those who work with these resources to create income and wealth. Many socialists believe, however, that the state-owned industries in many countries are now so large and bureaucratic that workers are able to exercise very little control over the way they are run.

Efficiency and pricing policy

Most of the nationalized industries are monopolies; they are the sole suppliers of the particular goods or services which they produce. They do not have to compete in the capital markets in order to raise the money they need for investment (they borrow from the government). It is, therefore, not possible to judge the efficiency of these industries against the performance of enterprises operating in competitive markets. Profits and losses are not necessarily a good guide to their efficiency. A monopoly is often able to raise prices and earn profits even though production is being carried on inefficiently. Similarly, losses do not necessarily indicate inefficiency, because, as we have mentioned earlier, they may be due to government policy which holds down the prices of the nationalized industries.

Table 9 Nationalized industries in the UK, 1978–79

	Turnover (£ million)	Capital employed (£ million)	Labour force (thousands)
British Aerospace	894	322	70
British Airports Authority	162	348	7
British Airways	1 640	793	58
British Gas	2 972	2 181	103
British National Oil Corporation	432	751	1
British Rail	1 979	1 743	243
British Shipbuilders	810	72	82
British Steel	3 288	4 020	186
British Transport Docks Board	120	177	12
British Waterways	12	13	3
Electricity Council and Boards	5 116	6 801	160
National Bus	437	199	64
National Coal Board	2 989	1 733	235
National Freight Corporation	394	91	36
North of Scotland Hydroelectric Board	173	556	4
Post Office	4 619	7 469	411
Scottish Transport	106	80	14
South of Scotland Electricity Board	463	713	14
	26 606	28 062	1 703

Source: *The Economist*, 15 March 1980.

Problems arise with regard to prices when nationalized industries are obliged, for social reasons, to operate uneconomic activities such as working uneconomic pits, running a loss-making railway line or operating a steelworks which is well below optimum size. These things are usually done in order to prevent a worsening of the unemployment situation in an assisted area; but who should bear the costs of these policies? If prices are raised throughout the industry so that total revenue covers total costs, the burdens of these social responsibilities would fall on the consumers of the particular goods or services.

For example, the burdens of maintaining employment in uneconomic collieries would fall on the consumers of coal. In the UK, it has now been accepted that these social costs should fall on the whole community and nationalized industries receive government subsidies to cover such costs.

As a means of stimulating economic efficiency in nationalized industries, the UK government has now decided to fix a financial target for each industry. Each public corporation is required to earn a surplus (or profit) equal to some given percentage of the value of the capital employed in the industry. For example, if an industry which employs net assets valued at £2000 million has a financial target of 5 per cent, it will be expected to earn an annual surplus of £100 million. Each nationalized industry has a different target; some are expected to do no more than break even.

Test paper 4

Short-answer questions

1   Give two examples of barriers to the growth of a small firm.

2   Although the motor car industry is dominated by a few giant firms, there are still many small firms making motor cars. Why do these small firms survive?

3   The marketing strategy of a supermarket is said to be based on the principle of 'very low margins and a very high turnover'. What does this mean?

4   A chocolate manufacturing firm is contemplating a merger with a firm making soft drinks. Some critics argue that the proposed merger does not make economic sense because the firms have nothing in common. Can you find arguments to answer these critics?

5   Although a single firm may account for 70 per cent of the total UK output of a commodity, it does not follow that this firm dominates the UK market. Why not?

6   Give (a) two advantages and (b) two disadvantages to the consumer of the small neighbourhood shop as compared with the large supermarket.

7   Why are interest charges such an important item of costs to the wholesaler?

8   In 1971 there were over 500 000 retail outlets in Britain; in 1980 there were less than 390 000. What were the major causes of this change?

9   A merger is proposed between two firms, each controlling a chain of clothing shops. Indicate some possible (a) marketing economies, (b) administrative economies and (c) financial economies, which might result from such a merger.

10   'The *ratios* in which land, labour and capital are combined in the operation of a supermarket are very different from those which apply in the corner shop.' Give examples to illustrate this comment.

11   What are likely to be the main influences on the choice of locations for new plants to manufacture (a) bricks, (b) high quality cutlery and (c) paper?

12   What kind of ancillary services might be provided by firms in an area where a furniture-making industry is heavily localized?

13   a   Why has the government provided each of the nationalized industries with a financial target?

b   'It is true that most nationalized industries are legal monopolies, but this does not mean that they are free from competition.' Explain.

14   Which major industries have declined and caused regional problems? Which areas of the UK have been particularly affected?

15   Give examples of government measures which are aimed at 'taking work to the workers'.

16   In the assisted areas, government assistance is available for improving the infrastructure. What is meant by the infrastructure?

17   A major car firm wishing to expand its plant in a well-established centre of the car industry (e.g. Coventry, Luton, Dagenham) is persuaded instead to open a branch factory on Humberside. What external economies of scale might be foregone as a result of this decision?

18   Why is the *net* cost of government assistance in development areas much less than the *gross* cost?

True or false?

19   **a**   Most firms in the UK are small firms and they also have (in total) more employees than large firms.
b   When the size of the firm is measured in terms of capital employed, the firms in the chemical industry will appear misleadingly small.
c   All the nationalized industries are labour-intensive industries.
d   Difficulties in obtaining Industrial Development Certificates may well have encouraged a number of take-overs and mergers.
e   The introduction of shrink-wrap packaging materials has been an important factor in changing the structure of the grocery trade.
f   In the UK, Marks and Spencer and Boots are typical examples of organizations described as 'multiples'.
g   In contrast to the situation in manufacturing, we find that, in retailing, small businesses still have a very large share of the total business.
h   External economies of scale are only available to the large firm.
i   The NEDC has powers to oblige firms to adopt the policies it recommends.
j   When an industry is described as *footloose* it means that its production costs are not significantly different in different locations.

Multiple-choice questions

20   Which of the following is/are nationalized?
1   BP (British Petroleum)
2   British Oxygen
3   British Rail
A   1, 2 and 3
B   1 and 2 only
C   2 and 3 only
D   1 only
E   3 only

21 Which of the following are recognized functions of wholesalers?
1 to supply retailers with products of different manufacturers
2 to provide retailers with information on, and samples of, the variety of goods available
3 to determine the prices charged by retailers
A 1, 2 and 3
B 1 and 2 only
C 2 and 3 only
D 1 only
E 3 only

Questions 22, 23 and 24 refer to the following terms.
A horizontal integration
B diversification
C rationalization
D vertical integration
E automation
Which of the above describe,
22 one of the incentives for a firm to develop into a multi-product enterprise?
23 the activities of a firm which is reducing its range of products and/or making more specialized use of its capital and labour?
24 the procedure when a chain of clothing stores takes over a hosiery factory?

25 In which of the following industries do a few very large firms account for the greater part of the total output?
A footwear
B clothing
C detergents
D book publishing
E furniture

26 The government expects the nationalized industries to
A maximize profits
B provide a public service and take no account of the losses incurred
C break even in each financial year
D earn a target rate of return (which is the same for each industry) on the net assets employed
E earn a target rate of return (which is different for each industry) on the net assets employed

Questions 27 and 28 refer to the following features of industrial location.
1 the availability of a skilled labour force
2 easily accessible deposits of the raw material required
3 firms in the locality providing repair and other technical services
4 adequate supplies of river water for use in the manufacturing process and for cooling

27 Which of the above are *acquired* advantages?

A 1, 2 and 3
B 2, 3 and 4
C 1 and 3 only
D 2 and 4 only
E 1 and 4 only

28 Which of the above are described as *external economies of scale*?

A 1, 2 and 3
B 2, 3 and 4
C 1 and 3 only
D 2 and 4 only
E 1 and 4 only

Data-response questions

29 'By the early 1970s, control of the brewing industry had been concentrated in a relatively small number of hands as a result of unprecedented and often frantic mergers in the previous decade. Between 1960 and 1970, the number of brewing companies was reduced from 247 to 96 and the number of breweries from 351 to 177. . . . Between 1966 and 1976, the number of brands of beer was halved. . . . In 1952 the largest six brewery companies owned 16 per cent of the nation's pubs; in 1976 they owned 56 per cent.'

Management Today, October 1979.

a What was (i) the number of establishments and (ii) the number of enterprises in the brewing industry in 1970?

b What would have been the main aims in reducing the number of brands of beer?

c Identify the types of integration referred to in the above passage.

d Can you provide any reasons for the remarkable increase in the concentration of ownership in the brewing industry?

30 '*Rising property values have put a premium on selling space*, so retail chains are tending to store their stocks well away from the High Street. This, in turn, has forced them to adopt sophisticated means of getting their goods delivered. They are bypassing wholesalers and dealing directly with manufacturers.'

The Economist, 1 December 1979.

a Explain the statement in italics.

b Can you provide some examples of 'the sophisticated means for getting their goods delivered'?

c Which of the diagrams on page 99 represents the pattern of distribution referred to in the passage? Explain your answer.

14 Population

World population

The population of the world now exceeds 4000 million and it is growing at about 1.8 per cent per annum. This means that the number of people in the world is increasing by more than 70 million every year. This is an exceptionally high rate of growth and has led to the widespread use of the term 'population explosion'.

The human race has been on earth for about one million years and for most of this period its numbers have increased very slowly. Throughout most of their history people lived without the benefits of agricultural technology or effective tools and with no adequate shelter and protection. Life was difficult and dangerous. Birth-rates were high but so were death-rates. Even as late as the eighteenth century life expectancy in Europe was very low, probably about 20 years and about one-quarter of the population died before they reached their first birthday.

Table 10 World population (estimated)

Year	Total population
1 000 000 BC	a few thousand
8000 BC	8 million
1 AD	300 million
1750	800 million
1900	1650 million
1970	3650 million
2000	6300 million

Source: *World Bank*, 1977.

The growth of population

The natural increase of population is measured by the difference between the birth-rate and the death-rate.

crude birth-rate	= number of births per annum per thousand of the population
crude death-rate	= number of deaths per annum per thousand of the population
natural rate of increase	= birth-rate – death-rate

If we take into account the effects of migration (the movement of people from one country to another), then the growth rate is measured as follows:

growth rate = birth-rate – death-rate + net migration

In Europe the rapid growth of population began in the eighteenth century as industrialization gathered momentum and technical progress led to large increases in productivity in both agriculture and industry. Higher real incomes, more adequate nutrition and improvements in transport, sanitation and medicine drastically reduced the extent of famine and disease. Improving living standards led to a fall in the death-rate and population began to grow because birth-rates remained relatively high. The population of Europe trebled during the period 1750 to 1914. Throughout the nineteenth century there was a steady fall in the death-rate, but the birth-rate did not begin to fall until the late 1870s. In the developed countries, the trend in the birth-rate has continued downwards until most of these countries have relatively stable populations with birth-rates only marginally higher than death-rates.

The present great upsurge in population is taking place chiefly in the less developed regions of Asia, Africa and Latin America. It is largely due to applications of medical science which have dramatically reduced the incidence of diseases such as cholera, typhoid, smallpox, and malaria. In these areas, death-rates have fallen much faster than they did in Europe. In the eight years from 1945 to 1953 the fall in the death-rate in Sri Lanka was as great as that which occurred in Sweden between 1771 and 1871. Not only are the growth rates in the less developed world much higher than they are in the developed countries, they are twice as large as the most rapid growth rates ever achieved in the developed world.

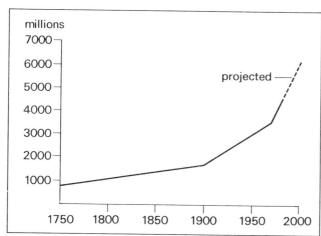

Fig. 14.1   The growth of world population

An examination of the experience of the more advanced countries reveals three stages in population development.
1   High birth-rates and high death-rates – populations growing very slowly.
2   High birth-rates and declining death-rates – populations growing relatively quickly.
3   Low birth-rates and low death-rates – near stationary populations.

The developed world as a whole took about 150 years to pass through these stages. If the less developed world takes about the same time to reach stage 3, the world's population could grow to about 15 000 million before it becomes stationary. This may not happen, of course, and many developing countries are attempting to limit population growth with programmes designed to encourage family planning. There is already evidence of falling birth-rates in many regions of the developing world.

The United Kingdom population

Table 11   UK population

Year	Total population (millions)
1700	6.5 (estimate)
1801	10.5
1851	22.5
1901	38.25
1951	50.2
1979	55.8
2001	57.5 (estimate)

In the nineteenth century, in common with other industrialized countries, the UK population grew fairly rapidly at a rate of about 1.5 per cent per annum. The rate of growth declined during the first half of the twentieth century to about 0.5 per cent per annum. The growth in the UK population was already apparent in the latter part of the eighteenth century and his observations of the conditions prevailing at this time led the Reverend Thomas Malthus to produce his theory of population in a book called *Essay on the Principle of Population* which he published in 1798. He held out a very gloomy prospect for the human race because he believed that the rate at which people are capable and desirous of reproducing themselves will always exceed the rate at which they are capable of increasing the output of goods and services. Malthus thought that, unless people took some *positive* steps to limit the size of their families then *natural* checks such as famine and disease would limit the growth of the population. Malthus's views were clearly based on the Law of Diminishing Returns, that is, an increasing population with limited resources would lead to a lower output per head. He did not forsee, however, the full extent of the technical revolution which offset the application of this law, neither did he foresee the fact that rising living standards eventually bring about a steady fall in the birth-rate. Nevertheless, conditions in many less developed parts of the world at the present time have led several commentators to use Malthus's ideas as a warning against the dangers of overpopulation.

Birth-rates, death-rates and migration

For most of the nineteenth century the UK birth-rate was about 35 per thousand. It began to fall in the last quarter of the nineteenth century and continued to fall until, in the 1930s, it was about 16 per thousand. During and after the Second World War, the birth-rate rose again, reaching 21 per thousand in 1947. It then fell once again, but in the late 1950s and early 1960s it rose until 1964 when a further decline in the birth-rate became apparent. The birth-rate began to rise again in the late 1970s and between 1977 and 1980 it rose from 11.8 to 13.5 per thousand.

The death-rate fell throughout the nineteenth century and the fall was particularly pronounced in the latter part of the century. In fact it offset the fall in the birth-rate so that the population continued to increase. In recent years, the death-rate has been fairly stable at about 12 per thousand (1979).

In the post-war period, natural increase has accounted for the greater part of the changes in the UK population. A further factor affecting the size of the population is migration. For the first thirty years of this century there was a small net outward flow (emigration) of people from Britain. In the 1930s and 1940s there was a small net inward flow (immigration) mainly from Europe and Ireland. In the 1950s the situation changed when the UK attracted immigrants from various Commonwealth countries, but especially from Asia, Africa and the West Indies. A peak was reached in 1961 when net immigration reached 160 000. The Commonwealth Immigration Act of 1962 placed restrictions on immigration and the number of immigrants gradually fell until in 1966 the UK once again became a net emigrant country. Fig. 14.2 provides a picture of the changes in the UK population, but note that the diagram uses the actual *numbers* of births and deaths and not the birth- and death-*rates*.

Sex distribution

The ratio of male births to female births varies little from 106:100 yet, in the total UK population there are more females than males. In 1980 there were approximately 105 females to every 100 males. But this overall figure is misleading. It arises because (a) historically, infant[1] mortality among male babies has been higher than among female babies and (b) the life expectancy of women is higher than it is for men.

A decrease in male infant mortality has brought about a significant change in the sex distribution of the population. Males now exceed females in every age group up to 50 years. On the other hand the increase in life expectancy is greater for women than men so that there are far more females in the older age groups. For every 100 men aged 70 years or more there are now about 180 women.

---

[1] Those aged 0–1 years.

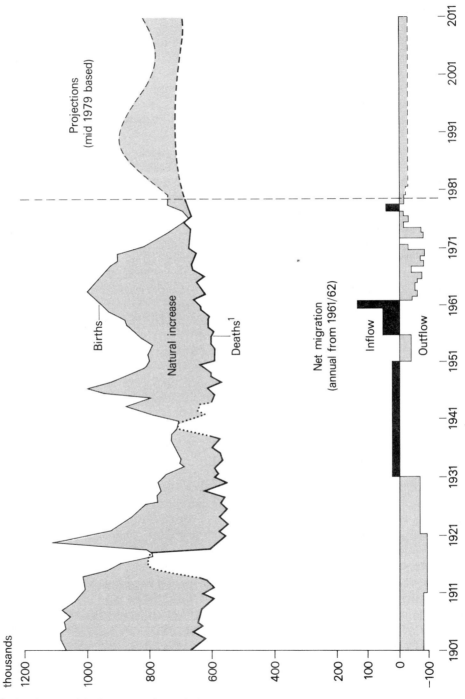

¹ The dots on this line cover the periods 1914–18 and 1939–45 which include deaths of non-civilians and merchant seamen who died outside the country.

Age distribution

The age distribution or age composition of a population provides information
on the percentages of the total population in each age group. This information
is important to economists because, as is explained below, it helps them to
work out the dependency ratio. The more important divisions of the
population by age are as follows.

1 *The working age groups*. In the UK these contain the people between 16
   years of age and 60 years (women) and 65 years (men). The number of
   people in the working age groups is *not* the same as the working population
   (see page 133).
2 *The dependent age groups*. These are the people below 16 years of age and
   those over 60 years of age (women) and 65 years of age (men).

The dependency ratio measures the relationship between the numbers in the
non-working age groups and the numbers in the working age groups. A simple
example should make this clear.

Age group	Number of people (millions)
Under 16 (males and females)	10 (non-working age group)
16–59 (women)	15 ⎱ (working age group)
16–64 (men)	19 ⎰
60+ (women)	6 ⎱ (non-working age group)
65+ (men)	4 ⎰

$$\text{Dependency ratio} \quad = \frac{20\text{m.}}{34\text{m.}} \times 100$$

$$= 58.8 \text{ per cent}$$

This means that for every 100 people in the working age groups there were
about 59 in the dependent age groups.

The age distribution of a country is usually illustrated by the type of bar
graph shown in Fig. 14.3. It is described as a population pyramid. The age
distribution of the UK population is fairly typical of developed countries with
low birth-rates and low death-rates and, hence, low growth rates. The shape of
the UK pyramid indicates a fairly high life expectancy since most people
survive into the older age groups. Life expectancy in the UK is about 70 years
for males and 76 years for females. The percentage in the working age groups
is expected to remain fairly constant at about 63 per cent for the remainder of
this century.

The population pyramid for the typical less developed country shows the
effects of a high birth-rate and a high growth rate. Such countries have high dependency ratios and a large proportion of the population is less than 15 years

Fig. 14.2 Population changes and projections, UK (annual averages)

Source: *Social Trends*, HMSO, 1980.

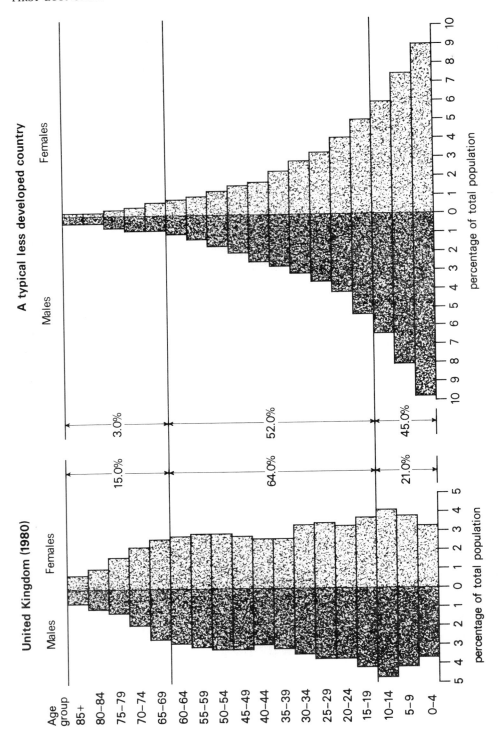

of age. In Africa, South Asia and Latin America there are approximately four young dependants for every five persons of working age, whereas in Europe the corresponding ratio is only two to five. On the other hand mortality rates are higher in the less developed countries and much smaller proportions of their populations consist of old-age dependants.

Regional distribution

The UK has a high population density averaging about 229 inhabitants per square kilometre, about the same as West Germany and India. Japan and Belgium have population densities one-third higher, while the population density of the USA is only one-ninth that of the UK. The population of the UK, however, is not evenly spread, almost 80 per cent of the people live in urban areas. The seven great conurbations of Greater London, Central Clydeside, Merseyside, Tyneside, South East Lancashire, West Midlands and West Yorkshire comprise less than 3 per cent of the land area of Great Britain but contain one-third of the total population. England is the most densely populated region of the UK with a population density of 355 inhabitants per square kilometre.

Before the process of industrialization began, the population of the British Isles was relatively small and widely dispersed. Apart from London, the only towns of any size were Norwich, York and Bristol. Industrialization led to a movement of people to the centres of industry in the North and Midlands. As towns developed around the centres of industry more and more people came to live in urban areas. The movement of population to the industrial areas of the North and Midlands continued until late in the nineteenth century when there was a drift to the southern counties and especially to the South East. This movement was due to the diminishing importance of coal as a source of power, the spread of electric power and the development of new industries attracted to the London area which, in addition to being a large potential market, was, and still is, the seat of government and the major financial and commercial centre. The drift to the South East continued for most of the present century, but in more recent years there has been some tendency (encouraged by the development of New Towns) for population to move out of London into the surrounding counties.

The working population

The working population consists of those people who are employed either as employees or on their own account plus those who have registered themselves as unemployed. In 1981 the working population of the UK was 26 million;

Fig. 14.3   Age distribution

equal to about 47 per cent of the population. The size of the working population depends upon:

a the size of the total population;

b the proportion of the population in the working age groups;

c the *activity rate* – the percentage of the numbers in the working age groups which is gainfully employed (or seeking work). The activity rate (or participation rate) depends upon:

  i the numbers in full-time further education;

  ii the numbers retiring early and the numbers of those who continue to work after reaching retirement age;

  iii the proportion of married women who take up jobs outside the home.

In 1972 the official school leaving age was raised from 15 years to 16 years and this removed about 0.4 per cent of the total population from the working age groups. In the last three decades there has been a large increase in the numbers of young people in full-time further education. For example, the number of full-time students in UK universities rose from 87 000 in 1951–52 to about 270 000 in 1977. There has been a similar expansion in other establishments of further education. The effect of this development has been to bring about a considerable decline in the activity rates of those under 19 years of age. The proportion of those who go on working after reaching retirement age has also been falling. On the other hand the 25–64 age group has increased its activity rate. This has been due to the increase in the numbers of married women taking up work outside the home. In 1931 the proportion was 10 per cent; it is now more than 50 per cent.

Occupational distribution

Over the past two decades the main trends in the occupational distribution of the labour force have been the fall in the numbers and the proportion employed in manufacturing, a sharp decline in the numbers engaged in the extractive industries and a large increase in the numbers employed in service industries.

In more recent years jobs which require very limited skills have been disappearing quite rapidly (600 000 were lost between 1971 and 1978). There has also been a falling away in the numbers of traditional craft jobs and a marked increase in the demand for technicians and technologists.

Falling employment has been most marked in the 'older' industries like steel, coal mining, textiles and shipbuilding. The 1970s saw a general decline in employment in the vehicles industry. The numbers employed in these industries have fallen partly because of falling output and partly because of increased productivity. Over the period covered by Table 12 some industries like chemicals and electrical engineering achieved increases in output, but there was no significant increase in employment; the extra output was due to greater productivity. Industries using advanced technology (e.g. electronics, computers, pharmaceuticals and some synthetic materials) increased employment.

Table 12 The changing pattern of employment in the UK

	1961		1980		
	Numbers (000s)	% of total	Numbers (000s)	% of total	% change 1961–80
Agriculture, forestry, fishing	1 098	4.5	638	2.6	−41.9
Mining and quarrying	728	3.0	345	1.4	−52.6
Manufacturing	8 636	35.3	6 940	28.0	−19.6
Construction	1 658	6.8	1 653	6.7	−0.3
Gas, water, electricity	389	1.6	347	1.4	−10.8
Transport and communications	1 724	7.0	1 577	6.4	−8.5
Other services	9 749	39.9	12 898	52.2	+32.3
HM Forces	474	1.9	322	1.3	−32.1
Total employed	24 456	100.0	24 720	100.0	

Sources: *Economic Progress Report*, HMSO, February 1980; *Economic Trends*, HMSO, December 1981.

Technical progress has been changing the pattern of the demand for labour. New machines and instruments have lessened the demand for some traditional crafts and for human supervision, but the construction, installation and maintenance of this advanced machinery and equipment has created demands for skilled labour. The major shift in the distribution of the labour force has been towards the service industries which now account for more than one-half of total employment (see Fig. 4.5). There have been large increases in the numbers employed in banking, insurance and other professional and financial services (e.g. accountancy). Two of the largest growth areas have been the educational and health services. Increasing real incomes and more leisure time have increased demands for services such as catering, hotels and tourism. There has also been a substantial increase in the number of workers employed by local authorities.

Table 12 gives details of changes in employment over a fairly long period of time. The severe recession experienced by the UK in the late 1970s and early 1980s led to a fall in employment in most sectors of the economy; manufacturing industries were particularly badly hit.

The changes in the occupational distribution of labour are, in part, a reflection of the increased employment of married women. A large percentage of the workers in service industries are females (e.g. 70 per cent of those in professional and scientific services). Additionally many married women work part-time and again we find that a large proportion of the employees in services are part-time workers (e.g. 50 per cent of the females working in education). Most of the trends outlined above are expected to continue well into the 1980s as Fig. 14.4 indicates.

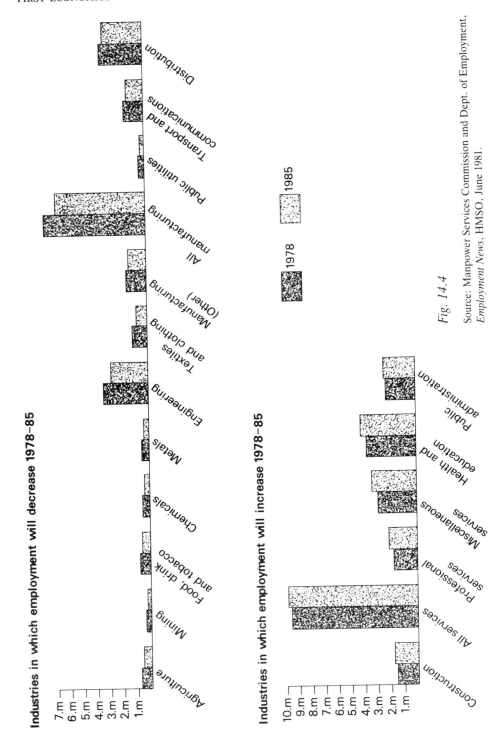

Industries in which employment will decrease 1978–85

Industries in which employment will increase 1978–85

1978   1985

Fig. 14.4

Source: Manpower Services Commission and Dept. of Employment, *Employment News*, HMSO, June 1981.

An optimum population

The density of population is a term which refers to the average number of persons per square kilometre. When economists refer to a country as *under-* or *over-populated*, however, they do not use population density as an indicator. The ability of a people to produce goods and services depends upon the supply of the other economic resources (land, capital and technical knowledge) available to them. Thus, a country which is largely desert and which has no valuable mineral deposits, very little in the way of capital equipment and a largely unskilled labour force, might be over-populated with 5 persons per square kilometre. On the other hand, a country richly endowed with fertile soil, mineral resources, large stocks of capital and a highly skilled labour force might be under-populated with 100 persons per square kilometre.

The idea that a population might be too small or too large has given rise to the concept of *an optimum population*. This is defined as 'that population which, with the existing stock of capital, land, technical knowledge and trading opportunities, maximizes output per head'. Fig. 14.5 helps to explain this idea. We can see that it is based on the laws of increasing and diminishing returns.

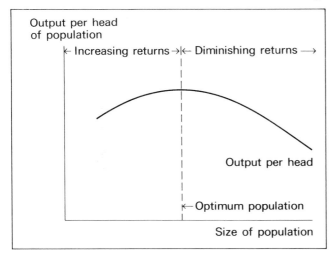

Fig. 14.5

When a country is experiencing increasing returns, population is below the optimum; when diminishing returns are being experienced, population is above the optimum. Unfortunately, it is not possible to make any accurate assessment of the optimum population for a country. First of all, we cannot experiment by adjusting the size of the population in order to see what happens to output per person. Secondly, the definition of optimum population is based on *the present situation* with regard to the stock of capital, the level of technical knowledge and the availability of trading opportunities, but these things are always changing. All we can do is to estimate what the economic effects would be if a population were expanding or declining.

137

An expanding population

The economic effects of changes in the size of the population depend upon the size of the existing population in relation to the supply of other economic resources. A population which is increasing because of an excess of births over deaths (rather than by immigration) is likely to contain an increasing proportion of younger persons. More resources will have to be devoted to the maintenance, education and training of the increasing number of young dependants. More resources will also be required to increase the stock of social capital (houses, schools etc.) as the population increases. Economic resources which might have been used to *raise* the standards of a *stationary* population will have to be used to *maintain* the standards of a *growing* population.

In the case of the UK, which imports about one-half of its food supplies and a large part of the raw materials used in industry, more food would have to be imported to feed the increasing numbers and more materials would have to be imported in order to provide more jobs as the labour force increases. To pay for these additional imports there would have to be a substantial increase in exports. An increasing population in a country as densely populated as the UK would increase the pressures on land (leading to higher land prices) and increase the problems of urban congestion.

On the other hand, a growing population means an increased demand for goods and services. This will encourage firms to expand production, invest in more machinery and take on more labour. If the population is below the optimum, an increase in the size of the population will enable many industries to take advantage of greater specialization and achieve more economies of large-scale production. With a larger percentage of younger people in the population, there will be more mobility in the labour force and expanding industries would be able to increase their labour forces from new recruits rather than by retraining workers from other industries.

A declining population

If the decline in the numbers of people is due to a fall in the birth-rate, the proportion of young dependants will be diminishing and, for a time, the *proportion* in the working age groups will be increasing. Thus, more resources can be devoted to raising living standards. But in the longer term, the proportion of older-age dependants will increase and the working population will have to provide relatively more income for pensioners and medical care for the aged.

As a population declines so does total demand for goods and services and this might lead to a more pessimistic outlook in the business world. There could be less investment and less incentive to start new enterprises. If the population is falling below the optimum, then average costs of production could well increase as the large capital-intensive industries begin to lose some of the advantages of large-scale production. On the other hand, a declining population could bring the benefit of a reduced dependence on imports.

Test paper 5

Short-answer questions

1 At the beginning of Year 1 a country has a population of 10 million. The crude birth-rate is 35 per thousand and the crude death-rate is 15 per thousand. Net immigration is at the rate of 100 000 per annum. What will be the size of the population at the end of Year 2?

2 In what circumstances may a country be experiencing a steadily falling birth-rate *and* a steadily increasing population? Assume there is no migration.

3 What are the *main* reasons for the high rates of population growth now being experienced in the less developed world?

4 Which of the following countries have extremely low population growth rates (a) Brazil (b) Sweden (c) West Germany (d) India (e) Mexico?

5 If a country's population continues to grow at a rate of 3 per cent per annum, how long, approximately, would it take to double in size?

6 Malthus thought that population had a tendency to increase at a *geometric* rate while food production, he thought, could, at best, only be increased at an *arithmetic* rate. Explain the terms in italics.

7 What is the current annual percentage rate of growth of the UK population?

8 The question is based on the following details of a country's population.

Age group	No. of people (millions)
under 10	8
10–15	6
16–29	9
30–49	14
50–64	13
over 65	10

The official school leaving age is 16 years and the retirement age for both men and women is 65 years. The activity ratio is 80 per cent.
a What is the dependency ratio?
b What is the size of the working population?

9 Why is it important for purposes of economic planning to have accurate population statistics showing the numbers in the different age groups?

10 In Fig. 14.3 (UK) the numbers in the age groups between 35 years and 45 years are smaller than the numbers in the age groups which precede them and follow them. What is the explanation for this situation?

11 Suggest some possible reasons for the steady increase, in the UK over the past 50 years, in the proportion of married women taking up work outside the home.

12 A study of the trends in the working population has led some people to declare that the UK is undergoing a process of 'de-industrialization'. What do you think they mean by this term and what might have led them to make such an observation?

True or false?

13 a The economic activity rate is much higher for men than it is for women.
b The economist describes a country as under-populated when it has a very low population density.
c The UK birth-rate has followed a steady downward trend throughout the present century.
d Females outnumber males in the UK population because there are more female births than male births.
e The average age of the population is very much lower in developing countries than in developed countries.
f A constant birth-rate and a falling death-rate will increase the dependency ratio.

Multiple-choice questions

14 The size of the UK population predicted for the end of this century has varied between 50 million and 70 million. These wide differences have been due mainly to errors in forecasting
1 migration
2 movements in the death-rate
3 movements in the birth-rate
A 1, 2 and 3
B 1 and 2 only
C 2 and 3 only
D 1 only
E 3 only

15 The numbers in the working age groups are influenced by all of the following *except*
A the age composition of the population
B migration
C the numbers in full-time further education
D the official retirement age
E the official school leaving age

16 In the UK the proportion of married women now going out to work is
A less than 10%
B between 10% and 25%
C between 25% and 40%
D between 40% and 50%
E between 50% and 60%

17 In which of the following industrial groups has employment risen over the past 25 years?
1 manufacturing
2 gas, water, electricity
3 distribution
A 1, 2 and 3
B 1 and 2 only
C 2 and 3 only
D 1 only
E 3 only

18 The present size of the world's population is
A between 2 and 3 billion
B between 3 and 4 billion
C between 4 and 5 billion   (1 billion = 1000 million)
D between 5 and 6 billion
E between 6 and 7 billion

19 Which of the following UK planning regions has the smallest population?
A East Midlands
B West Midlands
C North West
D East Anglia
E South West

Data-response question

20 A recent (1979) study of population trends indicated that the likely changes over the next twenty-five years could be favourable to the UK. Some of the main points from this study are set out below.
1 The numbers passing into the working age groups at adolescence will exceed the numbers reaching retirement age.
2 The number of births (on current trends) will be less than the numbers in the school leaving year.
3 The number of people retiring will be falling and is expected to fall faster than the death-rate.
If these projections are proved accurate,
a What will happen to the dependency ratio?
b Describe some of the economic consequences of the changes in the age structure of the population.

15 Prices and markets

Value

Price is a measure of value, but, in economics, the word 'value' has a restricted meaning; it refers to *value in exchange*. In other words, we measure the value of a good or service in terms of the things for which it will exchange. Nowadays practically all exchanges make use of money and economic goods have money prices. This makes it easy for us to find a commodity's value in exchange. All we have to do is to compare its price with the prices of other commodities. If one hour of labour is 'priced' at £4, then the exchange value of that hour of labour is the variety of goods which could be bought for £4.

Prices are sometimes fixed by the state or by powerful firms which dominate markets, but most prices are still determined by what are known as the market forces of supply and demand. Even when prices are set by authorities such as the state, the forces of supply and demand still play an important part in the setting of those prices. In order to study the operation of market forces we must know something about markets.

Markets

The traditional market is a place where buyers and sellers meet in order to do business with one another. Most of our towns have market squares or market halls where buying and selling takes place in a manner which has changed little for centuries. In the modern world, however, a market can take many forms. It is best defined as an arrangement which allows buyers and sellers to make effective contact with one another so that prices can be established and exchange transactions can take place. Buyers and sellers do not have to meet face to face; the telephone network can provide an efficient link between them and so can the 'small ads' columns in the local newspaper. The foreign exchange market is an efficient arrangement for the buying and selling of foreign currencies, but the dealers in this market are separated, often, by thousands of miles. Telecommunications networks keep them in constant touch with one another and they can do business just as effectively as if they were in the same room.

Traditionally markets were mainly local, but the development of improved transport facilities, better communications and the use of advertising has created national markets for most goods and services. These same developments have also led to the establishment of international markets for many goods and services. There are world markets for primary products such as rubber, non-ferrous metals, oil and foodstuffs such as wheat, sugar and meat. The products of advanced technology such as artificial fibres, electronic equipment, computers, motor cars and aeroplanes are sold on world markets. And we must

Markets for labour ▶

◀ A market for livestock sales by auction

A traditional market ▼

A market for foreign ▲ currencies

Local markets ▶

Fig. 15.1

not overlook the fact that many services such as banking and insurance are also bought and sold on a world-wide scale.

The existence of a market allows the willingness and ability of people to buy (i.e. demand) to interact with the willingness and ability of people to sell (i.e. supply) in such a way that a price is established which balances these forces of supply and demand.

Demand

Demand does not simply measure the strength of people's wants or desires. The desire to possess a commodity will have no effect on the price of that commodity unless it is supported by an ability to buy that good. Demand in economics means effective demand and refers to the willingness and ability to buy. In a market economy goods and services are only produced if there is a demand for them. In some areas of the world there is a great deal of want, but very little demand because the people are so poor. Demand is usually defined as, *'the quantity demanded at any given price over some given period of time'*.

The amount of a good demanded depends upon the price and, for the great majority of goods and services, the quantity demanded increases as the price decreases. This fact is normally stated in the form of a 'law' of supply and demand, thus, *'other things being equal, more will be demanded at lower prices than at higher prices'*. We can state with some certainty that more of a good will be demanded at a lower price only if we make the assumption that no other changes take place. We assume, for example, that things such as consumers' income, consumers' taste and the prices of other goods and services all remain unchanged. Thus, the phrase 'other things being equal' is a very important part of the statement about demand. The same reasoning applies of course when we refer to the effects of an increase in price which will cause less to be demanded.

The demand curve

The relationship between the price of a good and the quantity demanded is usually expressed in the form of a demand schedule or demand curve as illustrated in Fig. 15.2. The normal demand curve slopes downwards from left to right according to the law of demand quoted above. There are several ways of explaining the shape of the demand curve; we shall consider two of them.

The income and substitution effects

If the price of a commodity falls while consumers' income and the prices of

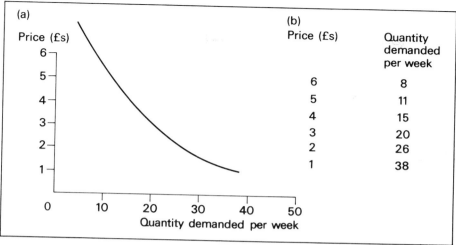

Fig. 15.2(a) Demand curve

Fig. 15.2(b) Demand schedule

other goods and services remain unchanged, then people's real income will increase, that is, the purchasing power of their money incomes will be greater. This will probably encourage existing buyers of the commodity to buy more and some people who were unwilling or unable to buy at the previous price will now be prepared to buy at the lower price. This is known as *the income effect*. The opposite income effect will operate when the price of a commodity rises.

If other things do not change, a fall in the price of a commodity will make it *relatively* cheaper when compared with the goods for which it can be substituted. For example, a fall in the price of butter will persuade many people to buy more butter and less margarine. Note that butter does not have to become cheaper than margarine for this effect to take place; when choosing between different goods, it is relative prices which people take into account. They may not be prepared to pay 100p per kilogram more for Commodity A than Commodity B, but they might be quite happy to pay 50p per kilogram more for it. When a price change causes people to buy more of one good and less of another, it is described as *the substitution effect*.

Diminishing marginal utility

Another explanation of the downward slope of the demand curve makes use of the obvious fact that consumers demand goods and services because they obtain satisfaction from them. The satisfaction, pleasure or benefit derived from consuming goods and services is described as *utility*. The amount of utility obtained from the consumption of a good or service cannot be measured because it is a personal sensation; the same commodity will render different amounts of utility to different people. A smoker will obtain great utility from the consumption of tobacco, but the same commodity provides no utility (or probably negative utility) to the non-smoker. Thus, we cannot say that a particular thing possesses so much utility; the amount of utility it yields is a purely personal experience.

Although utility cannot be measured we can still make use of the idea. It is possible, by observing human behaviour, to say whether a person obtains more utility from one thing than from another. The sacrifices which people are prepared to make in order to obtain different goods gives a fairly good idea of whether they get more utility from one good than another. For example, if someone is prepared to pay £5 for a unit of Commodity X, but will not pay more than £3 for a unit of Commodity Y, we must accept the fact that the unit of X provides that person with more utility than the unit of Y.

There is one relationship between consumption and utility which seems to be true for most people, and for most goods and services. This refers to the way in which total utility or satisfaction increases as one consumes more and more units of some particular commodity. The amount by which the consumption of one more unit increases total utility is described as marginal utility. *The Law of Diminishing Marginal Utility* states that, 'the utility derived by a person from the consumption of a commodity increases as consumption increases, but each additional unit of the commodity adds less and less to his or her total utility'. In other words, the extra satisfaction obtained from the consumption of additional units tends to decline as the quantity consumed increases.

For example, after a session of heavy manual work, the first cup of tea will probably provide a person with a great deal of utility; a second cup will also be very welcome but not so enjoyable as the first. More cups of tea will yield smaller and smaller amounts of utility. *Total utility* is increasing, but *marginal utility* is diminishing. Of course a point may be reached where marginal utility becomes negative (one can have too much of a good thing) and if this happens, total utility will begin to decline.

Fig. 15.3 illustrates the Law of Diminishing Marginal Utility. For this purpose we have assumed that utility can be measured in units which we have called 'utils'. The individual 'pillars' show the additions to total utility derived from the consumption of one more unit. The sum of these pillars (i.e. the shaded area) represents total utility.

Marginal utility and demand

Since marginal utility diminishes, it is clear that a person will only be persuaded to buy additional units of a commodity if he or she is asked to make smaller and smaller sacrifices in order to obtain those extra units. The price of a commodity is a measure of the opportunity cost of that commodity, because price measures the value of the things we have to go without in order to buy a unit of that commodity. Suppose a family buys 2 kilograms of beef each week when the price is £3 per kilogram. The marginal utility of a third kilogram must be less than the utility obtained by spending £3 on other goods and services. If,

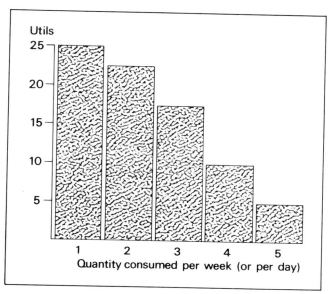

Fig. 15.3   Marginal utility

however, the price of beef were to fall to £2.50 per kilogram, the family may be persuaded to buy 3 kilograms per week. Spending £2.50 on a third kilogram of beef may yield more utility than could be obtained by spending that £2.50 on other goods and services.

What we are saying is that the amount of a commodity which people buy depends upon its marginal utility and its price. If other things do not change, price must fall in order to make the purchase of additional units worthwhile. This means that the individual's demand curve for any good will slope downwards from left to right. For any particular good, different people will have different demand curves according to their tastes and incomes, but they will all slope downwards from left to right. The total demand curve for a commodity therefore must also slope downwards from left to right.

Changes in the conditions of demand

Students beginning the study of supply and demand are often puzzled and confused by the expression 'changes in demand'. Unfortunately this term is often used to describe both (a) a movement *along* the demand curve and (b) a movement *of* the demand curve. In fact these two movements have entirely different causes and it is wise to use different expressions to describe the different movements. Table 13 and Fig. 15.4 are included in an attempt to avoid any misunderstanding.

Table 13

Price (£s)	Quantity demanded per week	Quantity demanded per week after increase in demand
10	20	50
9	30	70
8	50	90
7	70	110
6	90	140
5	120	170
4	150	220
3	190	270
2	240	340

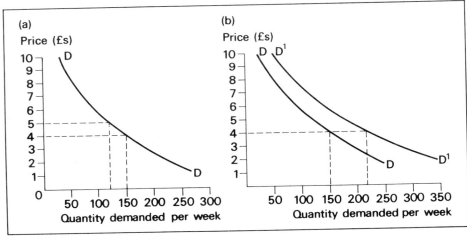

Fig. 15.4(a)   *Fig. 15.4(b)*

The first two columns in Table 13 represent a normal demand curve and this is shown as DD in Fig. 15.4(a) and Fig. 15.4(b). DD is drawn on the assumption than when the price of the product changes, other things do not change. Thus a change in price causes a movement *along* the demand curve. A fall in price leads to an *extension of demand*. For example, when price falls from £5 to £4, the quantity demanded increases from 120 units to 150 units (Fig. 15.4(a)). Similarly a rise in price leads to a *contraction of* demand. When price increases from £4 to £5, the quantity demanded falls from 150 units to 120 units.

An entirely different situation is shown in Fig. 15.4(b). In this case, the whole demand curve has shifted. A movement of the demand curve from DD to D¹D¹ is described as *an increase in demand*, because more is demanded at each and every price. Thus, whereas a quantity of 150 units was previously de-manded at price £4, the quantity demanded at this price is now 220 units. The same diagram can be used to demonstrate *a fall in demand* which means that less is demanded at each and every price. All we need to do is assume that the demand curve has shifted from D^1D^1 to DD. To summarize:

1 An increase in demand means that the demand curve moves to the right causing more to be demanded at each price.

2 A fall in demand means that the demand curve moves to the left causing less to be demanded at each price.

Causes of movements of the demand curve

A demand curve describes what happens to quantity demanded when the price changes and other things remain unchanged. These 'other things', however, do change. They are described as the *conditions of demand* and it is changes in these conditions which cause the demand curve to move. The main causes of changes in demand are set out below.

1 Incomes
Our ability to buy goods and services depends mainly on the level of our real incomes. An increase in real income will, in most cases, increase the demand for goods and services; a fall in real income will cause the demand for most things to fall. Strictly speaking it is changes in *disposable* real income which affect demand. Disposable income is the amount of money we have to spend after taking into account deductions for income tax and national insurance contributions as well as any benefits received in the form of pensions, unemployment pay, child benefits and so on. Thus, a change in the rate of income tax may change the position of demand curves even though the gross pay of individuals may not have changed.

There are, however, circumstances where an increase in real income might cause the demand for a product to fall. Some commodities are described as *inferior goods* because a rise in real income causes people to buy less of them and to buy more of the superior substitutes. Which goods happen to be 'inferior' depends upon the standard of living of the community. In Western Europe and North America, public transport has suffered a serious decline in demand as incomes have risen and more people have been able to afford motor cars. In these regions the demand for bread has also been falling for a number of years. As standards of living have risen, bread has become a supplement to a meal instead of providing a major part of people's diet. An increase in real income will reduce the demand for 'inferior' goods (moving the demand curves to the left) and increase the demand for superior goods.

2 The prices of other goods and services
Many of the things we buy have close *substitutes* and a change in the price of a commodity will affect the demands for its substitutes. For example, the different brands of petrol are close substitutes for one another. An increase in the price of one brand will undoubtedly lead to increases in the demand for other

brands (we are continuing to assume that other things remain unchanged). A fall in the price of pork might well reduce the demand for beef. In general, an increase in the price of a commodity will tend to increase the demand for its substitutes. The reverse will apply when the price of a commodity falls.

The demand for some commodities will also be affected by changes in the prices of their *complements*. Goods are complementary when they are jointly demanded; the use of one good requiring the use of another. Cassette players and cassettes, cameras and films, and cars and petrol are examples of complementary goods. In this case a fall in the price of a commodity will increase the demand for its complement. A fall in the price of record players will tend to increase the demand for records. An increase in the price of a good will tend to reduce the demand for its complement.

3   Tastes and fashion

Some changes in demand are often unpredictable. These are the variations in demand due to changes in taste and fashion. Industries which are particularly affected by such changes are those producing clothing, footwear and entertainment, but processed foods and beverages are also subject to these influences (note the very large increase in the demand for lager at the expense of beer during the 1970s).

4   Advertising

The main aim of most advertising campaigns is to increase the demand for the advertised product, that is, to shift the demand curve to the right. If a successful advertising campaign is carried out on behalf of a good which has a number of closely competing substitutes (e.g. instant coffee) it will also have the effect of shifting the demand curves for the competing goods to the left. This may not happen, of course, where the *total* market is growing very rapidly.

5   Hire-purchase

The sales of many durable consumer goods are heavily dependent on hire-purchase facilities. If hire-purchase terms are made easier (e.g. by smaller deposits and longer periods for repayment), the demand curves for many goods will move to the right. The demands for motor cars, electrical appliances and furniture are particularly susceptible to changes in hire-purchase terms.

Supply

Supply does not mean the existing stock of a commodity; it refers to the amounts which traders are prepared to offer for sale over some period of time. More precisely supply is defined as, *'the quantity of a commodity which is supplied at any given price over some given period of time'*.

The amounts offered for sale will depend upon the prices consumers are prepared to pay. When farmers consider market prices to be too low, they will sometimes plough in vegetables or leave fruit to rot in the orchards rather than take these products to the market. In such cases the fruit and vegetables were not part of the *supply* of these commodities because they were not offered for sale.

Another of the laws of supply and demand states that, *'more will be supplied at higher prices than at lower prices'*. This law is usually illustrated by a supply schedule or a supply curve as in Fig. 15.5

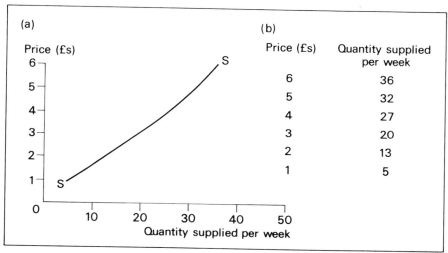

(a)

Price (£s)

(b)

Price (£s)	Quantity supplied per week
6	36
5	32
4	27
3	20
2	13
1	5

Quantity supplied per week

Fig. 15.5(a) *Supply curve*   Fig. 15.5(b) *Supply schedule*

As mentioned earlier, we assume that firms in the private sector aim to maximize their profits. This assumption helps us to understand why supply curves slope upwards from left to right, that is, why traders are prepared to supply more at higher prices. If an increase in demand causes the price of a commodity to rise, production will become more profitable. The amount supplied will increase because existing firms will be encouraged to increase their outputs and new firms will be attracted into the industry. We saw earlier (page 40) that the firm's cost curves tend to turn upwards as production increases. This is a further reason why it will require higher prices to persuade firms to supply more.

A fall in the demand for a product leads to a fall in market price so that production becomes less profitable. The quantity supplied will fall as firms cut back on production (in an attempt to reduce average and marginal costs). The fall in price may also drive some of the less efficient firms out of business.

Changes in the conditions of supply

We can use the same reasoning when dealing with changes in supply as we did when dealing with changes in demand. A movement along the supply curve is caused by changes in the price of the product and such a movement is based on the assumption that other things which might affect supply do not change. Movements along the supply curve are described as *extensions or contractions of supply*.

Fig. 15.6(a) illustrates the effect of a change in price. If price falls from OP to OP¹, the quantity supplied falls from OQ to OQ¹ (i.e. a contraction of supply). The same diagram may be used to illustrate an extension of supply.

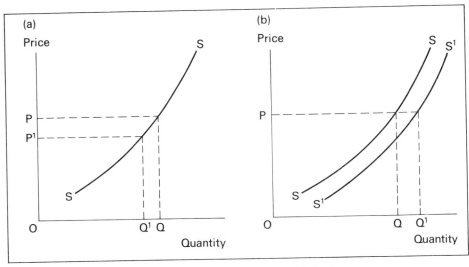

Fig. 15.6(a)   *Fig. 15.6(b)*

A movement *of* the supply curve comes about when the conditions of supply change and this movement is referred to as a *change in supply*. An increase in supply means that more is supplied at each and every price and is illustrated by a movement of the supply curve to the right. In Fig. 15.6(b), a movement of the supply curve from SS to S¹S¹ represents an increase in supply.

A fall in supply means that less is supplied at each and every price and the supply curve moves to the left. In Fig. 15.6(b), a movement of the supply curve from S¹S¹ to SS represents a fall in supply.

The changes which cause the supply curve to move its position must be changes which affect the costs of production. If a firm is prepared to supply more at the existing price it indicates that some change has taken place which enables it to produce at a lower cost. Similarly, when a firm is prepared to supply less at any existing price[1] some development must have caused its costs of production to rise. The following are the more likely causes of movement of the supply curve.

1 Changes in the prices of the factors of production
The prices paid for labour (i.e. wages), land (i.e. rent) and capital (i.e. in-

[1] Or, alternatively, a higher price is required to persuade the firm to supply any given quantity.

terest) are clearly costs to the entrepreneur. Any changes in these prices, assuming other things do not change (e.g. techniques of production) will obviously move the firm's cost curve and hence its supply curve. For example, an increase in wage rates (when productivity remains unchanged) will raise production costs and shift the supply curve to the left while a fall in the rate of interest will reduce costs and move the supply curve to the right.

2 Technical progress

Changes in the techniques of production, such as the use of more efficient machinery, better organization at work, or the introduction of a new technology (e.g. robots), will also affect the costs of production because such developments influence productivity. If the productivity of labour rises faster than the wage rate then labour costs per unit will fall. Improvements in productivity (other things remaining equal) will lower production costs and move the supply curve to the right.

3 Weather conditions

The outputs of farmers are very much influenced by variations in the climate. The yields from the land are to some extent independent of the area cultivated and the costs incurred in ploughing and planting. Extremely favourable weather conditions will lead to bumper crops and unfavourable weather will have the opposite effect. Such variations in weather conditions change the average costs of production. If good weather increases the number of tonnes of barley yielded by one hectare of land, it means that the costs of producing each tonne have fallen; the supply curve will move to the right. The opposite applies when unfavourable weather reduces the yield per hectare.

4 Taxes and subsidies

The costs of bringing goods to market can be changed by imposing taxes on, or granting subsidies to, producers. Placing a tax on a good or service (e.g. VAT) has a similar effect to an increase in the costs of production and moves the supply curve to the left. When the government grants a subsidy to producers it has the same effect as a decrease in the costs of production and the supply curve moves to the right.

Market price

If we now bring together the supply and demand curves on one diagram we find that they intersect at only one price. This is the *market* or *equilibrium price*. The market price is arrived at by a gradual process. Shortages and surpluses at prices other than market prices will cause the price to move until it settles at a price where the market is in equilibrium, that is, where the quantity demanded is equal to the quantity supplied. For example, in Fig. 15.7, if suppliers began to trade at a price of £4 the quantity supplied per week (27 units) would exceed the quantity demanded (15 units). The surplus (12 units per

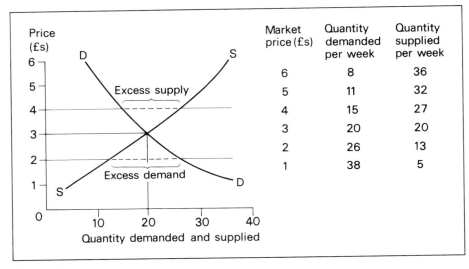

	Market price (£s)	Quantity demanded per week	Quantity supplied per week
	6	8	36
	5	11	32
	4	15	27
	3	20	20
	2	26	13
	1	38	5

Fig. 15.7

week) would force down the price as suppliers tried to dispose of their stocks. If suppliers began to trade at a price of £2, the quantity demanded (26 units) would exceed the quantity supplied (13 units) and the resulting shortage would cause the price to be bid upwards. Only at a price of £3 is the quantity supplied equal to the quantity demanded.

Changes in market prices

1 When demand changes

We can examine the effects of a change in demand by assuming that the supply conditions do not change. For this purpose we make use of Fig. 15.8. The diagram can be used to explain the effects of an increase or a decrease in demand. Assuming DD to be the original demand curve, a movement of the curve to D^1D^1 represents an increase in demand. The immediate effect of the change is to cause a shortage at the existing price (OP). This shortage, shown by the dotted line, will force price upwards. As the price rises, more will be supplied and eventually a new market price will be established at OP^1.

Now assume that D^1D^1 is the original demand. A movement of the curve to DD represents a fall in demand. The immediate effect is to cause a surplus at the existing price (OP^1) shown by the heavier section of the price line. This surplus will cause suppliers to lower prices and reduce the quantity supplied. As the price falls, the quantity demanded increases. Eventually a new equilibrium price of OP will be established.

The effects of a change in demand may be summarized as follows.

a   *'Other things being equal, an increase in demand will raise the price and increase the quantity supplied.'*

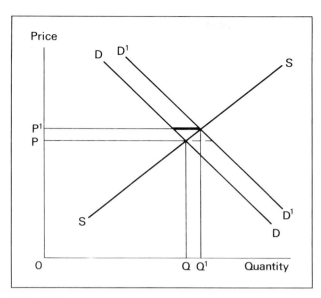

Fig. 15.8

b *'Other things being equal, a fall in demand will lower the price and reduce the quantity supplied.'*

2 When supply changes
Fig. 15.9 illustrates the effects of a movement of the supply curve.

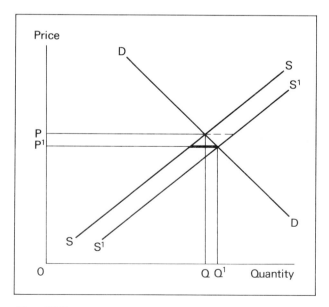

Fig. 15.9

Assume that the line SS is the original supply curve and that supply increases from SS to S^1S^1. The immediate effect is to cause a surplus at the existing price (OP). This surplus is represented by the dotted line and suppliers faced with the prospect of unsold stocks will be obliged to reduce their prices. As price falls the quantity demanded increases until a new market price of OP^1 is established. If S^1S^1 is taken to be the original supply curve, the diagram can be used to show the effects of a fall in supply (S^1S^1 to SS). It can be seen that this particular change would cause a shortage at the existing price (OP^1). This shortage, shown by the heavier section of the price line, will cause price to rise and the quantity demanded to fall until the price settles at OP.

The effects of a change in supply are summarized below.

a *'Other things being equal, an increase in supply will lower the price and increase the quantity demanded.'*

b *'Other things being equal, a fall in supply will raise the price and reduce the quantity demanded.'*

Points to note

It is important to be clear on the changes described above. An *increase* in price may be associated with *an increase or a decrease* in quantity demanded. It all depends on what caused the price to change. An increase in demand (see Fig. 15.8) will lead to more being demanded at a higher price. A fall in supply (see Fig. 15.9) will lead to less being demanded at a higher price. The same diagrams can also be used to demonstrate that a fall in demand leads to less being demanded at a lower price while an increase in supply leads to more being demanded at a lower price. We can draw no conclusions about the effect of a price change unless we know whether it was a change in supply or a change in demand which caused the change in price.

Elasticity of demand

Firms are well aware of the fact that with a given demand curve, more will be demanded at lower prices and less will be demanded at higher prices. Of more interest to the firm, however, is how the changes in price will affect total revenue. Will the change in price increase or decrease total revenue? For example, in the two demand situations shown below, a fall in price reduces total revenue in (a), but increases total revenue in (b).

a	Price	Quantity demanded per week	Total revenue
	80p	100	8000p
	60p	120	7200p

b **Price**   **Quantity demanded per week**   **Total revenue**
   80p   100   8000p
   60p   150   9000p

The extent to which total revenue changes when price changes depends upon the elasticity of demand. This is a technical term which describes the responsiveness of quantity demanded to a change in price. If a small change in price causes a relatively large change in the quantity demanded, we say that demand is *elastic*. If a small change in price causes a relatively small change in the quantity demanded, we say that demand is *inelastic*. Elasticity of demand can be measured by the formula,

$$\text{Elasticity of demand} = \frac{\text{percentage change in quantity demanded}}{\text{percentage change in price}}$$

a   If the numerical value of elasticity is greater than 1, demand is said to be elastic. The change in quantity will be proportionately greater than the change in price. This is the case in example 2 below.
b   If the numerical value of elasticity is less than 1, demand is said to be inelastic. The change in quantity will be proportionately less than the change in price. This is the case in example 1 below.
c   If the numerical value of elasticity is equal to 1, demand has unit elasticity. The proportionate change in quantity is equal to the proportionate change in price.

Examples
1   If, when price increases from 8p to 10p, the quantity demanded per week falls from 100 units to 90 units.

$$\text{Elasticity of demand} = \frac{10\%}{20\%} = 0.5$$

2   If, when price falls from £5 to £4, the quantity demanded per week increases from 100 units to 130 units,

$$\text{Elasticity of demand} = \frac{30\%}{20\%} = 1.5$$

The purpose of Fig. 15.10 is to draw attention to the fact that for virtually all demand curves, elasticity of demand is different at different prices. The following two examples from Fig. 15.10 demonstrate this.
a   When price rises from £4 to £5 (i.e. by 25 per cent), quantity demanded falls from 30 units to 20 units (i.e. by 33⅓ per cent). In this price range, elasticity of demand is 1.33, i.e. demand is elastic.
b   When price falls from £2 to £1 (i.e. by 50 per cent), quantity demanded increases from 50 units to 60 units (i.e. by 20 per cent). In this price range, elasticity of demand is 0.4, i.e. demand is inelastic.

157

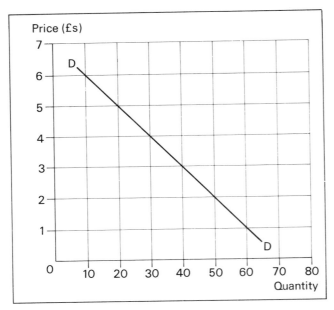

Fig. 15.10

Elasticity of demand and total revenue

It is important to know whether demand is elastic or inelastic at any particular price because this information tells us what happens to total revenue when price changes.

1　*When demand is elastic*, the percentage change in quantity demanded will be greater than the percentage change in the price. Thus, if price falls by 10 per cent, quantity demanded will rise by more than 10 per cent and total revenue will increase. On the other hand, if price rises by 10 per cent, quantity demanded will fall by more than 10 per cent and total revenue will fall. In general terms, therefore, when demand is elastic, a price reduction will increase total revenue and a price increase will reduce total revenue.

2　*When demand is inelastic*, the percentage change in the quantity demanded is less than the percentage change in price. Thus, if price falls by 10 per cent, the quantity demanded will increase by less than 10 per cent and the total revenue will fall. If, however, price is increased by 10 per cent, the quantity demanded will fall by less than 10 per cent and total revenue will increase. It is apparent, therefore, that when demand is inelastic, a price reduction will reduce total revenue and a price increase will increase total revenue.

Fig. 15.11(a) and Fig. 15.11(b) illustrate the relationship between elasticity of demand and total revenue. The amount of total revenue at any price is de-

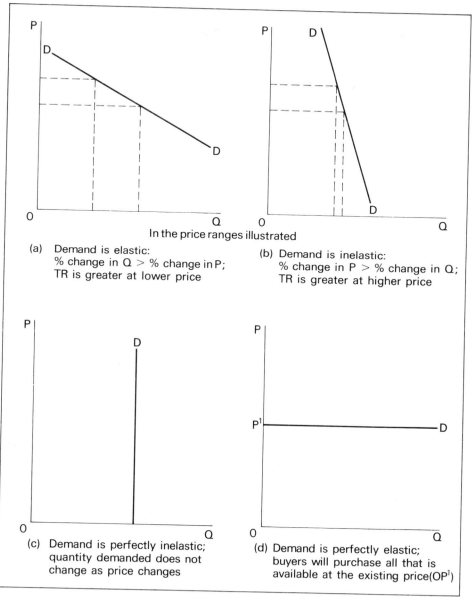

Fig. 15.11

picted by the rectangle under the demand curve (shown by dotted lines in these diagrams). The height of such a rectangle is a measure of the price, and the breadth of the rectangle measures the quantity demanded. Since total revenue = quantity sold × price, the area of the rectangle is a representation of total revenue.

In Fig. 15.11(a) it is clear that demand is elastic in the price range illustrated because total revenue is greater at the lower price.

In Fig. 15.11(b), total revenue is obviously greater at the higher price and demand is inelastic in the price range illustrated.

Fig. 15.11(c) and (d) illustrate two extreme cases. In Fig. 15.11(c) demand is perfectly inelastic. There is no change in the quantity demanded as price changes and elasticity of demand is zero at all prices.

In Fig. 15.11(d) we have a perfectly elastic demand curve. In the case there is an unlimited demand at the ruling price and elasticity of demand is infinity.

The determinants of elasticity of demand

1   The availability of substitutes

If a commodity has a number of close substitutes all selling within a narrow price range, we must expect the demand to be elastic. If the price of such a commodity were raised and other things did not change, many consumers would switch to the *relatively* cheaper substitute. Similarly, if the price of the commodity were reduced, it would attract many buyers who were formerly buying the now relatively dearer substitutes. In both cases a change in price would lead to a more than proportionate change in the quantity demanded. In markets where there are several closely competing brands such as those for cigarettes, petrol, beer and detergents, the demand for any one brand will be elastic.

Where a commodity has no close substitute, demand is likely to be inelastic. There will be no opportunity for consumers to switch to, or from, substitutes when the price of the commodity changes. There will be a relatively small change in the quantity demanded when price changes. Athough the demand for any one brand of petrol may be elastic, the total demand for petrol will be inelastic, because it has no *close* substitute. Similarly, the demand for any one brand of paint will be elastic but the demand for paint will be inelastic. An interesting example of a product which has both an elastic and inelastic demand is electricity. In the market for lighting, the demand for electricity is inelastic; it has no close substitute. In the market for heating, however, it has competition from oil and gas and its demand will be elastic.

2   The proportion of income spent on the commodity

Where the total spending (per week or per month) on a good or service accounts for a very small fraction of consumers' income, the demand for it will tend to be inelastic. A relatively large change in the price of matches or table salt will have little effect on the quantities demanded.

3   Habit-forming goods

People can become addicted to certain products; tobacco and alcohol are obvious examples. Where this is the case, demand will be inelastic because, to the addict, such goods have no close substitutes.

4 'Luxuries' and 'necessities'

It is often said that the demands for necessities are inelastic and the demands for luxuries are elastic. It is certainly true that the demands for necessities such as food, water and shelter are inelastic, but so are the demands for petrol, tobacco and alcoholic drinks. The problem here is the meaning of the word 'necessities'. As standards of living rise, what was a luxury to one generation often becomes a necessity to the next. For example, domestic electrical appliances such as electric irons and washing machines are widely regarded as necessities in most developed countries. All we can say is that demands will tend to be inelastic for those commodities which are generally regarded as necessities.

Elasticity of supply

This term refers to the manner in which the quantity supplied responds to a change in price. Elasticity of supply can be treated in very much the same way as elasticity of demand, remembering, in this case, that the quantity moves in the same direction as price. It can be measured by the formula,

$$\text{Elasticity of supply} = \frac{\text{percentage change in the quantity supplied}}{\text{percentage change in the price}}$$

If the numerical value of elasticity is greater than 1, supply is elastic.
If the numerical value of elasticity is less than 1, supply is inelastic.
If the numerical value of elasticity is equal to 1, supply has unit elasticity.
Supply is elastic when a change in price leads to a more than proportionate change in the quantity supplied. It is inelastic when a change in price leads to a less than proportionate change in the quantity supplied.

Examples
1 If an increase in price from 10p to 11p (i.e. 10 per cent) causes the quantity supplied per week to increase from 1000 units to 1300 units (i.e. 30 per cent), elasticity of supply is 3 (i.e. supply is elastic).
2 If a fall in price from £5 to £4 (i.e. 20 per cent), causes the quantity supplied to decrease from 200 units to 180 units per week (i.e. 10 per cent), elasticity of supply is 0.5 (i.e. supply is inelastic).

Fig. 15.12 illustrates situations where supply is (a) inelastic, (b) elastic, (c) perfectly inelastic and (d) perfectly elastic.

The determinants of elasticity of supply

When changes in demand bring about changes in market prices, firms try to respond to these price changes by increasing or decreasing their outputs. If price

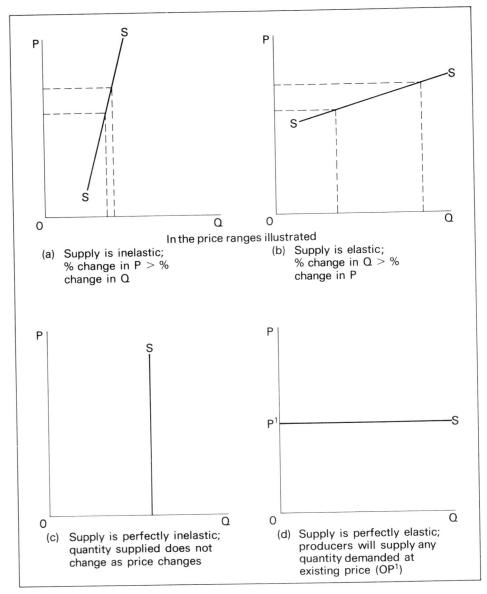

Fig. 15.12

rises they will try to produce more, if price falls and production becomes less profitable, they will react by reducing their outputs. If firms have little difficulty in increasing or decreasing their levels of production, supply, in the short run, will be elastic. If, however, they find it difficult to adjust their outputs, then, in the short run, supply will be inelastic. Problems of inelastic supply tend to be short-run problems. In the long run, the outputs of most commodities can be increased. More labour can be trained, more capital can be created, more land can be brought into cultivation and so on. Problems can arise, however, even in the long run, in the case of non-replaceable resources such as oil and certain minerals. Elasticity of supply is concerned with the time it takes to adjust supply to changes in demand and the main factors governing the ability of firms to adjust their supplies are set out below.

1 Availability of resources

When an industry is working below capacity, that is, machines are lying idle and labour is unemployed, an increase in demand can usually be met fairly easily by taking on more labour and putting the idle machines to work. Supply will be elastic. If the industry is fully employed, however, an increase in demand cannot be met in the short run. It may take a long time to extend factories and install new machinery. Supply in the short run will be inelastic. For example, it takes a long time to expand the capacities of mining industries and the industries producing electricity, steel and chemicals. The shortage of a particular type of labour may cause supply to be inelastic in the short run. In the 1970s some British industries found it difficult to expand output because of a shortage of skilled labour although total unemployment was relatively high.

2 The level of stocks

If an industry is holding large stocks of finished goods or raw materials, an increase in demand for these commodities can be met by running down stocks. While they last, supply will be elastic.

3 Farm and plantation products

In the case of agricultural products, the elasticity of supply is largely governed by the length of the growing season. For things like vegetables and cereals no great change in supply can be brought about for at least a year. In the case of beef and dairy products it will take even longer because it may take several years to increase the size of beef and dairy herds.

Some plantation products, such as natural rubber, tea, coffee and cocoa, will be inelastic in supply over fairly long periods of time because it takes several years for the trees or bushes to reach maturity. Industries producing commodities such as these also face difficulties when demand falls. There will inevitably be surpluses because the trees will continue to produce their crops. Growers may have to accept very drastic reductions in price in order to dispose of these surpluses and they will be very reluctant to cut down valuable trees unless they are certain that the fall in demand is permanent.

In general, the supplies of manufactured goods tend to be more elastic than the supplies of primary products. In manufacturing it is often possible to deal with a fall in demand by dismissing labour and switching off machinery while an increase in demand may be met by putting idle capacity to work or by working overtime. In the case of agriculture, there are problems associated with the length of the growing season and, in mining, geological difficulties may make it difficult to carry out a substantial increase in output in the short run. Note, however, that techniques such as deep freezing have made the supply of many foodstuffs more elastic; this year's supply is not limited to this year's crop.

Applications of supply and demand analysis

1 Non-market prices

In some cases the price of a good or service is fixed by the state (or other authority) at a level which is higher or lower than the true market price. We can illustrate the effects of such price fixing by taking two examples.

1 Holding down food prices during an emergency
The free market price for this commodity (say, butter) is OP, but the government makes an order fixing the maximum price at OP¹. At the price OP¹ there is a shortage equal to Q¹Q² and in order to avoid a situation where some people will be unable to obtain any supplies, the government will be obliged to introduce some form of physical rationing. Note that the fixing of a maximum price above OP would have no effect if demand and supply conditions remain unchanged.

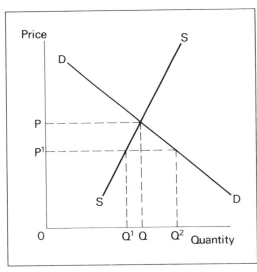

Fig. 15.13

2 Offering farmers a guaranteed price higher than the free market price
The free market price for this commodity (say, wheat), is OP, but the government guarantees that farmers will receive a minimum price of OP¹. At this

price there is a market surplus of Q^1Q^2 and the government will be obliged to purchase this surplus and place it in stock. It may hold this stock in order to relieve some future shortage or it may sell it on the open market at a loss.

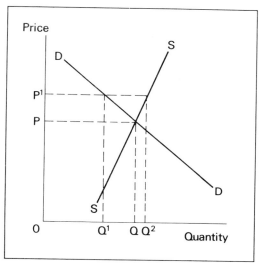

Fig. 15.14

2   A fixed supply

1   Cup Final Tickets

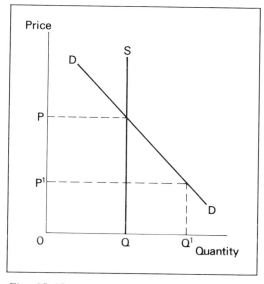

Fig. 15.15

This is really another example of price fixing. The supply of Cup Final tickets is strictly limited to the capacity of Wembley Stadium (i.e. supply is perfectly in-elastic). The free market price of tickets is OP, but the Football Association (FA) set a price well below this at OP¹. At the fixed price there is a shortage (QQ¹) and the FA is forced to apply some system of physical rationing.

2 Site values

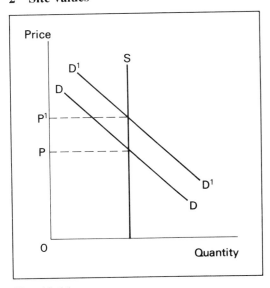

Fig. 15.16

The geographical immobility of land gives rise to some interesting applications of supply and demand analysis. For example, the number of sites for shops, cafes, banks and offices in the High Street is strictly limited. Any increase in demand for such sites cannot bring forth a greater supply. Fig. 15.16 shows that an increase in demand will cause price to rise by the full extent of the change in demand. Increasing site values help to explain the 'high rise' developments in the centres of cities.

3 Effects of changes in the markets for other commodities

In Fig. 15.17 the heavier lines show the original demand and supply curves for a manufactured product X. The initial equilibrium position, therefore, is *a*. In order to simplify the diagram the price and quantity lines from the equilibrium position are not drawn. The other supply and demand curves represent possi-ble changes in costs of production and market demand. We can use the dia-gram to explain various changes in market conditions, starting from DD and SS each time.

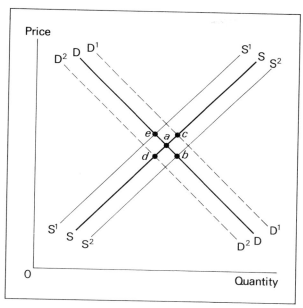

Fig. 15.17

1   An increase in the productivity of the workers producing X
If we assume that the wage rate remains unchanged, the effect will be to reduce the costs of producing X and the supply curve will move to S²S². The new
equilibrium position will be *b*.

2   An increase in the price of a substitute for X
An increase in the price of a substitute will increase the demand for X. The demand curve will move to D¹D¹ and the new equilibrium position will be *c*.

3   A rise in the price of a complementary good
This will have the effect of reducing the demand for X. The demand curve will
move to D²D² and the new equilibrium position will be *d*.

4   The imposition of a tax on X
This has the same effect as an increase in the costs of production. The supply
curve will move to S¹S¹ and the new equilibrium position will be *e*.

16 Competition and monopoly

Competition can take many forms. Firms compete by using such techniques as (a) advertising, (b) more attractive packaging, (c) offering improved services such as delivery and after-sales services, (d) creating more attractive sales outlets and (e) providing better hire-purchase facilities. The main form of competition, however, is price competition where firms try to 'underprice' their competitors.

Perfect competition

Economists have created a theoretical model of pure or perfect competition which is based on price competition. It is a model of a market where no single buyer or seller can exercise any influence on the market price and there is no government activity in the market. In the model of a perfectly competitive market certain conditions are assumed to exist.

1 There are many buyers and sellers and their individual purchases and sales are too small to have any influence on the market price.
2 Each of the firms in the industry supplies exactly the same product. In other words, the products of one firm are perfect substitutes for the products of other firms in the industry.
3 There are no barriers to the movement of firms into and out of the industry.
4 All the buyers and sellers are assumed to have perfect knowledge of what is happening in the market.

If these conditions prevail, competition between sellers will give rise to one uniform market price. Since all firms are selling identical products and buyers know exactly what is happening in the market, they will always deal with the supplier quoting the lowest market price. Similarly suppliers will be aware of the demand conditions and price will be adjusted until there are no shortages or surpluses. Competition, therefore, will force the price down to a level which makes it just worthwhile for the firm to continue in business. Variations in an individual firm's output will have no influence on the price at which it sells its product. Under these conditions the firm is described as a *price-taker*; it has to take the price as given by forces beyond its control.

The model of perfect competition is a creation of economic theory. In the real world, however, we can find some situations which have several features of the perfect market. In agriculture, the individual farmer is a price-taker; no single farmer can influence the prices of farm products. In some manufacturing industries there are many small producers each supplying goods very similar to those produced by other firms. Each firm sees itself selling in a market where the price of its product is largely beyond its control. In the footwear industry, for example, a firm producing fairly standard types of shoes may describe itself as 'producing for the £15 market'. It knows that there are many other firms supplying shoes which are very close substitutes for its own products and that competition between these firms has established a market price of £15. The Stock Exchange also provides an example of a market where there is perfect knowledge (there is close personal contact between buyers and sellers) and homogeneous commodities (one £5 share in Company A is exactly like any other £5 share).

Monopoly

At the other extreme from perfect competition is the monopolized industry. Several important features of monopoly are summarized below and then, later, explained in more detail.

1　Monopolists are sole suppliers.
2　Since a monopolist supplies the entire market, the demand curve for his product is the total or market demand curve. A monopolist, therefore, faces a downward sloping demand curve. He will have to reduce his price in order to increase the quantity he sells.
3　A monopolist has considerable market power, but cannot determine both the price of the product *and* the quantity he sells. If he decides on the price of the product, the demand curve then determines the quantity sold. If he decides to place a certain quantity of goods on the market each week, the demand curve determines the price at which he can dispose of this quantity.
4　A supplier can only exercise monopoly power if he has some effective way of preventing other firms from entering the market.
5　A monopolist's power to control the *market* supply means that, by deliberately restricting this supply, he *can* charge higher prices and make greater profits than would be the case in a very competitive industry. He may not do so.
6　A monopoly is not necessarily a single firm or single *producer*. A monopoly situation exists where there is a single *supplier*. If several producers are marketing their products through a single selling agency (e.g. the Milk Marketing Board) there is a monopoly situation.

Price and marginal revenue

A firm contemplating an increase in its production will try to estimate the profitability of the increased output. It will clearly be profitable to produce more goods if they add more to the firm's revenue than to its costs. The amount by which a firm's total costs increase when its production increases by one more unit is described as marginal cost (see page 38). The amount by which its revenue increases when it sells one more unit is described as marginal revenue. Thus, we can see that a firm will be tempted to increase output if it estimates that marginal revenue will be greater than marginal cost. The relationships between the different types of revenue are set out in Table 14.

Total revenue is quite simply the amount of money received from the sale of a given quantity of output.

Average revenue is the total revenue divided by the quantity of goods sold. It is, in fact, another name for price. Thus, if a firm obtains a total revenue of £10 000 from the sale of 2000 units, the average revenue (or price) equals £5.

Marginal revenue is the change in total revenue when the quantity sold is varied by one unit. In Table 14, when the monopolist reduces price from £9 to £8, sales increase by one unit and the total revenue rises from £18 to £24. The marginal revenue yielded by the sale of the third unit is £6.

Table 14

Monopoly

Price (average revenue)	Quantity demanded	Total revenue	Marginal revenue
£10	1	£10	£10
£9	2	£18	£8
£8	3	£24	£6
£7	4	£28	£4
£6	5	£30	£2
£5	6	£30	0
£4	7	£28	−£2

Individual firm under perfect competition

Price (average revenue)	Quantity demanded	Total revenue	Marginal revenue
£5	1	£5	£5
£5	2	£10	£5
£5	3	£15	£5
£5	4	£20	£5
£5	5	£25	£5
£5	6	£30	£5
£5	7	£35	£5

For the firm under perfect competition, marginal revenue is always equal to price (i.e. average revenue). This must be so because price does not change when the firm varies its output. The sale of one more unit will increase total revenue by the price of that unit. This is made clear in Table 14.

Under monopoly, however, marginal revenue is always less than price: the sale of an additional unit does not increase total revenue by the price of that unit. This is due to the fact that monopolists have to reduce price if they wish to increase the quantity sold. In Table 14 it can be seen that a fall in price from £8 to £7 causes the quantity demanded to increase from 3 units to 4 units. The extra unit sells for £7, but total revenue only increases by £4. This is because the 3 units previously selling at £8 each, now sell at £7 each. When the demand curve slopes downwards from left to right, marginal revenue is always less than price. Fig. 16.1 (based on Table 14) illustrates the relationships between average revenue (i.e. price) and marginal revenue under monopoly (Fig. 16.1(a)) and for a firm operating under conditions of perfect competition (Fig. 16.1(b)).

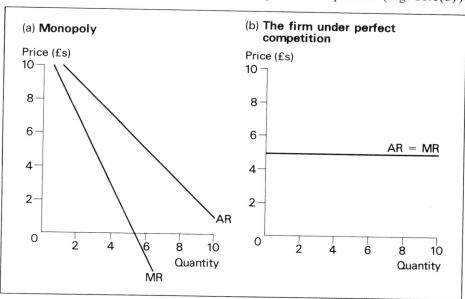

Fig. 16.1 Price and marginal revenue

In Fig. 16.1(a), the values for marginal revenue have been plotted at the mid-points on the quantity axis because MR refers to the *change* in total revenue when the quantity demanded changes by one unit.

Barriers to the entry of new firms

A monopoly can only continue to exist if there are some effective means of preventing other firms from entering the industry. Remember that a monopoly is not only a firm, it is also the industry. These restrictions or barriers to entry can take several forms.

1 The Law

Competition may be restricted by law and legal restrictions on competition have a long history. In the past, the Crown granted sole trading rights in certain parts of the world to great trading companies such as the East India Company and the Hudson's Bay Company. More recently we have the example of several nationalized industries being granted monopoly powers by law. For example, the industries supplying electricity, gas and coal and those supplying rail and postal services in the UK all have monopoly powers conferred on them by the state.

The law relating to patents also grants monopoly powers. A firm which has a patent duly accepted and registered is granted monopoly powers; no other firm is allowed to supply a product which is clearly a copy of the patented article. Patent rights are normally granted for a limited period.

2 Geographical barriers

Where workable deposits of certain minerals are heavily concentrated in a particular region, the owners of such deposits clearly have a degree of monopoly power although this power will be seriously weakened by the discovery of new deposits or the development of a substitute. The heavy concentration of oil deposits in the Middle East provides a good example of this basis of monopoly power. Some commodities such as wine (e.g. Burgundy and Champagne) or cheeses (e.g. Camembert and Gruyère) are associated with particular geographical areas. The genuine articles can only be supplied by firms located in those areas. Transport costs also create geographical barriers. The village shop, for example, enjoys some degree of monopoly power because the costs and inconvenience of travelling to the larger city-centre stores might outweigh the advantages of lower prices in the city.

3 Technical barriers

It will be very difficult for new firms to enter industries which are dominated by large firms using vast amounts of expensive capital equipment. Such large capital-intensive firms will be enjoying important economies of scale which any new, smaller firm entering the industry will not be able to match. Its average costs of production would be well above those achieved by the existing large firms. New firms will also find it difficult to enter industries where there are established firms producing goods with nationally-known brand names. Intensive advertising of such products provides a formidable barrier to the entry of new firms. In order to break into such a market a new entrant would have to undertake a very costly and risky campaign to promote a new product (e.g. detergents, instant coffee).

Types of monopoly

The fact that there is a single supplier of a commodity does not mean, necessarily, that there is a single producer. The single firm type of monopoly is found in some industries (e.g. some nationalized industries) but a monopoly may also consist of an organization of independent firms. If the firms in an industry come to some arrangement whereby they agree not to compete with one another on the basis of price, or they limit competition in some other way (e.g. by sharing the total market on some kind of geographical basis), consumers are, in effect, facing a sole supplier. Before the introduction of legislation to control monopoly (see pages 177–80), this type of monopoly organization was a fairly common feature of British industry.

Agreements between firms which are designed to restrict competition are described as *restrictive trade practices* or *monopolistic practices*. Although many of these practices have been abandoned as a result of legislation, a look at a few of the more common types and the way they operate will help us to understand the nature of monopoly in the real world.

1 Exclusive dealing and collective boycott
The firms in an industry (or the main producers) form an association and agree to supply only those market outlets (e.g. shops, garages) which stock, exclusively, the goods produced by firms belonging to the association. If any of these market outlets decides to sell goods produced by a firm which is not a member of the trade association, it will be boycotted. All the firms in the trade association will refuse to supply the offending wholesaler or retailer. This is a most effective restriction on competition because any new producers will find it very difficult to market their goods.

2 Price agreements
Price competition may be eliminated by an agreement between the firms in an industry to charge common prices. This arrangement is only feasible when the firms are making virtually identical products. A good example of the way in which price competition may be restricted was provided by the practice of *resale price maintenance* (RPM) which was widespread in the UK until 1964. Under the system of RPM, manufacturers were able to fix the resale prices of their products so that retailers could not compete on the basis of price – the same good sold at the same price wherever it was sold. The Resale Prices Act of 1964 led to the almost complete abandonment of this practice and we have seen earlier how this, in turn, led to severe price competition at the retail stage. Even where producers are charging different prices for their products they can still restrict competition between themselves by arranging that they will all move their prices at the same time and to the same extent.

3 Output agreements
Producers may collaborate to restrict total supply. The aim of such agreements is to keep prices higher than they would be otherwise. Each firm may be given an annual output quota and be subject to penalties if it exceeds its quota. Output quotas are commonly used as part of national or international marketing schemes in order to prevent the emergence of large surpluses which would drastically lower prices.

4 Restrictions on the supply of materials

Firms will be unable to enter an industry if they cannot obtain essential raw materials, components or capital equipment. The existing firms in an industry might make an agreement with their suppliers to withhold supplies of such materials from any firm which is not party to the agreement. For example, Commodity X can only be made by using highly specialized machinery and this, say, is only manufactured by two firms. The producers of Commodity X may sign an agreement with the two firms who make the machinery such that these machinery manufacturers agree not to supply their equipment to any new firms wishing to enter the industry.

The advantages and disadvantages of monopoly

In most developed countries, the state has devised some machinery for the regulation of monopolies. In the UK, as in several other countries, private monopolies have not been banned. It is recognized that although monopoly can, and sometimes does, operate to the disadvantage of consumers, some features of monopoly may be advantageous.

Possible disadvantages of monopoly

1   Monopolists control the *total* supply of a good or service and will tend to use this power to restrict supply in order to maximize profit. Prices will tend to be higher and output lower than would be the case if the industry were made up of many competing firms.
2   Monopolists are not under constant pressure from competitors and will, therefore, tend to be less efficient and have less incentive to introduce new techniques than will firms in highly competitive markets.
3   When an industry is monopolized, the variety of goods available to consumers will be much smaller than that supplied by a number of competing firms.
4   The barriers to entry prevent the emergence of new firms. This may slow down the rate of economic development since the flow of new ideas and new products (which are often introduced by new firms) will be restricted. It may mean that young and able people with ambitions to succeed in the business world will be denied the opportunity to become entrepreneurs.

Some arguments for monopoly

1   In some industries such as the public utilities (gas, water, electricity, telecommunications) large amounts of fixed capital are required in order to supply consumers. Competition in these industries would lead to a wasteful duplication of capital (e.g. gas and water mains) and average fixed costs would be much higher in a competitive industry than under monopoly.
2   Where monopoly takes the form of a large dominant firm, it will be able to achieve economies of scale which a number of small competing firms could not obtain. These lower costs, of course, might be used to increase monopoly profit rather than to lower prices.

3 It can be argued that there is likely to be more research and development carried out by a monopolist than by a number of competing firms. A monopolist will obtain all the profits from a successful new technology, but, in a competitive market, the advantages to any firm introducing a new technique will be short-lived because other firms in the industry will quickly adopt the new ideas.

4 In some industries, competition might lead to an excessive variety of products with many firms all trying to produce something different from the goods made by their competitors. In the case of some technical products (e.g. motor cars and electrical appliances) such variety would mean small-scale and high-cost production of each design or model. When an industry is monopolized, variety is reduced, there is more standardization, the scale of production of each model is increased, production costs per unit are reduced and consumers usually have a much wider availability of spare parts.

Imperfect or monopolistic competition

The models of perfect competition and pure monopoly are extremes. In the real world the markets for most goods and services lie somewhere between these two extremes. The majority of firms operate in what are described as imperfectly competitive markets. These markets have some of the features of both monopoly and perfect competition.

The main characteristic of such markets is product differentiation. The goods made by the firms in a particular industry are not identical. Each firm tries to distinguish its product from those of its rivals by such things as differences in design and packaging, but especially by the use of such techniques as branding and advertising. The use of trade marks and brand names gives producers some degree of monopoly power. Each firm is a sole supplier of the goods bearing a particular brand name. But this monopoly power will be very limited because each firm will have to face competition from several other firms making close substitutes. The markets for footwear and clothing provide examples of this type of competition and the world market for motor cars is also highly competitive with many close substitutes in the medium-price range. The fact that each firm is a sole supplier of a particular brand has led to the use of the term monopolistic competition to describe this type of market situation.

In many markets, the goods produced by the different firms and marketed under different brand names are, in fact, technically very similar. This has led to the widespread use of advertising as a means of persuading the consumer that the various brands are fundamentally very different. This is discussed in the next section.

A particular form of imperfect competition, known as *oligopoly*, is a feature of several major industries. Oligopoly exists when an industry is dominated by a few large and powerful firms. The oil, tyre and tobacco industries are examples of oligopolies. Each firm distinguishes its product from those of its rivals by branding and advertising, but in this case each firm is powerful enough to influence the total market. If one firm cuts its price, there will be a major effect on the sales of other firms who will almost certainly have to follow suit. Oligopolists, therefore, will be reluctant to indulge in damaging price wars and the rivalry between them usually takes the form of *non-price competition* which includes large-scale advertising, 'special offers', free gifts, competitions, more attractive retail outlets and so on.

Advertising

Any account of markets and prices which is related to the real world must recognize the important role played by advertising. In most industrialized countries advertising is a large industry. In the UK, in 1980, the total annual expenditure on advertising was more than £2500 million. This is a very large figure although it accounted for less than 2 per cent of total consumers' expenditure. Advertising uses a variety of media and it is probably something of a surprise to most people to learn that advertising on television is by no means the most important form of advertising. Fig. 16.2 shows the distribution of advertising expenditure over the different media and it clearly demonstrates the predominance of newspapers, journals and magazines as an advertising medium.

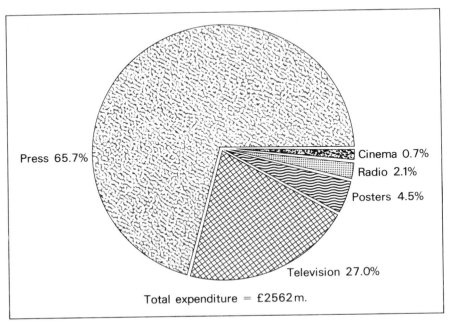

Fig. 16.2   Total advertising expenditure, UK, 1980

Source: The Advertising Association, May 1981.

The main aim of advertising in the commercial world is to move the demand curve for a good or service to the right and there is no doubt that a well-planned and cleverly presented advertising campaign can increase the demand for the product. But producers are keen to point out that an increase in demand can only be sustained if the consumers are satisfied with the product. Many of the most intensively advertised products are those which consumers buy every day or every week (e.g. cigarettes, beer, processed food, detergents, coffee, toothpaste and so on). Producers of such products maintain that consumers will not continue to buy a well-advertised product which does not live up to consumers' expectations.

Advertising also aims to make the demand for the product more inelastic. It attempts to develop an intense brand loyalty to a particular product by convincing consumers that the competing goods are *not* close substitutes.

There is a widely held view that advertising is simply an additional cost of production and must, therefore, have the effect of keeping prices higher than they would be if the products were not advertised. The supporters of advertising reply that advertising can reduce average costs of production because it can lead to increased sales which enable producers to produce on a larger scale. But where Firm A advertises to steal customers from Firm B, and Firm B advertises to offset the effects of A's advertising, the net result may be that market shares will be little changed and the effect will be an increase in average costs.

Some advertising is essential. Without it consumers would be unaware of the variety of goods and services available and their choices would be restricted. It is also necessary to inform consumers of the availability and features of new products as they become available. Economists refer to this advertising as *informative* advertising and its importance is seen in the fact that the government spends very large sums on this type of advertising (e.g. providing information about social services and so on). Critics of advertising, however, argue that much advertising is merely persuasive and does not add to consumers' knowledge of the market. Moreover, it is argued that exaggerated claims can mislead the consumer, but we must bear in mind that the Trade Descriptions Act (see page 181) offers consumers some protection against misleading advertising.

As mentioned earlier the intensive advertising of branded products may also act as a barrier to the entry of new firms into an industry. Against this, the advertising industry argues that advertising is a most powerful instrument of competition and its use is a spur to greater efficiency.

The control of monopoly in the UK

The first UK legislation aimed at controlling monopolies was passed in 1948. Since that time, controls have been extended by a number of Acts of Parliament, but the basis of the present arrangements for dealing with monopolies is the Fair Trading Act of 1973[1]. Overall responsibility for the operation of government policy on monopolies rests with the Director-General of Fair Trading. The Director-General's department, the Office of Fair Trading, acts as a central point for the collection of information on market conditions and for recommending action against companies or trade associations which might be acting against the public interest. There are two particularly important agencies concerned with the investigation and control of monopolies: the Monopolies and Mergers Commission and the Restrictive Practices Court.

The Monopolies and Mergers Commission (MMC)

The job of the MMC is to investigate and report on monopoly situations or suspected monopoly situations. The Commission cannot take any action until a case is referred to it by the Minister responsible (at present the Secretary of State for Trade) or by the Director-General of Fair Trading. The 1973 Act defined monopoly as a situation where 25 per cent or more of the total supply of a good or service is controlled by a single firm or group of firms acting together so as to restrict competition. The ability to control at least a quarter of the total market is considered to be sufficient to enable a supplier to exercise some degree of monopoly power.

When requested to do so, the MMC conducts a detailed investigation into all aspects of the supply of a particular good or service in the UK (or part of the UK). It has powers to demand all the information it requires from the firms under investigation. The MMC is obliged to present a report on its findings and to say whether it thinks the firms (or firm) in that industry are acting against the public interest. It must also set out its recommendations on what changes, if any, it would like to see carried out in respect of such matters as ownership, production methods, marketing methods, pricing policies and so on. The MMC has no powers to order firms to change their practices, it can only recommend that some action be taken. The Minister to whom the MMC is responsible does have powers to order firms to change their policies and practices.

Where the Commission finds that a monopoly is operating against the public interest, it is normal for the Secretary of State to ask the Director-General to negotiate with the firms concerned and get them to remedy the situation. In addition to its work on monopolies, the MMC also has powers to investigate and report on proposed mergers when these are referred to it by the appropriate Minister. It is the Director-General's responsibility to advise the Minister on whether a proposed merger should be referred to the Commission. It is the job of the MMC to say whether it believes the proposed merger would operate against the public interest. The Minister has powers to veto any proposed merger where it is considered its effects would be harmful to the public interest

[1] Subsequently extended by further legislation, namely the Competition Act of 1980.

(e.g. where it would unduly increase monopoly power or adversely affect consumer choice).

The Restrictive Practices Court

This is a branch of the High Court presided over by a judge who is assisted by persons with experience in industry and commerce. It came into being as a result of the Restrictive Practices Act of 1956. Subsequent legislation extended the scope of this Act and the powers to control restrictive trade practices (see page 173) are now contained in the Restrictive Trade Practices Act of 1976.

Associations of firms which make agreements to restrict competition in the supply of goods and services are obliged to place such agreements on the register maintained by the Director-General of Fair Trading. The law assumes that the restrictive trade agreements on the register are harmful to the public interest. In other words they lead to higher prices, restrict consumer choice, lead to lower output and higher unemployment or prevent the development of new products and more efficient methods of production.

The task of the Court is to look into the operation of such agreements and then decide whether they are harmful to the public interest. The Director-General selects agreements for the consideration of the Court and it is then the responsibility of the firms operating these agreements to prove that they do not adversely affect the public interest. Unlike the MMC the Restrictive Practices Court makes rulings which are legally enforceable.

Although the Court has ruled that some restrictive trade agreements do not operate against the public interest, it has condemned most of those which it has considered. In addition many hundreds of such agreements have been voluntarily abandoned. In the case of resale price maintenance, only two categories of goods have survived to continue the practice – books and proprietary medicines. The great majority of firms operating this practice chose to abandon it rather than defend it before the Court.

Both the MMC and the Restrictive Practices Court have to decide whether a particular monopoly situation is harmful to the public interest. This is often a difficult decision to make because, in many of the cases considered, there are both advantages and disadvantages. A monopoly in the UK may be restricting consumer choice, but its size and freedom from competition at home may enable it to compete more successfully in foreign markets. A restrictive trade agreement between several firms may be keeping prices relatively high and maintaining a number of relatively inefficient firms in business. Breaking this agreement may lead to severe competition, a much more streamlined industry but a much lower level of employment in that industry. A firm with a dominant position in an industry may be charging prices well above its costs of production. But these high prices may well allow several smaller firms to survive in that industry. Forcing the large firm to lower its prices will benefit consumers but these lower prices will probably drive the small firms out of business. These are typical of the problems faced by the MMC and the Court.

Protecting the consumer

In a perfectly free market, individual consumers are in a relatively weak position in their dealings with suppliers. The law assumes that both parties to a contract are equally well informed and equally experienced. In respect of the sale of goods and services, however, the individual buyer does not have the knowledge of the product, the experience of business practices or the knowledge of commercial law which is usually possessed by the firm supplying the goods and services. This fact has become increasingly obvious as more and more of our income is spent on sophisticated and technical goods and services (e.g. motor cars, domestic appliances and holidays abroad).

In recent years, governments have acted in several ways to protect the interests of consumers. They have:

a   passed laws to extend the rights of consumers;

b   provided consumers with facilities for obtaining advice on all kinds of problems through local Consumer Advice Centres and Citizens' Advice Bureaux.

c   published an extensive range of booklets and pamphlets containing information on consumers' rights.

Overall responsibility for safeguarding the interests of consumers rests with the Director-General of Fair Trading. The Director-General proposes new laws to end unfair trading practices, encourages trade associations to adopt codes of practice for their members to follow, and deals with manufacturers and traders who persistently commit offences.

The major Acts of Parliament affecting consumers in the market place are as follows.

The Sale of Goods Act

This imposes three main legal obligations on the seller.

1   The goods supplied must be of merchantable quality. If a person buys a pre-packed garment and finds a hole in it when it is unpacked the buyer has the right to return the garment.

2   The goods must be fit for the purpose for which goods of that kind are normally used (a lawn mower should be able to cut grass!).

3   The goods must be as described on the package, on a display sign or by the seller.

If any of these obligations are not met, the seller has broken the contract and the buyer has the right to claim back the money spent. But the buyer must exercise due care. If the goods were thoroughly examined on purchase and the faults should have been apparent, or the feature of which he or she complains was pointed out by the seller, the buyer has no rights against the seller.

The Unsolicited Goods and Services Act

This Act makes it an offence for traders to demand payment for goods which people have not ordered. Such goods are often sent through the post.

The Trade Descriptions Act

The Act makes it a criminal offence for a trader to describe inaccurately the goods being sold or the services offered. A spoken false description is just as much an offence as a written one. Under this Act a 'price mark-down' may be an offence. For example, if a shopkeeper simply crosses out £10 on a price ticket and adds £8, the goods must have been sold at £10 for at least twenty-eight consecutive days in the last six months or, if not, this must be made clear. For instance the ticket may be marked, 'last week's price £10, now £8'.

The Weights and Measures Act

Nowadays many goods, especially groceries, are pre-packed instead of being weighed out at the time of purchase. This Act applies to most items and makes it an offence if the weight or some other indication of quantity is not marked on the packet, tin or bottle. It is also an offence to give a wrong indication of the weight or quantity.

The Food and Drugs Act

Under this Act, it is an offence to sell unfit food, or to describe food falsely, or to mislead people about its nature, substance or quality. The regulations cover food hygiene wherever it is sold, food labelling and food composition.

The Consumer Protection Act

This Act gives the government powers to make regulations for any type of goods in order to prevent or reduce the risk of death and personal injury. Regulations have been made in respect of such things as electrical appliances, oil heaters, cooking utensils, and the flammability of clothing materials.

The Consumer Credit Act

This is a far-reaching measure covering all aspects of the sale of goods and services on credit. All firms concerned with the provision of consumer credit must be licensed with the Director-General of Fair Trading who is responsible for the working of the Act. This legislation makes it compulsory for traders to provide far more information about their credit and hire transactions than was formerly the case. Consumers also have the right to ask a court for relief if they think they are being charged an extortionately high amount for credit.

Test paper 6

Short-answer questions

1 'The best price I could get for my car was £2500, but it was worth at least £2750.' Distinguish between these two measures of value.

2 'The quantity demanded of Commodity X at a price of 50p is 1000 units.' Why is this an incomplete statement of demand?

3 'There is bound to be a strong demand for food and clothing because there are so many poor people living there.' This observation was made about a particular country. Is it a sensible statement?

4 One particular individual was observed to purchase less of a commodity when its price fell. Does this mean that the 'laws' of demand are invalid?

5 'Utility cannot be measured.' Why not?

6 When marginal utility falls to zero what can be said about total utility?

7 Which of the following will cause a movement *of* the demand curve for Commodity X?
 a a fall in the price of X
 b a fall in the costs of producing X
 c the development of a close substitute for X

8 'At the present time it is not worthwhile taking apples to the market.' Show how this statement by a farmer illustrates the difference between *stock* and *supply*.

9 At a price of £10 producers are willing to offer 1000 pairs of shoes for sale each week. At a price of £11 they are willing to offer 1500 pairs. Is supply elastic or inelastic?

10 'Monopoly refers to a market situation where there is a sole supplier; it does not mean necessarily that there is a sole producer.' Explain.

11 Extremely favourable weather conditions will not affect a farmer's fixed costs. Why then will it reduce a farmer's average costs?

12 When the price of a commodity increased, more units of the commodity were sold. What was the likely cause of the price increase?

13 A manufacturer calculates that the elasticity of demand for automatic dishwashers is 2. It is decided to lower the price of a dishwasher from £250 to £225. At this lower price sales increase to 240 per month. Calculate the quantity sold per month at the original price.

14 When the price of a commodity was reduced from 10p to 8p, the total weekly revenue fell from £100 to £80. What was the elasticity of demand in the price range 10p to 8p?

15 If an increase in the demand for electricity occurs when,
 a generating plants are working below capacity,
 b generating plants are working at full capacity,
 in which situation would supply be inelastic? Give reasons for your answer.

16 Under what circumstances is a black market likely to flourish?

17 The free market equilibrium price for a commodity is 80p. The government fixes a statutory minimum price of £1. Does this mean that suppliers will experience a large increase in their sales revenues?

18 The newspapers declare that the high price of tomatoes is due to a severe shortage caused by the widespread effects of a plant disease. Shoppers notice that most fruit and vegetable shops have stocks of tomatoes and many of them refuse to believe that there is a shortage. Use elementary supply and demand analysis to explain these conflicting views.

19 What are the most obvious imperfections in the market for petrol when it is compared to the model of perfect competition?

20 Why is it misleading to define a monopolist as a single producer?

21 What exactly is being restricted when firms are operating a restrictive trade practice?

True or false?

22 **a** Perfect competition means that the price of a commodity does not change.

b Cameras and films are complementary goods.

c If supply is perfectly elastic, an increase in demand will leave price unchanged.

d An increase in real income will increase the demands for all consumer goods.

e Other things being equal, an increase in the weekly wage rate in an industry will move the industry's supply curve to the left.

f If a commodity has a close substitute, it is very likely that the demand for it will be inelastic.

g In a free market, a shortage simply means that the existing price is too low.

h Monopolists have the power to determine both the price of a commodity and the quantity they wish to sell.

i By increasing brand loyalty, advertising can make the demand for a commodity more inelastic.

j The Monopolies and Mergers Commission has the power to break up monopolies which are operating against the public interest.

Multiple-choice questions

Questions 23, 24 and 25 refer to the following details of the market for a commodity. Each question refers to the original situation given overleaf.

Price	Quantity demanded per week (000s)	Quantity supplied per week (000s)
10p	100	300
9p	120	240
8p	140	200
7p	160	160
6p	180	120
5p	200	100

23 If demand doubled at all prices, what would be the new equilibrium price?
 A 10p
 B 9p
 C 8p
 D 7p
 E 6p

24 If supply fell by 50 per cent at all prices, what would be the new equilibrium price?
 A 9p
 B 8p
 C 7p
 D 6p
 E 5p

25 If the government guarantees producers a price of 8p and is prepared to buy any surplus, what would be the cost per week to the government?
 A £2000
 B £4800
 C £6000
 D £11 200
 E £16 000

Questions 26, 27 and 28 refer to the following details of the revenues and costs of an individual firm which is *not* operating in a perfect market.

Quantity demanded per week	Total revenue	Average cost
1	£100	£120
2	£180	£ 80
3	£240	£ 60
4	£280	£ 50
5	£300	£ 50

26 Which is the most profitable weekly output?
 A 1 unit
 B 2 units
 C 3 units
 D 4 units
 E 5 units

27 What is the marginal revenue when output increase from 3 units to 4 units?

A £ 10
B –£ 40
C £ 40
D £240
E £240

28 What is the marginal cost when output increases from 3 units to 4 units?

A –£ 10
B £ 10
C £ 20
D £180
E £200

Data-response questions

29 An arena has a seating capacity of 4000 people. An internationally re-nowned 'pop' group is booked to appear in this venue for one night. The demand schedule for tickets is estimated to be as follows.

Price	£12	£10	£8	£6	£4	£2
No. of seats demanded	1000	2000	3000	4000	5000	6000

a Draw the demand and supply curves on a sheet of graph paper. What is the equilibrium price?
b If the organizers of the concert were to fix the price of tickets at £5 what will be the extent of the shortage or surplus of tickets (assuming the above demand conditions apply)?
c Now assume that before the tickets go on sale, it is announced that the very popular lead singer will not be appearing. This causes demand to fall by 20 per cent at all prices.
  i What is the new equilibrium price?
  ii What will be the extent of the shortage or surplus at the fixed price of £5?

30 An individual firm faces the following demand conditions.

Price	£10	£9	£8	£7	£6	£5
Quantity demanded per week	1000	2000	3000	4000	5000	6000

The firm's fixed costs are £2000 per week and variable costs are constant at £5 per unit. It is estimated that an annual advertising campaign costing £52 000 per annum would raise demand by 20 per cent at all prices. Would you advise the firm to undertake such a campaign?

17　The national income

Economic activity results in the production and consumption of a great variety of goods and services. Every day enormous quantities of different goods and services are produced and consumed. Because production is going on all the time, the amount produced can only be measured over some given period of time and it is usual for the national output to be measured over a period of one year. What is being measured is a *flow* of goods and services and not a stock. Economists attempt to measure the rate at which production is taking place (i.e. the annual national product) in order to see what is happening to living standards and to find out which sectors of the economy are expanding and which are contracting. The value of the annual output of goods and services is referred to as the *national product* or the *national income*.

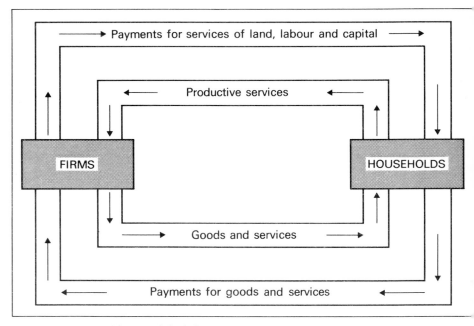

Fig. 17.1　A highly simplified diagram of the flow of income

Fig. 17.1 illustrates the nature of economic activity in a very simple economy which has only two sectors: households and firms. Members of households sell factor services to firms, that is, they sell the services of labour, land and capital. Firms make payments for these services in the form of wages, rent, interest and profits; these payments represent incomes to households. These two flows are shown in the upper 'pipes' in Fig. 17.1

The incomes received by households are spent on goods and services produced by firms. The flow of output and the flow of spending on this output are shown in the two lower 'pipes' in Fig. 17.1. In this very simple economy the value of the national output would be equal to the total flow of goods and services from firms to households in the course of one year.

The real world situation is more complicated than this, but Fig. 17.1 does help us to understand the basic reality of economic life as a series of flows of (a) goods and services (i.e. output) and (b) payments for these goods and services (i.e. income).

Measuring the national income – methods

It is not possible to add together the outputs of the different industries in physical terms. We cannot add units of footwear to tonnes of coal etc. Such things can only be added by using their monetary values. This presents little or no problem because most goods and services have money prices. The calculation of the national product is a formidable task and involves the collection and processing of a great mass of statistics. There will obviously be some errors and omissions in the final totals. Fortunately, the statisticians are able to make some checks on the accuracy of their calculations because they can measure the national product in three different ways.

1   *The output method* attempts to measure the value of the outputs of all the different industries.

2   *The income method* measures the value of total output by adding up all the incomes paid to factors of production for services rendered in producing the national product.

3   *The expenditure method* measures the amount of spending on the national product. It can be shown that these three methods should yield the same total.

1   Output = Income

The money value of the goods and services produced must be equal to the costs of production plus profits. These costs of production represent payments to the factors of production for services rendered, that is, they are incomes to the owners of the factors of production. Since profits also represent an income (to the entrepreneur) we can say that the value of total output is equal to the sum of the factor incomes, including profits. In other words, Output = Income.

2   Output = Expenditure

This equality is based on the obvious fact that whatever is produced must be sold or added to stocks. If we assume that the producers who are adding to stocks are, in fact, 'buying' some of their own output, we can say that all the goods and services produced are 'bought'. If total expenditure, therefore, includes additions to stocks, the value of total output must be equal to the total expenditure. Thus we can say that, Output = Expenditure.

Putting (a) and (b) together we have, Output = Income = Expenditure.

The income and expenditure aspects of the national income are illustrated in Fig. 17.2 and Table 15 (page 191) shows how the national income is measured using the output, income and expenditure methods.

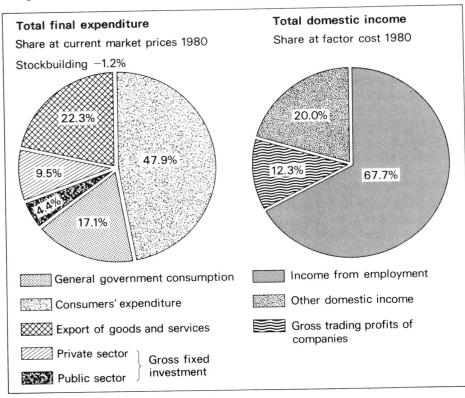

Fig. 17.2   Shares of income and expenditure

Source: *Economic Trends*, HMSO, August 1981.

Measuring the national income – problems

1   Public goods and services

National income is a measure of the money value of the national output, but many goods and services are provided by the state and do not have money prices. Obvious examples are education, health and police services. Such services are clearly part of the national output and use up scarce resources. They must, therefore, be given money values. The method chosen is to value them at *factor cost*; the costs of producing these services is taken as a measure of their market value. For example, the salaries of police officers, teachers, doctors and nurses are taken as measures of the values of their outputs.

2   Self-provided goods and services

The national income accounts understate the true national income to the extent that people produce things for their own use and consumption. A great deal of food is grown in household gardens and much repair work is done on a do-it-yourself basis. These activities add to the real national output, but, since there are no market transactions, the value of this production is not included in the national income accounts. The greatest omission of this type is the value of the services provided by housewives. This does not appear in the national income accounts because it is not possible to make any realistic estimate of the value of this output (although obviously it is very large indeed).

3   Double counting

The fact that the output of one firm is often the input of another means that there is a danger of double counting. If the value of the total output of the steel industry is added to the value of the output of the engineering industry, the value of the steel used to make machinery will be counted twice. Similarly, adding the output of flour-millers to that of the bakers will mean that the value of the flour used to make bread will be counted twice.

There are two ways of dealing with this problem, either (a) each firm's output must be measured in terms of *value added* or (b) only the values of *final products* must be counted. Both methods will produce the same total. This is made clear in the following example.

Stage of production	Value added
1 A lumber company fells trees and sells them to a saw mill for £500.	£500
2 The saw mill reduces the tree trunks to planks and boards which it sells to furniture manufacturers for £1000.	£500
3 The furniture manufacturers make cabinets which they sell to shops for £1500.	£500
4 Shops sell cabinets to the public for £2000.	£500
Value of final products = £2000 = sum of values added	£2000

4   Ownership of dwellings

Houses are an important part of the nation's stock of social capital. They produce services (shelter, comfort and convenience) for which people are prepared to pay a price (i.e. rent). The annual 'output' of the stock of houses, therefore, is included in the national income. Where houses are owner-occupied an estimated figure (equal to the rent they would earn if let) is included in the national income accounts.

5 Stock appreciation

This refers to changes in the value of stocks which are not due to changes in the quantities held, but to changes in prices. During inflation, the money value of goods held in stock will rise and this increase in value will mean higher profits for the firms selling these goods. Since this is a windfall gain and does not arise from any increase in output, a deduction is made from the income table so as to remove the effects of price changes (see Table 15).

6 Imports and exports

Some part of the spending of UK firms and households is devoted to foreign goods and services. Since this spending creates income abroad and not at home, it must be deducted from total spending in order to arrive at the national income. If a UK resident buys a Japanese car, the greater part of that expenditure creates income in Japan. Only that part of the spending which creates income in the UK (i.e. the wholesaling, retailing, and advertising of the car) will be included in the UK national income. Thus imports appear in Table 15 as a negative item. On the other hand some part of the national output is bought by overseas firms and residents. This spending creates income in the exporting country and the value of exports are added to the total spending in the home economy.

7 Transfer payments

In measuring the national income by the income method, care must be taken to include only *factor incomes*. Remember that we are trying to measure the value of the national product and must, therefore, include only those incomes paid out for services rendered in the production of goods and services. Many people receive incomes which are not of this type. Unemployment pay, sickness benefits and old age pensions are examples of incomes described as *transfer payments*. They are not included because they do not represent payments for contributions to the creation of the national product.

8 Expenditure taxes and subsidies

The statistics of total expenditure on goods and services record spending at *market prices* (the prices actually paid by the people making the purchases). For many goods and services, however, the market price includes an element of taxation (e.g. VAT) and the production of some goods and services is subsidized. In these cases, the market price is not a measure of the factor cost of the good or service. It does not measure the value of resources used up in the production of the good or service. National income is always measured at factor cost so that expenditure taxes are subtracted from total expenditure. Subsidies reduce market prices below factor cost and so they are added to total expenditure when the national income is being calculated.

Table 15   UK national income, 1980 (£ million)

Source: *National Income and Expenditure*, HMSO, 1981.

Output

Agriculture, forestry, fishing	4 296
Mining, quarrying, oil extraction	10 871
Manufacturing	48 060
Construction	13 025
Gas, water, electricity	5 803
Transport/communications	15 410
Distributive trades	19 328
Insurance, banking and financial services	18 288
Ownership of dwellings	11 996
Public administration and defence	13 987
Professional and scientific services	25 467
Other services	18 734
Errors and adjustments for some double counting	−11 777
Gross Domestic Product (at factor cost)	193 488
Net property income from abroad	−38
Gross National Product	193 450
Less Capital consumption	−27 045
National Income	166 405

Income

Income from employment	137 083
Income from self-employment	18 394
Gross trading profits of companies	24 979
Gross surpluses of public enterprises	6 185
Rent	13 231
Errors and adjustments	+93
Less Stock appreciation	−6 477
Gross Domestic Product (at factor cost)	193 488
Net property income from abroad	−38
Gross National Product	193 450
Less Capital consumption	−27 045
National Income	166 405

Expenditure

Consumers' expenditure	135 403
Government spending on consumer goods and services	48 337
Gross domestic fixed capital (investment)	40 050
Value of physical increase in stocks (investment)	−3 596
Total domestic spending at market prices	220 194
Plus Exports	63 198
Less Imports	−57 832
Less Taxes on expenditure	−37 287
Plus Subsidies	5 215
Gross Domestic Product (at factor cost)	193 488
Net property income from abroad	−38
Gross National Product	193 450
Less Capital consumption	−27 045
National Income	166 405

Some important terms

Gross Domestic Product (GDP)

This term is used to describe the value of the total output produced by the factors of production which are located within the country, whether these factors are owned by the residents of that country or by foreigners.

Gross National Product (GNP)

This is the value of the total output produced by nationally-owned factors of production wherever they happen to be located, whether at home or abroad. In the UK, as in most non-communist countries, there are foreign-owned enterprises. Some part of the income (e.g. profits and interest) created by these firms will be taken out of the country by the foreign owners. On the other hand, many UK firms own enterprises which are located overseas and some of the profits from these overseas activities will return to the parent company in the UK. The national income accounts show the difference between these two flows of income as follows:

Property income earned abroad – property income paid abroad
= net property income from abroad.

This item, of course, may be negative. Thus,
Gross Domestic Product + net property income from abroad
= *Gross National Product*

National income

The national income of the UK may be seen as the total value of goods and services becoming available to the British people during the course of a year, either for purposes of consumption or as additions to the nation's stock of capital. This is not the same thing as the GNP, because, in the process of production, *capital is consumed*; it becomes worn out or obsolete. The GNP figure includes the total output of capital, but the national income only includes the additions to the capital stock. The difference between the two, therefore, is the value of the capital which has been consumed, otherwise known as *depreciation*. Thus,

Gross National Product – depreciation = *National Income*
(net national product)

National income and the standard of living

There is no way of obtaining a precise measurement of the standard of living because so many different things affect the welfare of human beings. People's standard of living will be influenced by such things as the amount of leisure they have and the extent to which they enjoy it, the environment in which they live and work, and the degree of political freedom they enjoy. The national income statistics do not provide information on such matters, but since the standard of living is very dependent on the quantities of material goods and services available to the people, changes in the national income are taken to be indicators of changes in the standard of living. For the following reasons, however, they must be used with some caution.

1   An increase in the national income may be due to a rise in prices rather than a rise in output. For example, the national income of the UK rose from about £36 000 million in 1969 to about £140 000 million in 1979 but the main cause of this very large increase was inflation. Over this period, the output of goods and services rose relatively slowly. To find out what has been happening to output (i.e. *real* income), the figures for money national income must be adjusted to remove the effects of rising prices. This is done by making use of an index number of prices which measures the extent to which prices, on average, have changed. The following example may help to make this clear.

	Year 1	**Year 4**
National income	£10 000 m.	£13 200 m.
Prices index	100	110

Money national income has increased by 32 per cent, but, over the same period, prices have risen by 10 per cent. The national income of Year 4, expressed in terms of the prices of Year 1

$$= \frac{£13\ 200\ \text{m.}}{1} \times \frac{100}{110} = £12\ 000\ \text{m.}$$

Put another way, it means that £13 200 million in Year 4 will buy the same quantities of goods and services that £12 000 million would have bought in Year 1. Hence *real* national income has risen by 20 per cent.

2   Another way in which an increase in national income may give a misleading impression of rising living standards is when population is also rising. If real national income rises by 5 per cent over a period of time when population increases by 8 per cent, living standards will fall. Thus, it is changes in real national income *per head* which must be used when changes in living standards are being assessed.

3   Income per head, however, is an average figure. A relatively high income per head may hide the fact that the national income is shared out very unequally. There may be a small number of people with very high incomes and a large number with very low incomes. It is necessary to know something about the distribution of the national income before any conclusions can be drawn about living standards.

4   The total national income figure tells us nothing about how the figure is made up. Standards of living depend very much on the output of consumer

goods and services. A large recorded increase in the national income may be due to a big expansion in the output of capital goods or of military equipment and, if this is so, there will be no corresponding increase in the standards of living in the years in which the increase is recorded.

5 The national income is measured at factor cost, but there are some 'costs' of production which do not appear in the prices we pay for goods and services. Industrial production creates problems of pollution, traffic congestion, loss of countryside and so on. These are costs which are borne by the whole community and not by firms producing goods and services. They are described as social costs and do not appear in the national income accounts. The money values of goods produced where there are heavy social costs do not provide a good indicator of their contributions to living standards.

Personal incomes

Having looked briefly at the problems of measuring what the community produces, we must now turn to the question of how it is shared out. How much of the national income goes to individuals depends upon the relative size of their money income. Economic goods have money prices so that money incomes may be seen as claims on the national output. People with larger money incomes have claims to greater shares of the national output than people with smaller incomes. Money incomes are acquired in different ways.

1 Wages and salaries .... payments for personal services
2 Rent, interest and profits .... incomes from property
3 Incomes from self-employment .... mixed incomes (i.e. 1 plus 2)
4 Social security benefits .... transfer payments

Table 16 gives brief details showing the relative importance of the different types of personal income in the UK.

Table 16 Total personal income, UK 1980

	percentage
Income from employment	68.3%
Income from self-employment	9.2%
Rent, interest and dividends	9.8%
Social security benefits	12.7%
	100.0%

Source: *National Income and Expenditure*, HMSO, 1981.

The greatest inequalities are found in the distribution of income from property and are due, of course, to the inequalities in the ownership of wealth, that is, in the ownership of such things as land, buildings, stocks and shares, government bonds and bank deposits. A table in the 1981 edition of *Social Trends* (HMSO) provides the following information on the distribution of personal wealth in the UK in 1978.

1% of the population owned 23% of total *marketable* wealth.
2% of the population owned 30% of total *marketable* wealth.
5% of the population owned 44% of total *marketable* wealth.
10% of the population owned 58% of total *marketable* wealth
25% of the population owned 83% of total *marketable* wealth.
50% of the population owned 95% of total *marketable* wealth.

By far the greater part of national income, however, takes the form of rewards to labour (see Table 16) and the next chapter looks at the reasons for differences in income in the labour market.

Money income and real income

A person's money income is the number of pounds he or she receives each week or each month. Real income refers to the quantities of goods and services which that money income will buy. When prices are rising or falling, a change in money income does not tell us what is happening to real income. A person who received a wage increase of 10 per cent during a period when prices rose by 15 per cent experienced an increase in money income but a fall in real income. In order to discover what is happening to real income it is necessary to make use of price index numbers as explained earlier.

Factor incomes

The incomes of the factors of production are classified as follows.
1 Wages and salaries are payments for the services of labour.
2 Interest is a payment for the services of capital.
3 Rent is a payment for the services of land.
4 Profit is a surplus over cost or a reward for bearing the risks of enterprise.
   Factor incomes are prices; they are the prices which must be paid in order to obtain the services of labour, capital, land and entrepreneurship. Just as there are markets for commodities so there are markets for the services of the factors of production where the prices of land, labour and capital are determined. In the next two chapters we look at the main influences on demand and supply in these factor markets. Attention is concentrated on the labour market, but much of what is said about the way in which wages are determined can be applied to the earnings of capital and land.

18 Wages

Wages and salaries account for about two-thirds of all factor incomes (see Fig. 17.2). The aspect of wages which excites most public attention and controversy seems to be that of wage differentials. We are all aware that there are great differences in wage rates between different occupations. Common sense tells us that these wage differences exist because different jobs demand different amounts of education, skill, experience and responsibility. As we shall see later these things do play a part in determining wage rates, but they are by no means the only reasons why wage differences exist and they do not explain why some of these wage differences persist.

Why, for example, is there no large-scale movement from low-wage occupations to high-wage occupations? What might happen if there were a high degree of occupational mobility is illustrated in Fig. 18.1

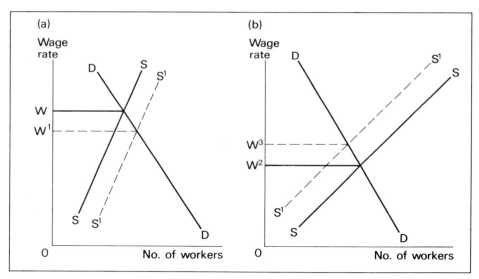

Fig. 18.1 Effects of greater mobility on wage differentials
(a) High-wage occupation   (b) Low-wage occupation

Assume that the two diagrams in Fig. 18.1 represent conditions in two labour markets and that, originally, OW and OW^2 were the wage rates in the two markets. If labour were very mobile occupationally, there would be a movement from the low-wage occupation to the high-wage occupation. This movement is represented by the movements of the supply curves in both markets from SS to S^1S^1. Falling supply in market (b) would cause the wage rate to rise and increasing supply in market (a) would cause the wage rate to fall. Such a movement would greatly reduce (or eliminate) the existing wage differentials.

The fact that in the real world, there are large differences in wage rates indicates the existence of serious barriers to the occupational mobility of labour. In other words there are many different markets for labour and it is often very difficult for a worker to move from one occupation to another. The prices (i.e. wage rates) in these different markets will not be the same because the supply and demand conditions will not be the same in each market. To understand the reasons why wage rates differ in this way we have to look at the things which determine the demand for and supply of labour.

The demand for labour

Firms will only employ labour when it is profitable for them to do so. The individual firm will take on workers as long as their employment adds more to the firm's revenue than to the firm's costs. This means that the firm must compare the value of what labour produces (per hour or per week) with what labour costs (per hour or per week). It is important to realize that high wages may not mean high labour costs and low wages do not necessarily mean that labour costs will be low. The following example should make this point clear. Both workers are producing the same commodity.

	Wage rate per hour	Hourly output (units)	Labour cost per unit of output
Worker A	£4	50	8p
Worker B	£3	30	10p

Worker A is more highly paid than Worker B but, because his productivity is greater, he produces goods at a lower cost than Worker B.

1 The demand for labour is a *derived* demand; it is derived from the demand for the product of labour. The services of the most conscientious and skilful workers will not be demanded if there is no demand for the goods they are trained to produce.

2 A firm's demand for labour will be influenced by the 'cost of labour' and this, as we have seen earlier, depends upon the wage rate and the productivity of labour.

3 The demand for labour will also be influenced by the prices of the goods and services produced by labour. If an increasing demand for the product increases its price, then, other things being equal, it will be more profitable to produce and the demand for labour will increase.

4 In capital-intensive industries, labour costs will be a relatively small percentage of total costs. Thus, an increase in wage-rates will have a relatively small effect on the price of the product and the demand for labour will be inelastic (see page 157). In labour-intensive industries, wages will be a high proportion of total costs and increases in the wage rates will have a relatively large effect on the price of the product. The demand for labour will tend to be elastic.

5 An important determinant of the demand for labour is the firm's ability to replace labour by machinery. The introduction of relatively low-cost labour-saving equipment will make the demand for labour more elastic. Rising labour costs will lead to an increasing substitution of capital for labour.

The demand curve for labour will be of the normal shape, sloping downwards from left to right. Other things being equal, an increase in the wage rate will reduce the amount of labour demanded. But if an increase in the wage rate is accompanied by a corresponding increase in productivity, labour costs will not increase and the amount of labour demanded will not fall.

The supply of labour

The determinants of the total supply of labour in a country were discussed on pages 133–4. At this point, it is the supply of labour to a particular occupation which concerns us. In other words, it is the factors which determine the supplies of architects, teachers, miners, nurses, typists and so on which are relevant when examining the reasons for differences in wages and salaries. To a great extent this is a question about the mobility of labour or the ability of labour to move from one occupation to another. Fig. 18.1 demonstrated that if labour were extremely mobile, any large differences in earnings between different occupations would tend to disappear. The fact that large wage differentials persist means that there must be severe restrictions on occupational mobility.

The ease or difficulty of entry to an occupation determines whether the supply of that type of labour is elastic or inelastic. For example, if a job requires a special kind of ability, high educational qualifications, or a long period of training, then, in the short run, the supply of that type of labour will be inelastic. A substantial increase in wages will bring forth a relatively small increase in supply. This reasoning does not apply of course if a large number of workers possessing the necessary qualifications are unemployed.

Where a job does not require any special aptitudes or specialized knowledge and the operations can be learned fairly quickly, supply will be elastic. A relatively small increase in the wage rate will bring about a relatively large increase in supply because workers from other jobs can move fairly easily into such an occupation.

In the long run, the supply of labour to most occupations will be elastic because, over a period of time, it is possible to educate and train more people for the jobs requiring specialist qualifications.

The individual's supply of labour

The supply of labour means the number of hours of work supplied per week or per month at any given wage rate. The supply curves used in this textbook have all been of the normal shape, that is, sloping upwards from left to right. Can we assume that the supply curve for labour is of the same shape? Will the individual worker offer more labour (i.e. more hours of work) when the wage rate increases? He or she may well do so when real wages are rather low, but experience seems to show that, for most people, as real income increases, leisure becomes more and more attractive. It is quite possible that a point is reached where an increase in the wage rate causes a worker to offer fewer hours of work. If this is so, it means that a point has been reached where, for that worker, the marginal utility derived from an extra hour's leisure exceeds that derived from the income obtained from an extra hour of work. This particular feature of individual behaviour is illustrated in Fig. 18.2.

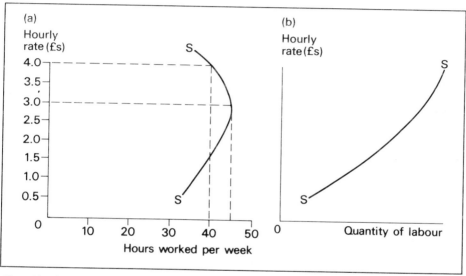

Fig. 18.2(a) An individual's supply curve   Fig. 18.2(b) Supply of labour to an occupation

It must be noted that the fact that the supply curve bends backwards does *not* mean that the person has chosen to have more leisure and less income; he or she can choose to have *more leisure and more income*. The following example illustrates this point.

When the wage rate is £3 per hour a person chooses to work 45 hours per week (i.e. her wages are £135 per week).

When the wage rate increases to £4 per hour she chooses to work 40 hours per week (i.e. her wages are £160 per week).

Most people, of course, are not free to choose the number of hours they work. Preferences for more leisure, however, reveal themselves in the claims made by trade unions and pressures for shorter working weeks have been very strong in recent years.

Supply of labour to an occupation

Although an individual's supply curve may bend backwards at some point, the total supply curve of labour to an occupation will be of the normal shape. People may opt for a shorter working week when real wages increase, but a rise in the wage rate in any one occupation or industry, other things being equal, will attract more people into that industry. In the long run more people will try to obtain the necessary qualifications and, in the short run, the higher wage rates may well increase the industry's labour force by attracting (a) people who may have left the industry to work elsewhere, (b) qualified married women who left the industry to stay at home, (c) people who have retired early and (d) people working in other jobs who have the necessary qualifications to enter this industry.

Net advantages

The amount of labour supplied does not depend solely upon the wage rate. There are many aspects of a job which affect people's willingness to offer their services. They will take account of such things as:

a   the opportunities for promotion;
b   the degree of job security;
c   the nature of the work – whether it is interesting and satisfying;
d   the physical conditions in which the work is carried out – whether they are pleasant or dirty and disagreeable;
e   the extent to which wages are supplemented by 'payments in kind' such as subsidized meals, subsidized transport, subsidized housing, 'company cars' and so on. These benefits are usually described as 'perks' and they provide another reason why differences in money incomes may give a misleading impression of differences in real incomes.

The amount of labour supplied in any given labour market, then, is determined by the monetary and non-monetary rewards being offered. Workers may accept relatively low wages in an occupation because of some compensating advantages which it enjoys over an occupation where money wages are higher. We can summarize by saying that it is the *net advantages* of an occupation which influence the willingness to supply labour.

Fig. 18.3 shows how supply and demand analysis might be used to help explain movements in wages and salaries. It shows what might happen in labour markets due to changes in the techniques of production. Assume that, in a particular industry, technical progress has resulted in the development of some very efficient automated machinery (e.g. robots) which can handle much of the process work and assembly work previously carried out by unskilled and semi-skilled labour. The demand for this type of labour will fall and, other things being equal, there will be some decline in the earnings of these workers (Fig. 18.3(a)). Supply being elastic, this type of labour will tend to move out of the industry into semi-skilled and unskilled work elsewhere. But the manufac-

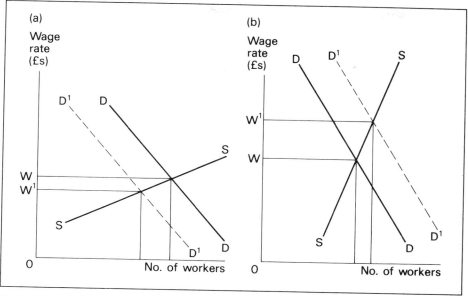

Fig. 18.3   Wage differences – an example
(*a*) *Unskilled job – demand falling*   (*b*) *Skilled job – demand rising*

ture, installation and maintenance of this new equipment will tend to increase the demand for skilled engineers (both mechanical and electrical). Supply of this type of labour is relatively inelastic and the increased demand could lead to a substantial rise in earnings (Fig. 18.3(b)).

Wage differences within an occupation

Quite apart from the differences in wage rates between occupations, there are often great variations in the rates of pay received by people in the same occupation. There are several reasons for this state of affairs.

1   Many occupations pay higher wages to those with greater experience and salary scales are arranged so that workers receive annual increases in pay.

2   In some jobs a 'payment by results' system is applied and workers' wages are linked directly to their outputs. Under this 'piece rate' system, the faster worker will obviously earn more than the slower worker.

3   Although the basic rate may be the same, the *earnings* of workers may differ from firm to firm because of differences in the amounts of overtime worked and because of variations in the type of bonuses paid for improvements in productivity, good time-keeping and low absenteeism.

4   The demand and supply conditions may be different in different parts of the country. Although there may be a nationally agreed minimum wage rate for the occupation, firms in areas where there is a labour shortage may offer higher wages.

5 Differences in the cost of living may also give rise to different wage rates within an occupation. A supplementary allowance is often paid to workers in the London area to compensate them for the relatively high cost of living in that area.

6 In the past, the most striking differences in the rates of remuneration within an occupation were the lower rates paid to women workers. The Equal Pay Act which came into force in 1976 made it illegal for employers to pay women less for doing the same work as men.

Trade unions

One does not have to be a student of economics to know that wage rates are not determined solely by the free play of market forces. It is common knowledge that the activities of trade unions and the government are a very important influence on the average level of wages and upon the differences in wage rates in different occupations.

Trade unions are associations of workers formed for the purposes of improving the pay and working conditions of their members. They aim to achieve these objectives by using their ability to control the supply of labour and by influencing Parliament to pass legislation which is favourable to their members. Unions have played an important part in the creation of laws which have given workers improvements in working conditions, protection against unfair dismissal, the right to compensation for injuries sustained at work, the right to redundancy payments and many other benefits. Many people, however, see the major role of trade unions as the representatives of workers in wage negotiations.

Types of trade union

In the UK, unions are organized in different ways. It is difficult to classify the unions because whatever classification is used there will be a great deal of overlapping. Nevertheless we can identify the main types of union.

1 Craft unions
These unions tend to restrict their membership to workers possessing certain skills (e.g. electricians, woodworkers, boilermakers). It has been traditional for such unions to recruit only those workers who have served a recognized apprenticeship in the particular craft represented by the union, although with the recent emphasis on the retraining of redundant workers this condition may not be enforced.

2 General unions
General unions recruit mainly unskilled and semi-skilled workers, but membership is open to all types of workers. They recruit members in all types of industries and, in the UK, these unions tend to be very large. The Transport

and General Workers' Union and the Union of General and Municipal Workers have 2 million and 1 million members respectively (see Table 17).

3 Industrial unions

The membership of an industrial union is based on an industry and it aims to recruit all the workers in a particular industry whether they are skilled or unskilled. This type of union is common in Western Europe and the USA, but not in the UK. Examples of this type of union in the UK are the National Union of Mineworkers and the National Union of Railwaymen.

4 'White collar' unions

The very large increase in the proportion of the working population engaged in service industries has led to a rapid growth in the membership of what are commonly referred to as 'white collar' unions. Unions representing teachers, health workers, civil servants, technical and managerial staff and so on are now among the largest unions in the UK (see Table 17).

One feature of the type of union organization which exists in the UK and which gives rise to some industrial problems is the fact that, in any one industry (or any one large firm), the workers will be members of different unions. The engineers will belong to the engineers' union, the electricians to the electricians' union, the unskilled workers to a general union, etc. Arrangements between management and workers over such matters as changes in working practices may require the agreement of many different unions before they can be implemented. It is a situation which also gives rise to what are known as *demarcation disputes*. These are disputes between unions which may arise when there is a proposed change in the techniques of production or some new material is being used (e.g. aluminium for windows instead of wood). Unions may disagree on the way the work is reallocated to members of different unions. For example, when ships are loaded with containers, should the containers be packed by dockers or by road haulage and railway workers?

Table 17   Trade unions in the UK – the ten largest unions, 1980

	Membership (thousands)
Transport Workers (TGWU)	2073
Engineers (AUEW)	1483
Municipal Workers (GMWU)	965
Local Government (NALGO)	729
Public Employees (NUPE)	712
Managerial Staff (ASTMS)	471
Shopworkers (USDAW)	462
Electricians (EEPTU)	420
Builders (UCATT)	320
Teachers (NUT)	291

Source: *The Economist*, 23 February 1980.

There are about 450 trade unions in the UK with a total membership of about 11.6 million (1981). The great majority of these unions are very small and the movement is dominated by a few very large unions. The ten unions in Table 17 have some 8 million members. Most of the trade unions are affiliated to the central body, the Trades Union Congress (TUC), which negotiates with the government on behalf of the whole trade union movement. But each union has complete freedom of action and its major role is to protect the interests of its own members.

Trade unions and wages

The fact that wages are settled as a result of negotiations between trade unions and employers does not mean that supply and demand analysis has no part to play in explaining the way in which wage rates are determined in the real world. Trade unions are able to exert an important influence on wage rates because they have the ability to control the supply of labour. They may do this by restricting entry into a trade or profession to those who have completed a recognized apprenticeship or some other course of training and, in some cases, unions may exercise direct control over recruitment. The 'closed shop' is a situation where only members of a particular trade union are permitted to work and the employer agrees to employ only members of that union. In these various ways trade unions are able to exercise a degree of monopoly power; they can restrict the supply of labour so as to influence its price (i.e. the wage rate). Ultimately the power of a union rests upon its ability to reduce the supply of labour to an industry (or industries) to zero, that is, to call a strike. The effectiveness of the strike weapon has steadily increased as industry has become more specialized and capital-intensive. When production is brought to a halt, firms still have to meet the heavy fixed costs. The specialized nature of production means that a relatively large industry can be brought to a halt by a strike which stops the production of some particular component.

Collective bargaining

Unions represent their members collectively and employers are also represented collectively by some kind of employers' association. In effect, a single seller of labour is negotiating with a single buyer of labour. This is the process of collective bargaining.

Trade unions' claims for higher pay tend to be based on one or more of the following arguments.

1 Comparability
It is a fairly common technique for union negotiators to draw up a kind of

'league table' showing the various occupations in order of their current wage rates. Unions will tend to press for a restoration of wage differentials when it seems as though their members have slipped down the league table or, if they are near the bottom, will demand some improvement in their position. This procedure can have inflationary consequences. If one or two powerful unions succeed in obtaining relatively large wage increases, other unions using the comparability argument will demand similar increases and the end result could be that wages in general rise much faster than the average increase in productivity.

2 Cost of living

Unions anxious to protect the real incomes of their members will claim a compensating wage increase whenever the cost of living rises. This could also have the effect of creating inflationary conditions (or worsening existing inflation). If the cause of the increase in the cost of living is 'external' (for example a rise in the prices of imported food or raw materials), a compensating wage increase, if it is not accompanied by a corresponding increase in productivity, can only result in a further rise in industry's costs of production.

3 Profitability

An increase in the profitability of an industry provides the unions with a case for an increase in wages. They argue, quite naturally, that the workers should share in the increased prosperity of the industry.

Unions, wages and employment

In pressing for better working conditions and higher wages, union negotiators cannot ignore the economic facts of life. They will consider the likely effects of higher wages on the level of employment. If an increase in the wage rate reduces the amount of labour demanded, some of their members will be better off, but others (those who lose their jobs) will be worse off. The trade unions will certainly take account of those things which determine the demand for labour (discussed earlier in the chapter). Remember that an increase in the wage rate does not *necessarily* mean that labour costs increase. If the wage rate rises by 5 per cent, but the productivity of labour also increases by 5 per cent, labour costs per unit of output will not change. Fig. 18.4 shows the possible effects of labour becoming unionized *in a competitive industry*.

In Fig. 18.4, DD and SS are the market demand and supply curves for labour. The free market wage rate is OW and, at this wage rate, OM workers are employed. If a trade union is formed which establishes a minimum wage rate of OW^1, the supply curve of labour to this industry now becomes the heavier line W^1S, because no labour will now be supplied at wage rates less than OW^1. In this particular case employment falls from OM to OM^1 workers.

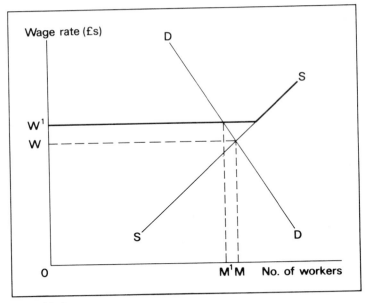

Fig. 18.4

This fall in employment, however, may not take place where employers have some degree of monopoly power and have been making excess profits by paying labour wages which were substantially less than the value of labour's product. In such cases unions may be able to raise wages at the expense of these profits and still maintain the existing level of employment. An increase in the wage rate may not lead to fewer workers being employed when it is accompanied by an agreement which leads to an increase in productivity. As explained earlier, the increase in productivity will offset the effects of the higher wage rate on labour costs. Trade unions may also believe that a higher wage rate may not lead to a reduced demand for labour because the increased costs can be passed on in the form of higher prices. If this is the case, money wages will rise but, if similar actions are taking place in other industries, real wages may not increase.

Real wages are a measure of what money wages will buy. If money wages are increasing, real wages will be increasing only if money wages are rising faster than prices. This happens when money wages are rising faster than the costs of production and it means that productivity must be increasing. In other words, real wages depend mainly on movements in productivity. Official statistics show that, in spite of the very large increases in money wages in the UK during the 1970s, real wages increased very much in line with increases in productivity. Trade unions can, however, increase the real income of their members independently of movements in productivity by taking a greater share of the national income. This might be done, for example, by reducing the share of profits in the national income.

The role of government

Because movements in wages, by affecting costs and prices, can have a serious influence on the national economic performance, the government, in recent years, has tended to play an increasing part in the procedures by which wages are determined. Generally speaking, this increased government intervention has been resisted by the trade unions who are strongly attached to the traditional methods of free collective bargaining, where the word 'free' means 'free from government interference'. The severe economic problems encountered in the 1960s and 1970s forced British governments to adopt policies to influence or control the rate at which the general level of wages was rising. These measures are described as incomes policies and are discussed on pages 332–4. But government intervention in the market for labour goes back much further than this.

Early this century the state set up wage regulating bodies for employees in industries and trades where trade union organization was very weak or where it was felt that collective bargaining on a voluntary basis was ineffective. Originally called Trade Boards, these bodies are now known as *Wages Councils* and they regulate the wages of about 3.5 million workers. There are some forty-six Wages Councils, each of which has equal numbers of employer and worker representatives and up to three independent members. A Wages Council submits its proposals on the minimum wage rate and annual holidays for a particular industry to the Secretary of State for Employment who can issue an order which makes these conditions of employment enforceable at law. In industries where there is a Wages Council, therefore, there is a legal minimum wage. Wages Councils cover such industries as catering, distribution, clothing, textiles and agriculture.

The state also provides machinery to assist in the settlement of disputes which inevitably arise where wages are decided by collective bargaining. In 1974 the government established the Advisory, Conciliation and Arbitration Service (ACAS). This body has many functions, but in connection with wage disputes it can offer, when asked to do so, the services of qualified staff to act as conciliators or it can appoint arbitrators.

19 Interest, rent and profits

Interest

Interest has been defined earlier as a payment for the services of capital. More strictly it is a payment which has to be made in order to borrow the funds needed to purchase capital goods. Since, however, people also borrow in order to buy consumer goods, it is better to define the rate of interest quite simply as the price of a loan.

People holding money have the ability to enjoy immediate consumption if they so wish. If they lend out this money they are foregoing the opportunity to 'consume now' and it is only natural that they will demand some kind of compensation for the sacrifice they are making. The payment of interest on their loans offers lenders a prospect of a higher level of *future* satisfaction. The rate of interest may be seen as a measure of the strength of a lender's preference for present rather than future satisfactions. If someone lends £100 for one year on condition that the borrower repays at least £110 at the end of the year, a rate of interest of 10 per cent is being demanded. Clearly anything less than £110 payable in one year's time would not compensate the lender for giving up the ability to consume £100 worth of goods and services now.

It is perhaps rather confusing to speak about *the* rate of interest when we all know that, at any given moment, there are many different rates of interest. There are a number of reasons why different borrowers are charged different rates of interest.

Why interest rates differ

1 There is always the risk of default by the borrower. In some cases, for example, loans to the government, this risk is negligible. In other cases, such as a loan to a brand new enterprise, the risk is considerable. Lenders will obviously demand higher interest rates where the risks are greater.
2 Lenders often demand some kind of security. For example, a loan in the form of a mortgage gives the lender a legal claim on the property of the borrower until such time as the loan is repaid. A lender will normally only accept as security some kind of asset which can easily be converted into money should the borrower default. The quality of the security offered by the borrower will influence the rate of interest being charged for a loan; the better the security, the lower the rate of interest which will have to be paid.
3 Another reason for differences in interest rates is the fact that loans are made for different periods of time. Generally speaking, long-term loans carry higher interest rates than short-term loans. This is because the risk element is greater the longer the duration of the loan; the longer the period, the greater the risks of 'things going wrong'.
4 Normally, the lender parts with the money and receives in return some kind

of IOU or promise to repay. Governments borrow by selling promises to repay in the form of government securities, and firms sell debentures. Many of these IOUs are marketable; they can be sold on the Stock Exchange or in the money markets. The people buying them, of course, will pay something less than the face values of the IOUs. For example, if someone pays £900 for an IOU which promises to pay £1000 in one year's time, that person is, in effect, charging £100 interest on a loan of £900. If a borrower is able to offer a lender an IOU which has a ready market, a loan will be obtained at a lower rate of interest than would have been charged had the IOU not been marketable.

In the real world, for the reasons set out above, there is a range of interest rates, but they all tend to move in the same direction. We talk of interest *rates* rising or falling. In discussing the factors which determine the rate of interest we are looking at those things which influence all interest rates.

The market rate of interest

Market rates of interest vary from day to day and hour by hour. The lowest of these rates is that at which the government is able to borrow money. The government is the most credit-worthy borrower. There is virtually no risk of the government defaulting on its debts because it has the powers to tax the income and wealth of the whole nation. The government borrows by issuing a variety of securities, most of which carry a fixed rate of interest. The buyers of these securities receive a fixed rate of interest based on the nominal or face value of the security. For example, the holder of a £1000 6 per cent government bond will receive an income of £60 per annum. The *market rate* of interest, however, is the *yield* on these government securities. Government securities are marketable and may change hands many times during their lifetimes. The market prices of such securities depend upon the strength of people's desire to hold money (which earns no income) relative to the attraction of holding securities (which do earn an income).

For example, if the bond (£1000 nominal value) mentioned above is selling in the open market for £800, the yield on this type of security is,

$$\frac{\text{guaranteed annual income}}{\text{market price}} \times \frac{100}{1} = \frac{£60}{£800} \times \frac{100}{1} = 7\frac{1}{2}\%$$

The fact that people are prepared to pay no more than £800 for a guaranteed annual income of £60 means that they will not part with their money unless they obtain a return of at least 7½ per cent. Thus, the market rate of interest, in this case, is 7½ per cent.

The demand for loans

The rate of interest is the price of a loan and must, therefore, be determined by the demand for and supply of loans. Loans are demanded:
a   by firms wishing to buy capital goods;

b by households wishing to buy houses (both new and second-hand);
c by households wishing to buy durable consumer goods (cars, furniture);
d by governments to finance expenditure which is not covered by taxation;
e by firms and households which have run into financial difficulties.

The provision of these loans is usually carried out by specialist financial institutions, many of which have already been discussed. The supply of loans to firms was discussed in Chapter 9. Loans for house purchase are supplied mainly by building societies while loans for the purchase of durable consumer goods are supplied mainly by finance houses specializing in hire-purchase finance, although banks also provide such loans. Loans to the government are provided by pension funds, insurance companies, banks, finance houses, and the general public.

The demand for loanable funds, therefore, is made up of several elements, but the relationship between the rate of interest and the demand for capital is a particularly important one.

The demand for capital

The demand for capital goods, like the demand for labour, depends upon its price and its productivity. The price of capital may be regarded as the rate of interest which has to be paid on the loans required for the purchase of the equipment. If a firm uses its own funds, the rate of interest still measures the cost of acquiring the capital because the firm will have to forego the interest it would have earned had it not bought the capital goods. The productivity of capital can be expressed in terms of the net profits it is expected to earn over its lifetime. This, too, can be measured in percentage terms. For example, if the installation of new machinery costing £200 000 is expected to bring about an increase in net profits of £20 000 per annum, we can say that the marginal productivity of capital is 10 per cent. Thus, both the cost of capital (the rate of interest) and the productivity of capital can be expressed in percentage terms.

A firm will be tempted to undertake investment if the expected profitability of the new capital exceeds its cost (i.e. the rate of interest). Referring back to the example above, if the firm were able to borrow money at 7 per cent, it might be tempted to undertake the investment. If, however, the rate of interest were 12 per cent, the project would not go forward. As the rate of interest falls, one would expect the amount of investment to increase. At lower rates of interest, some projects will appear profitable which would not have been profitable at higher rates of interest. Note, however, that investment (the purchase of capital goods) depends upon the *expected* profitability of capital – entrepreneurs cannot see into the future – they can only estimate future profitability. Expenditure on new capital, therefore, is likely to be very unstable because there are so many things which can change a firm's outlook on the future.

The supply of loans

The supply of loans comes from three main sources;

a   saving out of current income;
b   saving out of income earned in the past;
c   new money created by the state or the banking system (explained in Chapter 21).

Saving

Saving may be carried out by:
a   the government – the government may take in more revenue from taxation than it spends – in other words, it runs a budget surplus;
b   companies – in the form of retained profits;
c   private persons.

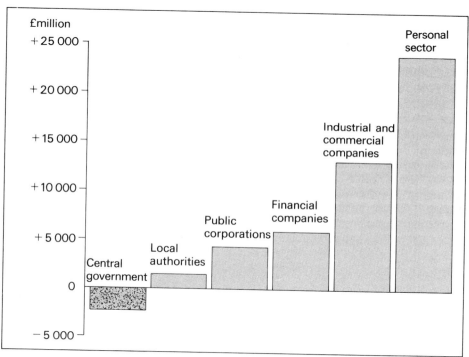

Fig. 19.1   Saving in the UK, 1980

Source: *Financial Statistics*, HMSO.

Saving provides the greater part of the money supplied as loans. These savings are collected by a variety of financial institutions and channelled to industry, households and government. But what determines the volume of saving?
1   The level of real income plays the most important part. As people become better off, they spend more, but spending does not usually rise at the same rate as income. As income rises, both spending and saving increase.
2   The social attitude towards thrift also plays a part. Other things being

equal, the proportion of income saved in a society where thrift is regarded as a virtue will be higher than in one where people place a higher value on 'living for the moment'.

3 The number and variety of savings institutions also influences the level of saving. In most developed countries, the people have access to, and are quite familiar with a wide range of savings schemes. Such facilities are not generally available in less developed countries so that the amount of actual saving may be much less than the amount of potential saving.

4 One might expect the rate of interest to have an important influence on the amount of saving. For most people this is the amount of reward they obtain for lending to banks and other financial institutions. As the rate of interest increases, therefore, one would expect the volume of this type of saving to increase. In fact, it appears that the rate of interest does not have a very large influence on the amount of saving. One reason for this is the fact that a large part of personal saving is *contractual*, that is, people sign some kind of agreement or contract which obliges them to make regular payments to pension funds, insurance companies, building societies and so on. Once such a contract is made, changes in the rate of interest will not influence the amount of saving.

Many people save in order to achieve some financial objective, such as the deposit for a house or the purchase price of a motor car. In this case, an increase in the rate of interest might well reduce the rate of saving because the sum required will be accumulating at a faster rate. The savings carried out by companies and governments are not likely to be much influenced by the rate of interest. Government saving takes the form of a budget surplus when it removes more income from the people than it returns to them in the form of public spending. In this case, the aim is to reduce total spending rather than to increase the wealth of the government. Companies save in order to finance expansion and the amounts of profit they retain are not likely to be influenced by the rate of interest.

Although the connection between the volume of saving and the rate of interest does not appear to be very strong, it seems generally agreed that there is some connection; higher rates of interest will tend to encourage some increase in saving.

The price of loans

It seems reasonable to assume that the demand curve for loans will be of the normal shape, sloping downwards from left to right. At lower prices (i.e. rates of interest), more loans will be demanded. We have seen earlier why, as the price of a loan falls, there will be more borrowing by firms wishing to buy capital goods. The same will be true of the demand for loans from people wishing to buy houses and durable consumer goods. A fall in the rate of interest reduces the total costs of equipment and property purchased with borrowed money.

The supply curve of loanable funds depends upon people's willingness and ability to lend and, other things being equal, higher rates of interest will increase the willingness to lend. The supply curve of loanable funds, therefore, will also be of the normal shape. Fig. 19.2 illustrates how the rate of interest is determined by the demand for, and the supply of, loanable funds.

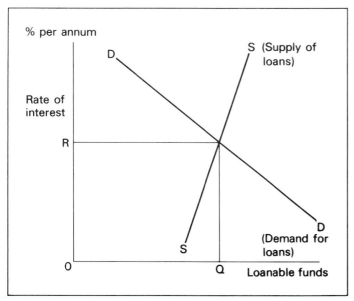

Fig. 19.2

It must be borne in mind, however, that the government is able to control the money supply and by increasing or decreasing the supply of money it can influence the supply of funds available for borrowing.

Economic rent

In ordinary speech, rent means a payment for the use of someone else's property. In the modern world it is possible to rent land, buildings, machines, motor cars, household appliances, in fact, almost any durable good. These rentals, however, include payments for the services of all the factors of production because the revenues received by the firms renting various types of property and equipment will be paid out as wages, rent, interest and profits. In economics the word 'rent' does not apply to this kind of payment. The fact that the economist uses the word 'rent' in a special sense is a source of some confusion to students and it is wise to use the term *economic rent* whenever the economist's idea of rent is being discussed.

213

As one might expect, the theory of rent developed from a study of the earnings of land and it is largely the work of David Ricardo whose ideas were published in 1817 in a book called *Principles of Political Economy and Taxation*. At this level it is only possible to give a very simplified outline of his views.

Ricardo pointed out that land is limited in supply, and because it is a gift of nature, it has no costs of production. This led him to the view that the income of landlords is a kind of 'unearned' surplus. He said that they were receiving income on an asset which had cost them nothing to create. No payment is necessary to call forth a supply of land. Since the supply of land is fixed, Ricardo saw the price of land (i.e. rent) as being determined solely by demand. If demand increased, price would rise by the full extent of the increase in demand; there could be no increase in supply to offset the increase in demand.

The demand for land is derived from the demand for the products of land. In Ricardo's time most people in the UK were employed in producing food from the land so that Ricardo saw the demand for land as being determined by the demand for food. He declared that high rents were due to high food prices – exactly the opposite to the general opinion which held that high food prices were due to the high rents being charged by landlords. Ricardo explained his ideas in the following manner. If the demand for wheat is high and rising, the price of wheat will be high and it will be profitable to grow wheat. The demand for wheat-growing land will rise and landlords will be able to charge higher rents. If the demand for wheat falls, the price of wheat will fall and farmers will only find it profitable to grow wheat if they can obtain land more cheaply. Landlords will charge lower rents because they will prefer to have some income from their land rather than leave it idle.

The essential idea of Ricardo's theory is that economic rent is a surplus; it is not a cost of production. It plays no part in determining the prices of agricultural products, but is, in fact, determined by these prices.

Economic rent and transfer earnings

Economists soon realised that the idea of rent as a surplus had much wider applications; it could be applied to the earnings of the other factors of production. They saw that some part of the earnings of labour, capital and the entrepreneur could, in many cases, be regarded as a surplus. Hence, the term economic rent came to be applied to that part of the earnings of a factor of production which is in excess of the payment required to keep it in its present employment. The payments made for the services of a factor have two elements.

1   *Transfer earnings*. This term describes the minimum payment which will maintain a factor in its present employment. If the earnings of a factor fall below its transfer earnings it will move to some other occupation. For example, if a lorry driver is earning £100 per week and he could earn £80 per week in the next best paid job he could obtain (say, bus driver), his transfer earnings, while he is employed as a lorry driver are £80 per week.

2   *Economic rent*. Any earnings over and above a factor's transfer earnings is economic rent. It represents that part of the earnings which is in excess of

the amount necessary to keep a factor in its present employment. In the example above, the lorry driver is receiving £20 per week as economic rent.

In the earlier discussion it was implied that all the earnings of land took the form of economic rent. This would be true if land had only one use, that is, if its transfer earnings were zero. But since most of the land occupied by the human race has more than one use, the whole of its earnings are not economic rent. Suppose that the highest bids for the use of an area of land come from Farmer A who is prepared to pay £30 per hectare and wants the land to grow potatoes, and Farmer B who offers £20 per hectare and wants the land to grow barley. Assuming that the highest bidder is successful, the transfer earnings of this plot of land will be £20 per hectare and the economic rent, £10 per hectare.

No. of employees	Weekly wage rate	Economic rent			
		1st employee	2nd employee	3rd employee	4th employee
1	£100	0	—	—	—
2	£110	£10	0	—	—
3	£120	£20	£10	0	—
4	£130	£30	£20	£10	0
5	£140	£40	£30	£20	£10

When 5 workers are employed, economic rent accounts for £100 of the total wage bill.

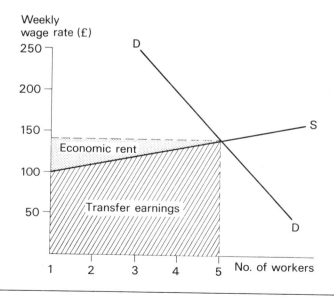

Fig. 19.3

215

Fig. 19.3 is included to demonstrate how economic rent arises in the labour market. It shows a situation where five workers are employed at a wage of £140 per week. As the demand for labour has increased so has the wage. The first person engaged was prepared to offer to work for £100 per week, the second for £110 per week and so on. But all five workers are receiving a wage of £140 per week because it has been necessary to bid up the wage rate in order to attract more workers. Thus the first four workers engaged are now receiving economic rent because the current wage rate exceeds their transfer earnings.

The most often quoted examples of economic rent in the earnings of labour are the very large incomes received by the 'stars' in the world of entertainment and in international sport. Their annual earnings are enormous by any standards. The greater part of these earnings take the form of economic rent because the transfer earnings of most 'stars' (i.e. the most they could earn in another job) will only be a small fraction of their current earnings.

Sometimes economic rent is of a temporary nature. For example, a large increase in world trade will lead to an increase in the demand for shipping space. In the short run, the supply of ships cannot be increased and there will be a large increase in freight rates. The increased earnings of the ships already working is economic rent, but, if the freight rates remain high, more ships will be built, freight rates will fall and the economic rent will be eliminated. Economic rent which is only temporary is described as *quasi-rent*.

Profits

Profit is usually described as a *residual* item; it is what remains of the firm's revenue when all expenses of production have been met. It can, therefore, be negative and a firm may make losses. In the business world, there are several ways in which a firm's profits may be expressed.

1 Profit margins
The profit margin is the excess of the selling price over the cost or buying price. It is usually calculated by expressing the amount of profit as a percentage of the cost price. For example,

Cost price £8, Selling price £10, Profit £2

$$\text{Profit margin} = \frac{£2}{£8} \times \frac{100}{1} = 25\%$$

The term *mark-up* is often used to describe the percentage profit per unit. Sometimes the profit margin is calculated as a percentage of the selling price. In this case the profit margin in the example above would be 20 per cent.

2 Total profits
This is quite simply the difference between total revenue and total costs. It is a

216

figure which is often given great publicity, but it tells us very little about a firm's performance. For example, a large firm might make total profits of several million pounds and such a large figure will attract a lot of attention, but no judgements can be made about the economic performance of the firm until these profits have been related to other features of the firm. How this might be done is demonstrated below.

3 Profit as a measure of performance

In order to estimate the degree of success which a firm is achieving, profits may be calculated as a percentage of the firm's *turnover* and/or of the *capital employed*. The turnover of a business is often used as another name for its sales. Profits are expressed as a percentage of turnover because this is one measure of how hard the firm is having to work in order to earn its profits; it shows what volume of sales it has to achieve in order to earn a given level of profits.

The economist is also interested in the ratio of profits to capital employed because this measurement provides a means of comparing the profitability of capital in different industries.

The example below should help to make these points a little clearer.

	Firm A	**Firm B**
Turnover	£500 000 000	£80 000
Profits	£25 000 000	£8 000
Capital employed	£250 000 000	£40 000

Profit as a percentage of turnover

Firm A $\dfrac{£25\ 000\ 000}{£500\ 000\ 000} \times \dfrac{100}{1} = 5\%$

Firm B $\dfrac{£8\ 000}{£80\ 000} \times \dfrac{100}{1} = 10\%$

Profit as a return on capital employed

Firm A $\dfrac{£25\ 000\ 000}{£250\ 000\ 000} \times \dfrac{100}{1} = 10\%$

Firm B $\dfrac{£8\ 000}{£40\ 000} \times \dfrac{100}{1} = 20\%$

Note that the very much larger profit figures of the larger firm represent a much smaller rate of return on capital employed.

The functions of profits

1 A reward for risk-bearing

Profit or the expectation of profit has a crucial role to play in the capitalist system. It is the prospect of profit which provides the incentive for people to set up in business or to expand existing businesses. It is the anticipation of profit which leads them to use their own savings or to borrow other people's savings to buy the services of land, labour and capital in order to produce goods and services. Such people take risks because there is no certainty that the enterprises will succeed. Profits, then, may be regarded as a reward for risk-taking.

2 A source of funds

As mentioned earlier, retained profits make up a large part of total saving. These retained profits, as was explained in Chapter 9, are a most important source of funds for investment purposes.

3 An indicator to investors

The purpose of economic activity is the satisfaction of wants and maximum satisfaction can only be achieved if resources are allocated to those uses which best meet the demands of consumers. In a competitive system, profits (and losses) serve as indicators of success in meeting these demands. Resources will tend to move into profitable industries and out of unprofitable industries. The trouble with this argument is that profits may be the result of a firm's monopoly power rather than of its superior efficiency.

4 An incentive to innovators

Economic growth depends to a great extent on the rate of technical and economic change. The introduction of new materials, new products, and new techniques of production is known as *innovation*. Profits provide a great stimulus to innovation because new developments offer prospects of large profits.

Test paper 7

Short-answer questions

1 The national income is a measure of the national output of goods and *services*. Why are services included in the national output and how do the statisticians measure the value of the services produced?

2 If a large number of motorists decided to stop washing their cars at home and to take them to the automatic car wash, what would happen to the national income?

3 If all the goods produced are not sold, how can national output = national expenditure?

4 What proportion of the national income represents payments for the services of labour?

5 Over a period of years, the average weekly wage increased from £100 to £150 and over the same period, prices increased by 25 per cent. What happened to real wages?

6 In an industry, a productivity agreement led to an increase in output-per-worker-hour of 20 per cent. The same agreement also increased the hourly wage rate from £2.00 to £2.50. What was the extent of the change in labour costs per unit of output?

7 The table below gives details of employment and output in an individual firm.

No. of workers	Total product (units per week)
1	100
2	300
3	540
4	700
5	800

If the price of the product is £1.00 per unit,

a What is the value of the marginal product of labour when the number of workers increases from 3 to 4?

b Assuming the firm tries to maximize its profits, how many workers will it employ when the weekly wage rate is £160?

8 The government publishes statistics showing (a) changes in the average weekly wage rate and (b) changes in average weekly earnings. What are the main reasons for the differences between these two measures of income?

9 A large firm declares a profit for the year of £1 000 000. Newspaper commentators describe it as a poor performance. In what sense might this be true?

10 'Interest is the price we have to pay in order to persuade people to sacrifice liquidity.' Explain this statement.

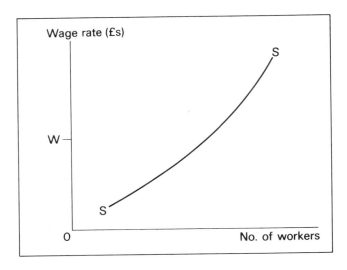

11   A shopkeeper is seeking a loan of £1000 for three months. Such a loan is offered by two firms. One firm demands an interest payment of £20, the other is demanding a rate of interest of 10 per cent per annum. Which offer should the shopkeeper accept?

12   Why is the rate of interest on a loan for house purchase lower than the rate charged on a loan for the purpose of setting up in business?

13   What is meant by *contractual* saving?

14   In what manner does the rent paid for a house differ from economic rent?

15   Distinguish between transfer earnings and transfer payments.

16   Give one example of how a piece of capital equipment (other than shipping) can earn economic rent.

17   What is meant by the expression 'ploughing back profits'?

18   In what fundamental ways do profits differ from wages and interest?

19   In the figure above, SS is the supply curve of labour to a particular industry. If a trade union is formed which is able to enforce a minimum wage of OW, what happens to the supply curve?

20   Distinguish between profits and dividends.

True or false?

21   a   Economic theory assumes that firms will try to maximize profit per unit of output.
b   It is possible for money national income to be rising while real national income is falling.
c   If all workers, over a period of years, obtain flat-rate wage increases, higher-paid workers are likely to complain about the erosion of wage differentials.

d In the UK, the growth in real wages has greatly exceeded the growth in productivity.

e An increase in wages must raise the average cost of production.

f In the UK, more working days are lost through strikes than through any other cause.

g Most British workers belong to industrial unions.

h The total profits of a firm which makes a profit of 10 per cent on each unit it sells must be greater than one which makes a profit of 5 per cent on each unit.

i Inflation might cause a firm to make what are known as 'windfall profits'.

j If a worker's current wage is equal to his or her transfer earnings no economic rent is being received.

Multiple-choice questions

22 The national income of the UK is equal to the annual value of
A   all the goods and services purchased by firms and households
B   the revenue of the central government
C   the total of all personal incomes
D   the national output measured at factor cost
E   the national output measured at market prices

23 The term *real wages* refers to
A   the basic wage rate plus any bonus payments
B   the gross wage minus income tax and other deductions
C   the gross wage minus any overtime payments
D   the amount of goods and services which the wage will buy
E   the wage rate negotiated by and accepted by the trade unions

24 Other things being equal, which of the following is/are likely to lead to a fall in interest rates?
1   an increase in the rate of saving
2   a large increase in government borrowing
3   an increase in consumption spending
A   1, 2 and 3
B   1 and 2 only
C   2 and 3 only
D   1 only
E   3 only

Questions 25, 26, 27 and 28 refer to the following terms.

    A transfer earnings
    B investment (or unearned) income
    C fringe benefits
    D transfer payments
    E disposable income

Which of the above describe,

25 a person's money wage *minus* the amount of economic rent he or she receives?

26 payments in kind?

27 remuneration in the form of grants or social security benefits?

28 wages or salary *minus* taxes on income *plus* any income received which is not a payment for services rendered?

Data-response questions

29 A wage-earning plumber decided to set up his own business. His annual wage as an employee was £6000. He had savings of £5000, earning interest at the rate of 10 per cent per annum, which he withdrew for the purchase of materials and equipment. He rented accommodation for £500 per annum and, in the first year, his administration and transport costs were £750 and he used up £1000 worth of materials. His gross income for the first year was £12 000.

The plumber declared that he had made a profit in his first year of £9750.

    a How did he arrive at this figure?

    b Would an economist agree with him? Explain your answer.

30 In the course of one year a firm:

    1 uses up materials which cost £10 000;

    2 pays out £15 000 in wages; £3000 in rent; £1000 in interest on loans, and £3000 in administrative expenses (clerical assistance);

    3 spends £4000 buying services from other firms (e.g. transport, repair work, advertising);

    4 sells goods to the value of £42 500.

    a What is the value added by this firm?

    b If, during the course of the year, the firm estimates that the value of its capital has depreciated by £1500, what is its contribution to the national income?

    c After making allowances for depreciation, the firm decides to pay out one-half of its profits in the form of dividends. Its share capital consists of 10 000 £1 ordinary shares. What rate of dividend will it declare?

20 Money

Money is something which plays an important part in all our daily lives, yet familiarity does not always imply understanding. Many people would find it rather difficult to give satisfactory answers to the questions, 'What is money?', and 'What kinds of things do we use as money?'. The majority of people would probably give the same answer to both questions, namely, 'Notes, coins and cheques'. But this would not be a good answer for several reasons. Firstly, notes and coin make up a relatively small part of the money supply. Secondly, cheques are not money and thirdly, the first question is really asking about the functions of money rather than its form.

Quite simply, money is whatever is generally acceptable in exchange for goods and services. If people are freely accepting a commodity as a means of payment, then that commodity is serving as money. Throughout history all kinds of commodities have been used as money, including beads, shells, hides, salt and, in more recent times, even cigarettes.

The functions of money

1 A medium of exchange

It has been explained earlier that specialized production can only develop if there is some easy and convenient way of exchanging goods and services. Specialist workers must be able to exchange their output for the goods and services produced by other specialist workers. The oldest and crudest system of exchange is *barter*, but this is a time-consuming and inconvenient method which proved to be a barrier to the extension of the division of labour. Under a barter system a person producing corn and wanting to acquire axes would have to find someone who wanted corn and at the same time, had a surplus of axes. The use of money as a medium of exchange removes the difficulties of the barter system. Producers sell their goods for money and then use the money to purchase whatever variety of goods and services they desire.

2 A measure of value

Even under a barter system, exchange can only take place when there is some agreement on what one thing is worth in terms of another. People would want to know, for instance, the 'price' of a camel in terms of goats, or the exchange rate between lengths of cloth and salt. In most societies these exchange values are now expressed in terms of money. When all goods have money prices it is very easy to discover the exchange rates between different commodities. If the price of one unit of X is £5 and the price of a unit of Y is £1, we know that, at the current rate of exchange, one unit of X is worth 5 units of Y.

3 A store of value

People may not wish to consume at the same rate as they produce. Workers may wish to accumulate the results of their present efforts and consume them in the future. In a system which does not use money they would have to store some of their output in a physical form. For example, a farmer might store grain and a carpenter might build up a stock of tables. But it is relatively costly to store things in this way and there are the added risks of damage and deterioration. In any case, people who are supplying services (e.g. doctors or lawyers) cannot accumulate or 'save up' the things they are producing. Money, however, removes most of these problems because we can sell whatever we are producing and hold the money. Holding wealth in the form of money is convenient because money is a *liquid asset*. Liquidity refers to the ease with which an asset can be converted into money. A liquid asset is one which can be converted into money without delay and with very little risk of any loss in value. Money, therefore, is the most liquid of all assets. The ability of money to act as a store of value is seriously affected when there is inflation because the *exchange* value of money is falling.

4 A standard of deferred payments

Just as it would be difficult to carry on trade in goods and services without using money, so borrowing and lending would be difficult to organize without the use of money. If money did not exist, borrowers would have to find people willing and able to lend them the actual goods they required and the debt would have to be repaid with similar goods. The use of money enables us to borrow 'purchasing power'; the borrowed money can be used to buy whatever goods and services are desired. Without money, the financing of large-scale industry with funds subscribed by thousands of people would have been impossible. Industry could not have been established by large numbers of people lending firms the physical items (buildings, machines, materials etc.) they need to set up in business.

The development of money

If money is to be widely used, the commodity chosen to serve as money must possess certain properties.
1   It must be *durable*. People will not accept as money something which is highly perishable or which rusts and deteriorates in other ways.
2   It must be *portable*. If people are to carry large amounts of purchasing power on their person, the commodity must have a high value relative to its weight and bulk.
3   It must be *divisible*. The commodity must be capable of subdivision into

small units without loss in value so that there is no problem in making both large and small payments.

4 It must be *homogeneous*. This means that any one unit of the commodity must be exactly like every other unit of that denomination. Imagine the problems if people thought that some 50p pieces were more valuable than other 50p pieces.

5 It must be *limited in supply*. Anything which is not limited in supply will have no economic value.

Although all kinds of commodities have been used as money at some time or other, the desirable qualities listed above explain why the precious metals, gold and silver, came to be widely adopted as money. In terms of durability, portability and divisibility they have great advantages over most other commodities which have been used as money. They also inspired confidence because they were (and are) highly valued for their own sake. The development of coinage enormously increased the convenience of using gold and silver as money and for centuries in most western countries they had virtually no competition from other kinds of money.

Paper money

The use of paper money developed during the seventeenth century when wealthier people began to leave gold and silver in the strongrooms of goldsmiths for safe-keeping. The goldsmiths issued certificates of deposit entitling the depositors to withdraw their bullion (precious metal) whenever they wished to do so. These certificates or receipts were promises to pay on demand (exactly the same promise still appears on our banknotes), and depositors gradually adopted the practice of using these certificates as a means of making payments. Instead of withdrawing gold and silver and handing it over in settlement of a debt, depositors began to hand over *claims* to gold and silver.

The first fully-developed banknotes came on the scene when (a) depositors began to ask for a number of separate receipts of convenient denominations (e.g. £1, £5, £10 and so on), and (b) the receipts or certificates were made *payable to bearer* so that anyone in possession of a banknote could exercise the right to convert it into gold or silver. These early banknotes were acceptable as a means of payment because they could be converted into gold on demand. At this stage, therefore, banknotes were *fully convertible* and had a 100 per cent backing in gold and silver. The goldsmiths limited the issue of notes to the value of precious metal in their vaults.

The next stage in the development of paper money came when the goldsmiths began to issue notes in excess of the value of bullion they were holding. They found that they could do this because the bulk of the gold and silver remained in their strongrooms. People were increasingly using banknotes to settle their debts and although each day some people would withdraw gold, others would be paying it in. The prospect of all depositors withdrawing their gold and silver on any one day seemed very remote. Thus, the total note issue was no longer backed by gold although all notes were fully convertible into gold. That part of a note issue not backed by gold is known as a *fiduciary issue*.

The goldsmith-bankers were, in fact, creating money and the money they created was used to make loans which brought them income in the form of interest. The granting of loans is still the most important and profitable activity of the banks. In the eighteenth and early nineteenth centuries, banking was subject to little or no regulation and anyone could establish themselves as bankers and issue banknotes. This was an unstable situation since many bankers were tempted to issue too many banknotes and found themselves unable to meet exceptional demands from people wishing to convert banknotes into gold. Depositors then found themselves holding notes which were worthless bits of paper, because news of a bank's failure made that bank's notes unacceptable. The state was obliged to regulate banking and the Bank of England is now the sole note-issuing authority in England and Wales. A few banks in Northern Ireland and Scotland still retain the right to issue banknotes.

Token money

Until the outbreak of the First World War, British banknotes were fully convertible into gold. Since that time a banknote has not been convertible although the wording on the notes has remained unchanged. The fact that the pieces of paper we now use as money are not backed by gold has in no way affected their acceptability. Once paper money without gold backing became generally acceptable, there was little point in maintaining a coinage of intrinsic value and the metallic value of present-day coinage is a tiny fraction of its money value. Our currency, both notes and coin, is entirely a token one.

Bank deposits

In developed countries, notes and coin account for a relatively small part of the total money supply. Table 18 gives brief details of the money supply in the UK.

Table 18   Money supply in the UK (20 January 1982)

	£ million
Notes and coin	10 405
Sterling bank deposits:	
Private sector	71 858
Public sector	1 825
	84 088

Source: *Bank of England Quarterly Bulletin*, March 1982.

It can be seen from Table 18 that bank deposits are the most important form of money. By far the greater part of total spending (by value) is carried out by the transfer of deposits using the cheque system. A cheque is not money; it is an order to a banker to transfer a sum of money from one bank deposit to another. Clearly a cheque drawn on account where the bank deposit is zero is worthless. Bank deposits are not a visible or tangible form of money, they consist of entries in bank accounts. Nowadays, in fact, they are mainly in the form of records on computer tapes.

Deposit money is a creation of the banking system. Just as the early bankers were able to create money by issuing bank notes in excess of the value of their holdings of gold, so modern bankers are able to increase the money supply by creating bank deposits in excess of their cash reserves. The early banknotes were claims to gold; they could be converted into gold. Bank deposits are claims to cash (notes and coin) because such deposits can be converted into cash. A person paying notes and coin into a bank will receive in return a bank deposit which can be spent by using a cheque book.

Since all bank deposits are convertible into cash (notes and coin), modern bankers must make sure that they are always in a position to meet depositors' demands for cash. They do not, however, need to keep a 100 per cent cash backing for the bank deposits they create. The widespread use of the cheque system means that on any one day only a small percentage of bank deposits will be converted into cash and these withdrawals are likely to be offset by people paying in cash. It is the likely *net* withdrawals of cash which bankers have to be concerned about. Bankers have found that they can safely create bank deposits greatly in excess of their cash reserves. Apart from the deposits which are created when customers pay in cash, deposits come into being when banks are making loans. People receiving bank loans will have their accounts credited (i.e. their deposits increased) by the amount of the loan. A highly simplified example might make this business of deposit creation a little clearer.

Suppose:
a   the banking system has discovered by long experience that depositors' net withdrawals of cash are most unlikely to exceed 10 per cent of total deposits;
b   on the basis of this experience, the banking system decides to operate with a 10 per cent cash ratio, that is, it does not allow its cash reserves to fall below 10 per cent of total deposits;
c   the amount of cash (i.e. notes and coin) in the banking system rises by £10 million due to an increased desire by the public to hold bank deposits.

The immediate effect of the intake of the additional cash is to increase bank deposits by £10 million because the people paying in this cash will have their deposits increased by this amount. But the additional £10 million of cash will serve as a 'backing' for deposits much greater than £10 million. It can, in fact be used to support bank deposits to the value of £100 million (with a 10 per cent cash ratio). The banking system, therefore, will be able to expand its deposits by a further £90 million. It will do this by increasing its lending.

Thus if the banks decide to maintain a 10 per cent cash ratio, bank deposits can be created up to a maximum of ten times the banks' holdings of cash. If the banks maintain a 20 per cent cash ratio, the maximum level of bank deposits will be five times their holdings of cash.

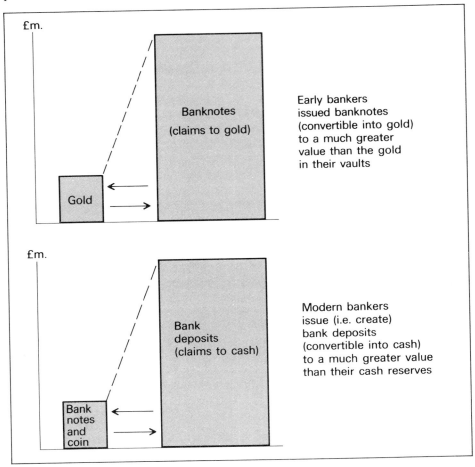

Fig. 20.1

Assets and liabilities

When a bank makes a loan, it increases its assets and liabilities by equal amounts. To the borrower, the bank deposit received is an asset because it represents purchasing power. The bank loan, however, is a liability; the money is owed to the bank. As far as the bank is concerned, the opposite applies. The bank deposit is a liability to the bank. It represents *a claim against the bank*. If depositors demand cash, the bank must supply it, while, if they draw cheques against the deposit, the bank must honour them. On the other hand, the bank sees the loan as an asset because it is a *claim against the borrower* who has a legal obligation to repay the loan. The bank may also ask the borrower to provide additional security in the form of some kind of claim against his or her property. If a bank makes a loan of £1000 it will affect its accounts as follows:

Liabilities		Assets	
Deposits	+£1000	Loans	+£1000

Legal tender

Legal tender describes the form of money which creditors must accept in settlement of debts. Bank deposits are not legal tender, they are claims to legal tender. In the UK, legal tender consists of:
a   bank notes up to an unlimited amount;
b   ½p, 1p and 2p coins up to 20p;
c   5p and 10p coins up to £5;
d   20p and 50p coins up to £10.
(The 20p coin came into circulation in June 1982; the £1 coin will be introduced in April 1983.)

Money and near money

Disputes still arise as to which assets should be counted as money. If we concentrate on the idea of money as a medium of exchange, that is, whatever is 'immediately spendable', then notes and coin and bank deposits on current account (those on which cheques can be drawn) are clearly money. If, however, we concentrate on the idea of money as a store of value, the money value of which is completely secure, we have to include in the supply of money, time deposits and other kinds of savings deposits. These latter deposits (e.g. building society deposits) do not serve as a medium of exchange, they cannot be spent in their present form, but most people would certainly include them in their total purchasing power. Savings deposits of various kinds are often described as *near money*.

The value of money

Prices tell us the rate at which money is exchanging for goods and services, that is, the value of goods and services in terms of money. Looked at another way, prices also tell us the value of money in terms of goods and services. If all prices rise, the value of money falls, because £1 will now exchange for a smaller quantity of goods and services. If we can measure what is happening to prices, therefore, we can also obtain a measure of what is happening to the value of money. For example, if prices rise, on average, by 25 per cent, that is in the ratio of 100:125, the value of money falls in the ratio 125:100, that is, by 20 per cent.

The task of measuring the extent to which prices are changing is not an easy one. Some of the difficulties are set out below and discussed more fully later on.

1   All prices do not move to the same extent or even in the same direction.
2   Some prices are much more important than others.
3   The same commodity may be sold at different prices in different kinds of shop or in different parts of the country.
4   In some cases an increase in price may not represent a fall in the value of money. If the quality of a good increases to the same extent as its price, the value of the money spent on this good will not have fallen.
5   There are many thousands of different goods and services and it is impossible to take account of all prices in a calculation of changes in the value of money.

A statistical device known as an index number is used to measure the average value of changes in such things as the prices of different goods and services, the outputs of different industries and the wages of different workers.

An index of prices

The first problem to present itself is 'What prices?'. For most people, of course, the retail prices of consumer goods and services are those which are of most concern and this is the index which is discussed in this section. It should be noted, however, that index numbers of export prices, import prices, wholesale prices and many other prices are also important.

An index number deals with percentage changes. In simple terms it is the average of the percentage changes in the prices of the various items included in the index.

Example 1

	Year 1		**Year 2**	
Commodity	**Price**	**Index**	**Price**	**Index**
A	10p	100	12p	120
B	£1.00	100	£1.25	125
C	£5.00	100	£4.50	90
	3) 300		3) 335	
	Price index = 100		Price index = 111.66	

In the base year the price of each commodity is given the value 100. The prices in subsequent years are expressed as changes on this base of 100. These numbers are described as price indices. Thus the price index for Commodity A is

100 in the base year and 120 in Year 2. In each year the index numbers for the commodities are totalled and then divided by the number of items. The index number of prices for the base year will be 100. In the example above the price index number for Year 2 is 111.66 which means that, on average, prices have risen by 11.66 per cent.

Unfortunately this type of index is misleading because it assumes that all the commodities are equally important. For example, a 10 per cent rise in the price of B would have exactly the same effect on the index as a 10 per cent rise in the price of C. But B may be some important and widely consumed foodstuff while C might be an article on which the average family spends a tiny fraction of its annual income. The value of a person's money depends upon the way in which that money is spent. Some goods and services account for a much higher proportion of total spending than other goods and services.

This particular difficulty is overcome by using a system of *weights*. Each commodity is given a weight, the size of which depends upon the percentage of total consumer spending devoted to that commodity. This system may be illustrated by re-working the above example with weighted commodities.

Example 2

		Year 1			Year 2		
Commodity	Weight	Price	Index	Weighted index	Price	Index	Weighted index
A	30	10p	100	3 000	12p	120	3 600
B	50	£1.00	100	5 000	£1.25	125	6 250
C	20	£5.00	100	2 000	£4.50	90	1 800
	100			100)10 000			100)11 650
			Price index = 100			Price index = 116.5	

The weights are allocated on the basis of consumers' spending habits and it has been assumed that 30 per cent of expenditure is devoted to Commodity A, 50 per cent to Commodity B and 20 per cent to Commodity C. The weights therefore are 30, 50 and 20. The procedure is similar to that in the first example, but the index numbers of prices are now multiplied by the weights. The weighted index numbers for each commodity are added together and divided by the total of the weights. The index calculated by this method shows that prices have increased by 16.5 per cent as against 11.66 per cent in the first example. The main reasons for this difference are that the commodity which had the largest price increase was the most heavily weighted and the commodity which fell in price had the smallest weight.

The Index of Retail Prices (RPI)

This important index is calculated each month and published by the Department of Employment. The main features of its construction are summarized below.

1   A representative sample of about 7000 households is selected each year and every fortnight about 270 of these are asked to keep a careful record of their expenditure over a two-week period.
2   These household budgets are analysed and the information is used to decide (a) composition of the goods and services to be included in the index and (b) the weights to be assigned to these goods and services.
3   A date is chosen as a base date and the prices on this date are given the value 100.
4   Around the middle of each month some 150 000 price quotations for about 350 different items are obtained from retail outlets throughout the country and from these quotations the changes in the prices of the various goods and services are estimated.
5   The index for each month is calculated in a similar manner to that illustrated in Example 2 above.

The Index of Retail Prices reflects the distribution of spending of about 85 per cent of the households in the UK. The two classes of household excluded from the sample survey are pensioner households and those households which have exceptionally high weekly incomes. It would be impossible to include all goods and services in the index, but the 350 individual items which are included are assumed to represent (in the way their prices move) all the goods and services bought by the average household.

There is a continuous development of new consumer goods and services and as time goes by consumers' spending habits change. This means that the items included in the index and the weights attached to them must be revised at regular intervals. This is done in January each year on the evidence obtained from the Family Expenditure Survey (see 1 above).

Table 19   Index of Retail Prices

	Weights used in 1981
Food	207
Alcoholic drinks	79
Tobacco	36
Housing	135
Fuel and light	62
Durable household goods	65
Clothing and footwear	81
Transport and vehicles	152
Miscellaneous goods	75
Services	66
Meals taken outside the home	42
	1000

Using the Index of Retail Prices

As noted earlier, the index gives a fairly accurate picture of the movements in those prices affecting the great majority of households, but it should be used with some caution.

Because the selection of commodities included and the weights assigned to them are adjusted at frequent intervals, the index cannot be used to give an accurate measurement of price changes over a long period of time. Over a period of, say, three or four years, the basis of the index will not change substantially and it will give a reasonably good account of what has been happening to the value of money. Comparisons over periods of, say, twenty years, using an index which has been subject to frequent adjustments, will not give a very accurate estimate of changes in the value of money.

The quality of goods changes over time. For example how can we measure the changes in the prices of motor cars? Is it reasonable to compare the price of a 1980 Cortina with a 1975 Cortina? This problem applies to most durable consumer goods and the statisticians attempt to deal with it by making some adjustment for quality changes when estimating the extent of the price change.

The index measures what is happening to the value of money being spent by the average family. If the spending pattern of a particular household is very different to that of the average household, the index will not give a really accurate account of what is happening to the value of that household's money.

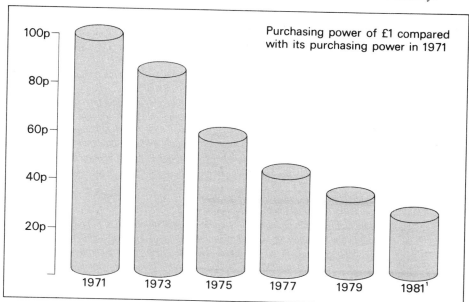

Fig. 20.2   Value of the pound

Source: *Dept. of Employment Gazette*, HMSO, 1981.

[1] 1 June

Changes in the value of money

Over the long period, the general trend of prices has been upwards, but it has not been a smooth continuous upward trend. There have been many periods when the general level of prices has fallen. For example, throughout most of the nineteenth century the trend of prices was downwards and the period between the First and Second World Wars was also a time of falling prices. In recent years, however, inflation has tended to become more persistent and widespread. Fig. 20.2 gives an indication of what happened to the value of money in the UK during the 1970s.

21 Banking

There are many kinds of banks, but in this chapter we shall be concerned mainly with the discount houses, the central bank and the commercial banks. We begin with an account of the way in which these institutions work together and of the various types of borrowing and lending which take place in what is known as the money market.

The London money market

The London money market deals with the provision of short-term loans. The financial institutions which play a major part in the operations of the money market are: the Bank of England; the commercial banks; the London offices of foreign banks; the accepting houses; the discount houses and a number of money brokers. The activities of the main institutions are explained later.

Discounting

Much of the business of the money market consists of buying and selling promises to pay (i.e. IOUs). Thus, when lenders provide borrowers with loans they *buy* the borrowers' promises to repay. These written promises are issued by such borrowers as the central government, local authorities, business firms and individuals. They are generally known as securities or bonds. A most common type of security traded on the money market is one which promises payment in one to six months (but normally three months) and is known as a bill of exchange. Money market institutions provide loans by discounting these bills. Discounting simply means buying a bill for less than its face value.

For example, suppose a bill carrying a promise to pay £100 in three months time is bought for £98. The purchaser of the bill is making a loan for three months. For this service a fee of £2 is being charged because, when the bill matures, £100 will be claimed from the person who signed the bill. The lender has, in effect, charged a rate of interest on the loan equal to,

$$\frac{2}{98} \times \frac{100}{1} \times \frac{4}{1} = 8.16\% \ per \ annum$$

Rates of interest are expressed on an annual basis.

Although this is the true rate of interest, the rate of discount is normally worked out on the face value of the security. Thus the *rate of discount* in the example above would be,

$$\frac{2}{100} \times \frac{100}{1} \times \frac{4}{1} = 8\% \ per \ annum$$

Bills of exchange

The bill of exchange has been used as a method of raising short-term loans since the seventeenth century. It is essentially a piece of paper which provides evidence of the indebtedness of one person to another. The person signing the bill is committed to pay a certain sum of money to a named person (or to the bearer) on a specified date. There are several types of bill of exchange.

1 Commercial bills

This is an important means by which traders in both home and overseas trade can obtain credit. For example, suppose a firm purchasing goods to the value of £100 000 does not wish to pay for them immediately; it might want three months credit. On the other hand, the firm selling the goods does not wish to extend credit to the purchaser. The bill of exchange was designed to overcome this problem. The seller of the goods will draw up a bill (see Fig. 21.1) and send it to the buyer. The seller of the goods is described as the *drawer* of the bill. The buyer of the goods will now write 'Accepted' on the bill, sign it and return it to the seller. The purchaser is described as the *drawee*. Thus, in the example shown in Fig. 21.1, ICI (the drawee) has agreed to pay £100 000 to the British Gas Corporation (the drawer) three months after accepting the bill.

The firm selling the goods now has a written promise from its debtor, and, if it does not wish to wait three months for its money, it can have the bill discounted. In this way the money market finances trade. The seller gets the money immediately, the buyer has three months in which to pay. The type of bill described above is a *trade bill*; it is drawn by one trader on another.

If the drawee is not well known in the banking world, the discount house may not be prepared to discount the bill without some added security. In this case the bill will need to be accepted by some financial institution. This work is carried out by firms known as Accepting Houses (normally merchant banks). For a fee, an accepting house will endorse the bill and in so doing it will guarantee payment should the person who originally signed the bill default on his or her promise.

Bills accepted by a bank (or accepting house) are described as *bank bills* (see Fig. 21.1). A purchaser of goods may make arrangements for a bank to accept on his behalf, bills drawn up to a maximum of, say, £100 000 at any given time. Thus, if Smith is selling to Jones, he may draw a bill of exchange directly on Jones's bank which, by accepting it, guarantees payment in three months' time. When such bills are drawn on banks of the highest standing, they are known as *fine bank bills*.

2 Treasury bills

Another important short-term security traded on the money market is the Treasury bill (see Fig. 21.1). These bills are issued by the government and have a life of ninety-one days. They are the means by which the government carries out its short-term borrowing and the people buying such bills are making loans to the government. Treasury bills are issued in denominations of £5000,

Local authority bill ▶

◀ Bank bill

Certificate of deposit ▶

◀ Trade bill

Treasury bill ▶

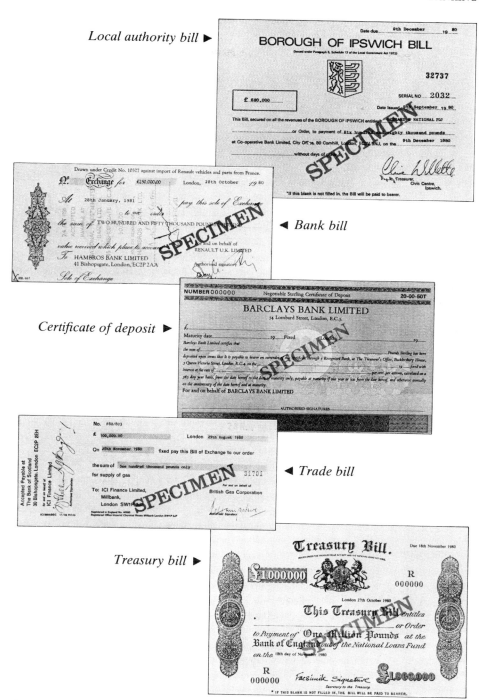

Fig. 21.1   Examples of securities discounted in the money market

£10 000, £25 000, £50 000, £100 000, £250 000, and £1 000 000 and are sold to the highest bidders at weekly auctions. Thus, if the average price paid at the weekly auction is £97.50 per £100 worth of Treasury bills, the government is paying a rate of interest of about 10.26 per cent per annum[1] because, when the bills fall due for repayment, the government redeems them at their face value. The discount houses and other financial institutions make bids for Treasury bills at these weekly auctions. The discount houses, in fact, guarantee, if necessary, to buy the entire issue.

3 Local authority bills
These (see Fig. 21.1) are very similar to Treasury bills and are issued by local authorities when they wish to obtain short-term loans. They are issued in denominations ranging from £5000 to £100 000.

4 Other money market securities
The discount houses and other money market institutions also deal in securities which have a rather longer life than bills of exchange. Most government borrowing is carried out by issuing long-term securities. As these securities approach the dates for repayment, they become, in effect, short-term securities and, as such, they are traded in the money market. The discount houses are major dealers in government securities which have less than five years to run to maturity. These securities are described as *short-dated gilt-edged stocks*. *Local authority bonds* with a life of one year are also bought and sold on the money market. The discount houses will also discount *certificates of deposit* (see page 242).

It should be noted that all the securities described above are marketable and the ownership of such securities can change hands several times during their lifetimes.

The operations of the discount houses

The discount houses are a special kind of institution which borrows money from various banks in the City of London and then uses these borrowed funds to discount the kind of securities described above. Much of the money is borrowed 'at call' or 'overnight' so that the banks can demand repayment of these loans immediately or at very short notice. Discount houses make profits because the interest rates they charge when discounting bills are normally higher than the interest rates they pay on their loans from the banks. But they are at risk because they are using funds which are repayable at call (or very short notice) to make loans for much longer periods of time (e.g. when discounting three-month bills). If the banks find that their cash reserves are running low,

[1] i.e. $\dfrac{2.5}{97.5} \times \dfrac{100}{1} \times \dfrac{4}{1} = 10.26\%$ approx.

they will take steps to rebuild these reserves by calling in some of their loans to the discount houses.

If only one or two banks are calling back their loans, there will be no real problem because the discount houses will be able to repay these loans by obtaining new loans from other banks. If, however, all the banks are experiencing a cash shortage and are calling in their money market loans, the discount houses will be in difficulties. They must honour their agreements to repay their loans on demand. In such a situation, the discount houses will be obliged to turn to *the lender of last resort* – the Bank of England. The central bank will provide the discount houses with the funds they need by rediscounting some of their bills, or by taking such bills as security for loans. The Bank of England will only accept first-class bills, that is, Treasury bills, local authority bills or commercial bills which have been accepted by certain reputable institutions. Although it will always lend to the discount houses, the central bank is free to set its own terms for such loans. Under some circumstances, it may supply loans at market rates of interest, but it may charge the discount houses what is known as *Minimum Lending Rate (MLR)*[1]. Since MLR is normally higher than the current market rates of interest, the discount houses will be making losses on these transactions. They will be paying higher rates of interest on their borrowings from the central bank than they have been earning on their lendings.

The Bank of England

The Bank of England is the central bank of the UK and has many important functions.
1   It is the government's bank and handles the government's income and expenditure.
2   It is the bankers' bank. The other banking institutions keep accounts at the central bank and use them to settle debts between themselves and for transactions between themselves and the central bank. Thus, if one bank makes a payment to another bank it will do so by drawing a cheque on its account at the central bank.
3   It is responsible for managing the national debt. The government's borrowing and lending is handled by the Bank of England which has the tasks of raising new loans by issuing government securities, arranging for the repayment of maturing securities and paying interest to the holders of existing securities.
4   It is the central note-issuing authority for the UK.
5   It is the lender of last resort (explained earlier).

---

[1] In August 1981 the Bank of England stated that it would cease the practice of making official declarations of its minimum lending rate; it will continue to influence interest rates by its market operations.

6 It is the government's agency in the foreign exchange market where it takes action to influence the external value of the pound (see page 273).

7 It is responsible for carrying out the government's monetary policy (see page 246).

The Bank of England is the agent which carries out the work described above, but the Treasury ultimately is responsible for putting the government's policies in respect of banking and the money supply into effect.

The central bank is divided into two departments, the Issue Department and the Banking Department. Both departments publish a weekly return which provides some guidance as to the work of the Bank of England.

Table 20   Bank of England weekly return (20 January 1982)

Liabilities	£ million	Assets	£ million
Issue Department			
Notes in circulation	10 642	Government securities	5 310
Notes in Banking Dept.	8	Other securities	5 340
	10 650		10 650
Banking Department			
Public deposits	43	Government securities	701
Special deposits	0	Advances and other accounts	1 055
Bankers' deposits	588	Premises and other securities	436
Reserves and other accounts	1 555	Notes and coin	8
Capital	14		
	2 200		2 200

Source: *Bank of England Quarterly Bulletin*, March 1982.

The Issue Department

This department is responsible for the note issue. It can be seen (Table 20) that the UK note issue is wholly fiduciary. The assets of the Issue Department contain no gold and the backing for the note issue consists entirely of government and other securities. The notes in circulation are those held by the rest of the banking system and by the general public.

The Banking Department

This department carries out all the other banking functions. The liabilities of the Banking Department are described briefly below.

1 Public deposits are the balances held by the government at the central bank. The relatively small balance shown in the weekly return is misleading because, every week, huge sums of money pass through this account.
2 Special deposits are assets belonging to the commercial banks; they are explained on page 247.
3 Bankers' deposits are the current accounts held by other banks and the discount houses.
4 Reserves and other accounts include deposits held by overseas banks, local authorities, public corporations and some international organizations.
5 Capital is the original capital of the Bank which was formerly a joint stock company.

The assets of the Banking Department consist of the following items.
1 Government securities include longer-term government and government-guaranteed securities and Treasury bills.
2 Advances and other accounts are the market loans to the discount houses and loans to other customers.
3 Premises, equipment and other securities comprise a variety of securities including some ordinary shares in companies, local authority bills and commercial bills, as well as the physical assets owned by the Bank.
4 Notes and coin are held in the Banking Department in order to meet the commercial banks' demands for currency.

More is said about the work of the Bank of England later in the chapter when the Bank's responsibility for the control of the money supply is discussed.

The commercial banks

These are the familiar High Street banks and, in the UK, the largest are Barclays, Lloyds, Midland and the National Westminster, each of which has several thousand branches. Commercial banks provide a variety of services.

1 Personal services
Among the services of a personal nature provided by the banks are:
a facilities for world-wide travel such as the supply of travellers' cheques and foreign currency;
b facilities for the safe deposit of money and other valuables;
c advice and help with the investment of funds (e.g. the purchase of securities);
d acting as an executor (i.e. dealing with the disposal of money and property left by a deceased person);
e acting as a trustee (a trust is an arrangement whereby the assets owned by an individual or family are administered by another group of people or a financial institution such as a bank).

2 Money transfer services

Banks assist in the transfer of money by supplying facilities such as:

a the cheque system and credit cards;
b the payment of bills by standing order (the bank will take over the responsibility for making regular payments on the due dates, e.g. annual subscriptions, rent payments, insurance premiums and so on);
c 24-hour cash dispensers and night safe facilities.

3 Investment and loan services

The banks are a most important source of loans. They lend to:

a central and local government;
b the nationalized industries;
c all types of firm in all industries in the private sector;
d individuals.

The banks are also important in the hire-purchase business because several of the larger finance houses which supply funds for hire-purchase are subsidiaries of the major banks.

The commercial banks are of particular interest to the economist because they manage the main payments system and, through their lending activities, they create money in the form of bank deposits. The operations of the commercial banks are quite complex and we shall do no more than sketch in an outline of their activities. This is best done by looking first at the items in a balance sheet of a commercial bank (Fig. 21.2).

A bank's liabilities

It has already been explained that the liabilities of a bank consist largely of its deposits. There are two main types of bank deposit.

1 *Current accounts.* Money held on current account can be withdrawn on demand, is subject to transfer by cheque, but does not earn interest.
2 *Deposit accounts.* These are sometimes described as time deposits. Money held in a deposit account cannot be transferred by cheque and can only be withdrawn after due notice (usually seven days). Interest is paid on deposit accounts.

Banks also accept large sums of money on longer-term deposit (from three months to five years). These deposits earn higher rates of interest and the bank acknowledges them by issuing depositors with *certificates of deposit* which are marketable; if the holders of such deposits run short of funds they can have the certificates discounted.

Capital appears as a liability because the commercial banks are joint stock companies and the share capital is a loan from the shareholders to the company. For a similar reason the item 'Reserves' appears as a liability. This consists of retained profits which are, in effect, a loan from the shareholders to the company.

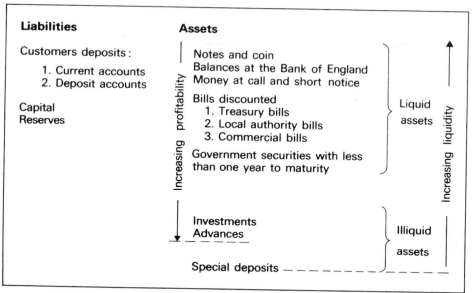

Fig. 21.2   A commercial bank's balance sheet

A bank's assets

The bank's assets consist mainly of loans and the assets side of the balance sheet shows how a bank derives its income. All the assets shown, except the first two items, consist of income-earning loans. The assets are arranged so that the least profitable are at the top and the most profitable (i.e. advances) are at the bottom (see Fig. 21.2). In terms of liquidity they are in the reverse order, the most liquid assets are at the top and the least liquid at the bottom. The most liquid asset of all, cash, earns no income and the short-term loans (liquid assets) earn lower rates of interest than the long-term loans (illiquid assets).

1 *Notes and coin.* These items are held in the bank's tills to meet depositors' demands for cash.

2 *Balances at the Bank of England.* All commercial banks keep current accounts at the central bank for reasons which have been explained earlier. Since these current accounts can be used to draw notes and coin on demand, the banks regard their deposits at the central bank as part of their cash reserves.

3 *Money at call and short notice.* These are the loans to the discount houses and other institutions in the money market. They are of a very short-term nature and earn relatively low rates of interest.

4 *Bills discounted.* These consist of Treasury bills, local authority bills and commercial bills which the banks purchase from the discount houses and other sources. The banks arrange their holdings of these bills so that some of them are maturing every week (or even every day).

5   *Government securities with less than one year to maturity*. These assets have been explained earlier.

All of the above are *liquid assets*, that is, they can be converted into cash quickly and easily. It is the existence of a highly developed money market in London which makes it possible for the banks to hold a variety of very liquid assets. The fact that they have such assets available means that the banks can operate with very small cash reserves. If they are faced with unexpectedly high demands from their depositors for cash, the banks can quickly obtain additional cash by (a) requesting the discount houses to repay their call loans and (b) selling some of their bills in the money market. The remaining assets are illiquid.

6   *Investments*. These are long-term government securities although most of those held by the banks have five years or less to run to maturity.

7   *Advances*. This is the banks' most profitable asset. It comprises the loans to households and firms. Traditionally banks have supplied firms with what is described as working capital – short-term loans for periods of six months to one year. In more recent years, however, the banks have greatly extended their lending for longer periods. There are two main ways in which a bank makes a loan.

a   A bank overdraft. This type of lending allows a depositor to overdraw his or her account by some agreed amount. Thus, if a firm is granted an overdraft facility of £5000, the bank will honour cheques drawn on the firm's account until it is £5000 'in the red'. Interest is only charged on the amount overdrawn. Business firms invariably use this form of borrowing because it is very flexible and a firm can never be absolutely sure of the amount it might have to borrow.

b   A bank loan. When an individual is granted a bank loan, the bank credits his or her account with the agreed amount, that is, the deposit is increased by the amount of the loan. Interest is charged on the full amount of the loan whether it is fully utilized or not.

8   *Special deposits*. These are deposits held at the Bank of England, but they cannot be withdrawn until the central bank decides to release them. Although they are held at the Bank of England, they do not count as part of the banks' cash reserves. Special deposits are explained more fully on page 247.

Liquidity and profitability

Banks are in business to make a profit which means that they have a strong incentive to build up the more profitable long-term loans. But they also have a responsibility to their depositors as well as to their shareholders. Banks must always be in a position to meet depositors' demands for notes and coin. They must, therefore, make certain that they have, at all times, sufficient cash (which earns no income) and an adequate supply of liquid assets (which earn low rates of interest). This need for liquidity, therefore, conflicts with the desire for profits and banks have to arrange their assets so as to achieve a satisfactory balance between the two objectives. As we shall see later, the banks are not completely free to choose the types and amounts of the assets they hold.

The London Clearing House

The fact that there are several different commercial banks means that the majority of payments made by cheque will require a transfer of money from one bank to another. If Miss A with an account in Barclays uses her cheque book to buy a radio from X and Co. which has an account with Lloyds, then a sum of money must be transferred from an account in Barclays to an account in Lloyds.

Many thousands of such cheques are drawn every day. To facilitate the settling of these inter-bank debts, the banks have established the London Clearing House. Cheques drawn on one bank but payable to another are sent to the clearing house where, each day, the amounts due from one bank to another are offset against each other. Thus, if the total value of cheques drawn on Barclays but payable to Lloyds is £500 million and the value of the cheques drawn on Lloyds but payable to Barclays is £450 million, a single payment of £50 million will settle the account. Barclays will use their account at the Bank of England to make this payment to Lloyds.

Controls on assets held by commercial banks

The Bank of England obliges the banks to keep a certain proportion of their total assets in the form of liquid assets. In 1971 the monetary authorities (the Treasury and the Bank of England) introduced regulations which obliged banks in the UK to maintain holdings of certain liquid assets, described as reserve assets, equal in value to at least 12½ per cent of their eligible liabilities.

Eligible liabilities correspond roughly to the banks' sterling deposits, that is deposits held on current and deposit account together with any large deposits placed with the banks for periods of up to two years. They also include any deposits against which the banks have issued certificates of deposit.

Reserve Assets were carefully defined by the authorities to include:
a   balances with the Bank of England (excluding special deposits);
b   money at call;
c   Treasury bills;
d   local authority bills;
e   commercial bills (up to a maximum of 2 per cent of eligible liabilities);
f   government securities with less than one year to run to maturity.
(Notice that notes and coin and money at short notice were not counted as reserve assets).

Since the ratio of reserve assets to total deposits could not fall below 1:8, the banks' ability to expand their deposits (by making loans) depended upon their ability to obtain reserve assets. Thus if a bank held £1000 million of reserve assets, it could not let its deposits exceed £12 500 million.

A most important regulation, also introduced in 1971, obliged the banks to maintain balances at the Bank of England equal to 1½ per cent of their total eligible liabilities.

In August 1981 the Bank of England abolished the 12½ per cent reserve assets ratio, but the obligation of banks to maintain balances at the Bank of England (now changed to ½ per cent of deposits) was extended to all banks in the UK (it had previously only applied to banks which were members of the London Clearing House). Although the 12½ per cent reserve asset ratio no longer applies, the Bank of England announced that banks would still be required to maintain certain ratios between liquid assets and total deposits. The idea of this requirement is to protect bank depositors by making sure that the banks always have sufficient liquid assets to meet all likely (and unlikely) demands for cash.

The central bank and monetary policy

Monetary policy aims to influence economic activity by acting on the total amount of spending in the economy. Total spending is obviously related to the amount of money in the economy and to the ease or difficulty with which households and firms can obtain loans. If the government's aim is to reduce the level of total spending, monetary policy will be used to increase the costs of borrowing and to make loans more difficult to obtain. The opposite measures will be used if the government wants to see an increase in total spending. The policy to be adopted is decided by the government, but the responsibility for carrying out the policy lies with the Bank of England.

Since the greater part of the money supply consists of bank deposits, any attempt to control the money supply must aim to control the level of bank deposits. The level of bank deposits is governed by the banks' ability to lend and the willingness and ability of the banks' customers to borrow. Thus, in order to be able to exercise some degree of control over the money supply, the central bank must have some means of influencing the banks' ability to lend and the willingness of households and firms to borrow. There are several measures it can use for this purpose.

1 Open market operations

The Bank of England operates as a buyer and seller in the markets for government securities. If it buys securities from households and firms, it will pay for them with cheques drawn on itself. The sellers of these securities will pay these cheques into their accounts at the commercial banks. The central bank will make payments on these cheques by increasing the bankers' balances in the Banking Department. This will lead to an increase in the cash reserves of the banks and they will be able to expand their lending and create additional bank deposits.

If the central bank sells securities in the open market, the buyers will pay for them with cheques drawn on their accounts in the commercial banks. The subsequent transfer of money from the commercial banks to the central bank will reduce the bankers' balances in the Banking Department. These transactions will reduce the cash reserves of the commercial banks and hence restrict their ability to create deposits.

2 Special deposits

The Bank of England can achieve similar results to those described above by making use of its powers to call for special deposits from the commercial banks. When such a call is made, money is transferred from the commercial banks' balances at the central bank into a special account where it earns interest but cannot be withdrawn. It does not, therefore, rank as a liquid asset. By making a call for special deposits the Bank of England can bring about an immediate reduction in the banks' cash reserves. If the Bank of England wishes to see an increase in the banks' ability to lend, it can release these special deposits and the banks' holdings of liquid assets will increase, because their current balances at the central bank will increase.

3 Directives

The Bank of England has powers to issue direct orders to the banks in respect of lending policies. It can, if it wishes, place a ceiling on the growth of bank deposits. It can also stipulate which type of lending it wishes to see reduced (e.g. loans to finance consumption and speculation). Although extensively used in the past, in more recent years the central bank has announced that it does not favour the use of this type of control.

4 Funding

Treasury bills make up an important part of the banks' holdings of liquid assets. If the government is borrowing very heavily by issuing Treasury bills, the banking system will be able to obtain a large supply of such bills. An increased holding of liquid assets increases the ability of the banks to create deposits by expanding their lending activities. One way in which the authorities might reduce the banks' holdings of liquid assets, therefore, is to reduce the issue of Treasury bills and borrow more on a long-term basis by issuing more long-term securities. The conversion of short-term debt into long-term debts is known as funding.

5 Interest rates

The extent of borrowing from the banks may be influenced by acting on the demand for loans. The quantity demanded of any commodity depends upon its price and this is probably equally true of loans. If the central bank can bring about an increase in interest rates, the growth of bank deposits will be reduced because the demand for loans will be reduced. One way in which this might be achieved is by open market operations. If the Bank of England carries out extensive selling of fixed interest securities in the open market, the prices of such securities will fall. When the market price of fixed interest securities falls, the rate of interest rises (see page 209). The Bank of England can also use its powers as a lender of last resort to raise the short-term market rate of interest. It can raise the rate of interest at which it lends and then make the money market short of funds (by selling securities). This will force the discount houses to borrow from the Bank of England at the higher rate of interest. This will tend to lead to an upward movement in the rates charged by the discount houses and by the commercial banks.

Measuring the money supply

We have seen that the supply of money consists of notes, coin and bank deposits. It should be fairly easy, therefore, to measure the supply of money. The fact is, however, that there are several different measures of the money supply and they differ according to the kinds of bank deposit included in the total. In the UK there are three important measures, M_1, Sterling M_3, and M_3.

M_1 is made up of all the notes and coin in circulation plus the sterling current accounts held by UK residents in the private sector.

Sterling M_3 consists of the notes and coin in circulation plus all bank deposits in both current and deposit account, in sterling, held by UK residents in both private and public sectors.

M_3 consists of Sterling M_3 plus the foreign currency deposits held by UK residents.

Table 21   UK money supply (20 January 1982)

	£million	
Notes and coin in circulation	10 405	
Private sector demand deposits	23 684	
	34 089	$= M_1$
Private sector time deposits	48 174	
Public sector deposits (time and current)	1 825	
	84 088	$=$ Sterling M_3
UK residents' foreign currency deposits	10 062	
	94 150	$= M_3$

Source: *Bank of England Quarterly Bulletin*, March 1982.

Some other banks

1 Savings Banks

The National Savings Bank operates through the Post Office. Depositors may pay in or withdraw money at any post office where savings bank business is transacted; there are about 21 000 such offices. Two types of account are available, (a) ordinary accounts where small sums can be withdrawn on demand and larger sums after a few days notice, and (b) investment accounts where one month's notice of withdrawal is required. Higher rates of interest are payable on investment accounts. Money deposited in the National Savings Bank is invested in government securities.

The Trustee Savings Banks are non-profit making institutions which are controlled by honorary local boards of trustees. There are about seventy-five Trustee Savings Banks with some 1500 offices. These banks also have ordinary and investment accounts which require different periods of notice for withdrawal and earn different rates of interest. The money deposited in these banks is invested in government and local authority securities. The Trustee Savings Banks also operate current account services (i.e. deposits can be transferred by cheque).

2 The National Giro

This commenced business in 1968. Its purpose is to provide a cheap and rapid means of transmitting money by making use of the extensive Post Office network. All the records are kept at a computerized centre at Bootle. People having Giro accounts are offered facilities for the following.

a Making payments to other people and firms with Giro accounts. This is done by posting a Giro transfer form to the computer centre. Transfers of this type are free, providing the account is in credit.

b Making deposits. These can be made in cash or by cheque at any post office.

c Making payments to non-account holders. This can be done by means of a postal cheque for which a small charge is made.

d Withdrawals. An account holder can withdraw cash at any post office.

e Making payments by standing order to other Giro account holders.

The National Giro now operates both current accounts and time deposits, it provides cheque guarantee cards and personal loans and limited overdraft facilities are also available.

Test paper 8

Short-answer questions

1 'Money is what money does.' As a definition of money this statement may be inadequate, but is it totally inaccurate?

2 What is meant by the term *a medium of exchange*?

3 Which particular function of money is most affected by inflation?

4 Give an example of something which might serve as money if banknotes and coins became worthless due to inflation, and explain why it would serve as money.

5 'The note issue of the UK is inconvertible.' Explain.

6 The unit of currency in a country is the crown. The note issue consists of 1 000 000 crowns and is fully convertible into gold. The backing for this note issue consists of gold (700 000 crowns), government securities (200 000 crowns) and other securities (100 000 crowns). What percentage of the note issue is fiduciary?

7 During a period of one month, the average value of bank deposits was £5 million. During the same period, the total value of cheques cleared was £15 million. Explain how this situation came about.

8 Why are deposits in building societies not included in the money supply?

9 What are the advantages of settling debts by making use of cheques?

10 Why do loans appear on the assets side of a bank's balance sheet?

11 Why would a 10 per cent increase in the price of bread have a much bigger effect on the Index of Retail Prices than a similar percentage increase in the price of salt?

12 Why is it necessary to carry out frequent changes in the weights used in the calculation of the Index of Retail Prices?

13 Name one class of good or service for which the weights used in the Index of Retail Prices have (a) increased and (b) decreased in recent years.

14 A bill of exchange for £5000 is taken to a discount house for discounting. It has three months to run to maturity and the discount house buys it for £4850. What is the rate of discount charged by the discount house?

15 'Treasury bills are issued *by tender* in the money market.' Explain the term in italics.

16 Why do commercial banks regard their balances at the Bank of England as a part of their cash reserves?

Questions 17, 18, 19 are based on the following table which shows the items on the assets side of a bank's balance sheet.

	£ million
Notes and coin held in the branches	100
Balances at the Bank of England	100
Money at call and short notice	150
Bills discounted	150
Investments	500
Advances	1000
	2000

17 What is the bank's present cash ratio?
18 What is the total value of the bank's holdings of liquid assets?
19 What would be the immediate effect on the assets side of the balance sheet if the bank were to draw £50 million in new notes from the Bank of England?
20 If a bank in the UK sells £50 million of its holdings of Treasury bills and then increases its lending to industry by £50 million what effects will the transactions have on the bank's
  a liquidity?
  b profitability?

True or false?

21 **a** Notes, coins and cheques are the principal form of money in the UK.
  b In the Index of Retail Prices the more expensive items are the most heavily weighted.
  c In the UK, only the Bank of England can create money.
  d The commercial banks' main source of income is the charges they make for handling cheques.
  e The special deposits held at the Bank of England are an important part of the banks' holdings of liquid assets.
  f If the Index of Retail Prices increases from 120 to 140, it means that retail prices, on average, have increased by 20 per cent.
  g When the Bank of England sells securities in the open market, the bankers' balances at the central bank will tend to fall.
  h If all prices were to double, the value of one commodity in terms of another would remain unchanged.
  i When a cheque is cashed, a bank's assets and liabilities fall by equal amounts.
  j Credit cards represent a new form of money.

Multiple-choice questions

Questions 22 and 23 refer to the following items.

1 postal orders
2 banknotes
3 cheques
4 bank deposits held on current account

22 In the UK, which of the above serve as a medium of exchange?
  A 1, 2 and 3
  B 1 and 2 only
  C 2, 3 and 4
  D 2 and 3 only
  E 2 and 4 only

23 Which of the above items are recognized as legal tender?
  A 1, 2 and 3
  B 1 and 2 only
  C 2 and 3 only
  D 3 and 4 only
  E 2 only

24 Which of the following characteristics *must* be possessed if a commodity is to serve as money?
  A durability
  B divisibility
  C portability
  D acceptability
  E homogeneity

25 Which of the following is/are recognized as liquid assets in the banking system?
  1 money at call and short notice
  2 bills of exchange
  3 special deposits held at the Bank of England
  A 1, 2 and 3
  B 1 and 2 only
  C 2 and 3 only
  D 1 only
  E 3 only

Questions 26 and 27 are based on the following list of bank assets.
  A balances at the Bank of England
  B money at call and short notice
  C bills discounted
  D investments
  E special deposits

26 Which one of the above is most likely to increase during a severe credit squeeze?

27 Which one of the above will increase as the direct result of the Bank of England buying securities in the open market?

Data-response questions

28 The question is based on the following data.

Commodity	Price (£)	Base Year Quantity purchased (units)	Year 4 Price (£)
A	1.00	1 000	1.20
B	0.50	12 000	0.55
C	2.00	1 000	3.00
D	0.10	10 000	0.11

Work out a weighted price index to show the movements in prices between the base year and Year 4. Use the total expenditures in the base year as the basis for the weights.

29 The questions are based on the following brief extract from an article on banking.

The National Giro does have advantages. It operates through 22 000 post offices up and down the country which are open from 9 am to 5 pm. The customer generally pays no *bank charges* and is given detailed information on the state of his account automatically after every credit. Until recently, however, the central computer *bounced* cheques if the account became temporarily *overdrawn* without any investigation of the *credit-worthiness* of the customer.

The Giro, however, has no *cash dispensers* or *credit cards*[1] and has only limited facilities for making personal loans.

a Explain the terms in italics.

b In this article the National Giro is being compared with the commercial banks. Explain why the statistics in the second sentence represent 'advantages'.

---

[1] The National Giro now provides cheque guarantee cards.

22 International trade and the balance of payments

International trade

International trade is the trade which crosses national frontiers. It is not strictly trade between 'nations', but between households and firms resident in different countries. Only in the communist world are governments themselves responsible for the trade between countries. There is one very important difference between domestic and foreign trade. The buying and selling of a good in international trade gives rise to two transactions, not one. A UK firm buying a machine from West Germany must (a) convert pounds into marks and then (b) exchange the marks for the machine. It is essential to keep this fact in mind because all the statistics relating to international trade will be recorded in the currency of the home country. For example, the value of the UK's exports and imports are given in pounds sterling, but these are simply the pound values of the foreign currency which has been earned and spent by UK residents.

Trade between nations has led to a great extension of the principle of specialization. The fact that human beings have different abilities, aptitudes, interests and personalities helps to explain why so much labour is specialized; people tend to do those jobs for which they are best suited. Similarly, the fact that economic resources are distributed unevenly throughout the world helps to explain why countries tend to specialize. Differences between countries in climatic conditions, in the nature of mineral deposits and in the ratios of labour to land are obvious reasons why some countries are more suited to some economic activities than others. International trade gives countries the opportunities to specialize in the things they do best.

The gains from trade

The advantages which countries might obtain from international trade are best explained by making use of a very simple model of a world where there are only two countries (A and B) and only two commodities are produced, say, tea and cloth. In spite of its simplicity, this model can be used to explain some of the important economic realities of international trade. In this simple model there are three possibilities.

1 *Each country has a total advantage in the production of one of the commodities.* For example, assume that Country A can produce tea but not cloth while Country B can produce cloth but not tea. In this case the gains from trading are self-evident because it will enable each country to increase the range of goods available to its citizens. This model explains the earliest

types of international trade which brought tropical products to Western Europe and manufactured goods to underdeveloped countries in Africa and Asia. In this early pattern of trade, countries were supplying each other with goods which they could not produce for themselves. This type of trade is still a relatively important part of total world trade, but by no means the most important part.

2   *Each country has an absolute advantage in the production of one of the commodities.* In this situation each country is capable of producing both tea and cloth, but each of them is more efficient than the other in producing one of these commodities. We shall assume that Country A is more efficient than Country B in the production of tea while Country B can produce cloth more efficiently than Country A. These conditions are illustrated in Fig. 22.1. Assume each country possesses 10 units of resources.

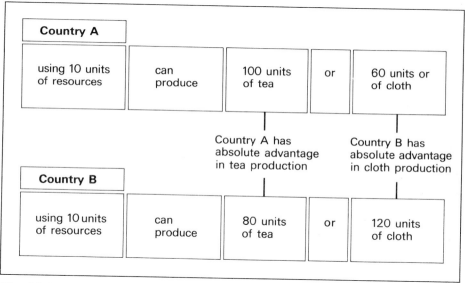

Fig. 22.1

In the absence of any opportunities to trade, each country would produce both commodities. Suppose that, in the absence of trading opportunities, each country devotes 5 units of resources to each industry. Then,

	Tea (units)		Cloth (units)
Country A will produce	50	and	30
Country B will produce	40	and	60
Total output	90	and	90

Now assume that trade becomes possible and each country specializes in producing the commodity which it produces more efficiently than the other country.

255

	Tea (units)		Cloth (units)
Country A will produce	100	and	0
Country B will produce	0	and	120
Total output	100	and	120

Specialization has increased total output and trade will enable each country to enjoy more of both commodities. Suppose 45 units of tea are exchanged for 40 units of cloth.

	Tea (units)		Cloth (units)
Country A can now consume	55	and	40
Country B can now consume	45	and	80
	100	and	120

3 *One country has an absolute advantage in the production of both commodities.* Let us now assume that Country A is more efficient than Country B in both industries. Thus, with the same input of resources (land, labour and capital), Country A can produce greater amounts of either tea or cloth than Country B. Under these circumstances it is much more difficult to see how *both* countries might gain from specialization and trade. Nevertheless it is possible for the total outputs of both commodities to be increased by specialization. The explanation which follows is known as the *theory of comparative advantage* (or comparative costs) and is based on Fig. 22.2. Assume each country has 10 units of resources.

It can be seen from Fig. 22.2 that Country A has an absolute advantage in both industries. In terms of the amounts of land, labour and capital used in production its costs of production are lower in both industries. The theory of comparative advantage, however, is based on differences in *opportunity costs*. In our particular example this means that the cost of a unit of tea is measured in terms of the amount of cloth which has to be foregone in order to produce that unit of tea. Similarly the cost of a unit of cloth is measured in terms of the amount of tea which its production causes to be foregone. The opportunity costs of tea and cloth in each country are clearly set out in Fig. 22.2.

When costs are measured in this way it can be seen that Country B has a *comparative* advantage in the production of tea because, in that country, a unit of tea only 'costs' half a unit of cloth whereas in Country A a unit of tea 'costs' four-fifths of a unit of cloth. Country A, on the other hand, has a comparative advantage in cloth production.

Providing the opportunity costs are different in the two countries, gains from specialization and trade are possible even when one country is more efficient than the other country in both industries. This can be demonstrated by another arithmetical example based on the information in Fig. 22.2. Proceeding as in the previous example, let us assume that, initially, no trade is taking place and each country devotes five units of resources to each industry.

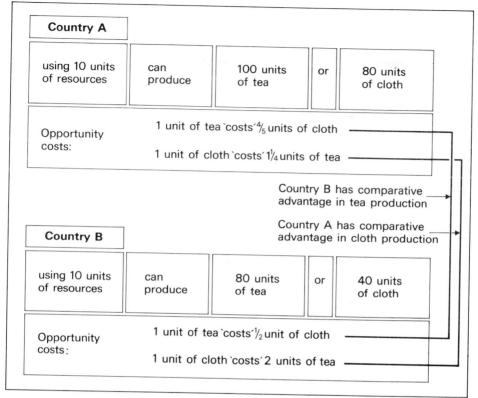

Fig. 22.2

	Tea (units)		**Cloth (units)**
Country A produces	50	and	40
Country B produces	40	and	20
Total output	90	and	60

Now assume that trading becomes possible and each country decides to specialize. It will concentrate its resources in the industry in which it has a comparative advantage. Country A will move resources from the tea industry to the cloth industry and Country B will move resources from the cloth industry to the tea industry.

If we allow each country to specialize one hundred per cent there is a problem because we find that while the total output of cloth increases, the total output of tea will fall. In spite of the fall in the output of tea, however, it can be shown that *the value* of the total outputs of tea and cloth would still be greater after specialization. This is so because, in both countries, the value of the increased output of cloth (measured in terms of tea) is greater than the foregone output of tea. The reader should check this by using the opportunity cost ratios.

This problem can be overcome if we assume that Country B specializes completely in the production of tea while Country A partially specializes, putting 2 units of resources to work in the tea industry and 8 units of resources to work in the cloth industry. Total output will be as follows.

	Tea (units)		Cloth (units)
Country A produces	20	and	64
Country B produces	80	and	0
Total output	100	and	64

Total output of both commodities has increased. If we now assume that 22 units of cloth are exchanged for 36 units of tea we find that,

	Tea (units)		Cloth (units)
Country A now consumes	56	and	42
Country B now consumes	44	and	22
	100	and	64

Both countries are better off than they were before they specialized and traded.

Some qualifications

The simple theory of comparative advantage outlined above does not take into account some of the features of the real world.
1 Although one country might be able to produce a good at a relatively lower cost than other countries, it will not be possible to obtain benefits from trade if transport costs outweigh its advantages in costs of production.
2 The arithmetical examples used above assume that average costs remain constant when output is varied. For example, we assume that in Country A every time a unit of resources is moved from the tea industry to the cloth industry, the output of tea falls by 10 units and the output of cloth increases by 8 units. This is not very likely because:
   a in some industries such as mining and agriculture, increasing output will encounter diminishing returns;
   b in industries such as manufacturing, increasing output is likely to yield economies of scale.
3 The simple theory of comparative advantage assumes that factors of production are very mobile. In our example we assumed that there were no problems in transferring resources from one industry to another. In fact, as we have seen earlier (pages 53–4), there are many barriers to this kind of mobility.
4 The theory is based on the assumption that countries are willing and able to trade with one another. In the real world we find that most countries erect various barriers to trade. These barriers are the subject of the next section.

Barriers to trade

1 Tariffs

These are taxes on foreign goods levied at the port of entry. They may be specific (e.g. £1 per tonne or per litre) or *ad valorem* (e.g. 10 per cent of the value of the good). Tariffs protect home industries by making foreign goods relatively dearer in the home market. Since tariffs are a form of taxation, they may be imposed in order to raise revenue for the government.

2 Quotas

These are very serious barriers to trade because they place a physical limit on the quantities of goods which may be imported into the country. For example, a country may decree that no more than 10 000 motor cars may be imported in any one year.

3 Exchange control

Imports must be purchased with foreign currencies and a system of exchange control limits the volume of imports by strictly controlling the supplies of foreign currencies made available to importers. Under this system, firms which export are obliged to surrender the foreign currency they earn to the central bank. In return they will receive the corresponding value in the home currency. The central bank then rations out these foreign currencies for the purchases of imports which are approved by the government.

4 Subsidies

A tariff makes the foreign good dearer in the home market; a subsidy makes the home-produced good cheaper in the home market. Subsidies to home producers, therefore, are a means of protecting them against foreign competition.

Reasons for barriers

There are many reasons why governments impose restrictions on imports.

1 To deal with a balance of payments deficit

A country with a serious and persistent deficit in its balance of payments may be forced to deal with it by restricting imports. The alternative measure of expanding exports will take quite a long time to come into effect and a cut-back in imports may be the only short-term solution available.

2 To protect an infant industry

A country may wish to establish an industry which, it is believed, when fully developed, could be very successful. This industry, however, may already be operating on a large scale in other countries. In its early stages of development the industry would be producing on a small scale with high average costs and would, therefore, in conditions of free trade, be unable to compete with the large industries in other countries. In order to allow such infant industry 'to grow up', it may be necessary to protect it from foreign competition. Once the industry reaches a size where it is obtaining the necessary economies of scale, the protection could be removed. In practice it might be difficult to remove the protective tariffs due to political pressures.

3   To eliminate or reduce 'unfair' competition

The argument here is that imports from low-wage countries represent unfair competition for domestic producers who are paying higher wages to their workers. The trouble with this argument is that it is not the level of wages which determine prices, but wage costs per unit of output. Some countries with relatively high wages, but enjoying high levels of labour productivity, have relatively low labour costs per unit of output. We should also bear in mind that if imports from low-wage countries are excluded, incomes in those countries will be depressed and wages could be driven even lower.

4   Strategic arguments

There are some industries which may be regarded as essential to a country's survival in times of war. Obvious examples are agriculture, steel, chemicals, and various types of engineering. In some countries these industries may not be efficient enough to survive in a world of free trade and they will, therefore, be protected by one or more of the measures described above.

Another type of strategic argument is used to justify the protection of home industries on the grounds that if a country specializes and becomes dependent on one or two major industries, it will be running great risks in a changing world. A fall in the demands for its major products could put such a country into serious economic difficulties. A country may wish to protect certain industries so that its people may be engaged in a wide variety of economic activities and not be dependent on the fortunes of one or two very large industries.

5   To assist a transfer of resources

A country may find that one or two of its old-established industries are losing the cost advantages which they have enjoyed in the past over industries in other countries. Under free trade these industries will lose their export markets and, quite possibly, their home markets. The resultant unemployment of capital and labour will impose harsh burdens on those dependent on these industries for their income. In order to alleviate these burdens a country may decide to protect such industries from foreign competition while they adjust to the changing situation (e.g. by closing down less efficient plants, merging and modernizing other plants, retraining labour for new jobs etc.).

Some likely economic effects of protection

The imposition of restrictions on international trade can have some adverse effects.

260

1   Consumers at home will be obliged to pay higher prices than those which would apply under free trade. Protection, therefore, may have inflationary consequences.

2   The use of measures to restrict imports will lead to lower incomes in other countries, because 'one country's imports are another country's exports'. This might lead to a general lowering of world trade.

3   The use of tariffs and quotas might lead to retaliation by the countries most affected. The end result could be a general increase in protection and a substantial fall in the volume of world trade.

4   An argument often used against protection is that, far from helping a home industry to improve its performance, the removal of foreign competition might make it less efficient.

The General Agreement on Tariffs and Trade (GATT)

The years since the Second World War have seen an unprecedented growth in the volume of world trade. There are many reasons for this development, but there seems little doubt that the work of international organizations set up to work for the removal of trade restrictions have played an important part in bringing about the expansion of world trade. GATT is one of these organizations. It began work in January 1948 and its membership now comprises most of the countries in the non-communist world. Representatives from member countries meet at regular intervals to negotiate agreements for the reduction of quotas, tariffs, and other barriers to trade. Although, to many observers, its progress appears to be slow, the organization has succeeded, over the years, in bringing about a significant liberalization of world trade. A basic principle of GATT is the 'most favoured nation' clause. This states that any tariff reductions agreed between any group of members must be extended to all other members of GATT. To some extent the work of GATT has been handicapped by the desire of some members to set up regional free trade blocs (explained in the next chapter) rather than work for free trade on a world-wide basis.

The terms of trade

If cars produced in the UK are sold in Canada for dollars and other UK firms then use Canadian dollars to buy wheat, we have, in effect, exchanged UK cars for Canadian wheat. The quantity of wheat which we can 'buy' with one motor car is obviously an important determinant of the standard of living. The terms of trade is an attempt to measure the rate at which a country's exports exchange for imports. So many different goods are exported and imported, however, that we cannot measure this exchange rate in physical terms. All that can be done is to use the movements in export and import prices to measure changes in the terms of trade.

The official calculation of the terms of trade makes use of index numbers as follows:

$$\text{The terms of trade} = \frac{\text{Index of export prices}}{\text{Index of import prices}} \times \frac{100}{1}$$

Since both the import and export price indexes will start in the same base year, the terms of trade for that year will be equal to 100. Table 22 provides some examples of movements in the terms of trade.

Table 22   Movements in the terms of trade

Year	Index of export prices	Index of import prices	Terms of trade	
1	100	100	100.00	
				} favourable
2	110	105	104.76	
				} unfavourable
3	115	116	99.13	
				} favourable
4	110	108	101.80	
				} unfavourable
5	104	105	99.05	

If the numerical value of the terms of trade increases, it means that export prices have risen *relative* to import prices. This is described as *favourable movement* because it means that any given quantity of exports will now exchange for a greater volume of imports. Conversely, a fall in the terms of trade means that import prices have risen relative to export prices. This is described as an *unfavourable movement* because any given volume of exports now exchanges for a smaller volume of imports.

Notice that it is relative price movements which affect the terms of trade. For example in Table 22 it can be seen that a favourable movement can arise when:
a   the prices of exports and imports are both rising but there is a greater percentage rise in export prices;
b   when both sets of prices are falling, but there is a greater percentage fall in the prices of imports;
The reader should reason out the various combinations of price movements which can result in (i) favourable movements and (ii) unfavourable movements in the terms of trade.

The use of the words 'favourable' and 'unfavourable' to describe movements in the terms of trade can be very misleading. It is only the *price* movements which are being referred to when these terms are being used. The terms of trade do not tell us anything about changes in the *volumes* of exports and imports. A favourable movement in the *terms of trade* may or may not lead to a favourable movement in the *balance of trade* and the same is true of an unfavourable movement in the terms of trade. Two simple examples should make this important point a little clearer.

1 Assume export prices rise by 10 per cent and import prices remain constant. This is a favourable movement in the terms of trade. Now the quantity of exports will fall. If it falls by more than 10 per cent (i.e. demand is elastic) less foreign currency will be earned from exports and if spending on imports remains unchanged, the balance of trade will be adversely affected.

2 Assume that export prices remain constant and the *foreign prices* of imports rise by 10 per cent. This is an unfavourable movement in the terms of trade. If, however, the quantity of imports falls by more than 10 per cent (i.e. demand is elastic), less foreign currency will be spent on imports. If export earnings remain unchanged, there will be a favourable movement in the balance of trade. Thus, the way in which changes in the terms of trade affect the balance of trade depends to a large extent on the elasticities of demand for exports and imports.

The balance of payments

The balance of payments is an account of a country's financial transactions with the rest of the world. Like most balance sheets it contains details of the financial results of trading over a period of one year although it is usual for countries to publish quarterly figures in addition to the annual accounts. The balance of payments is best explained by referring to an actual example and for this purpose we make use of Table 23 overleaf.

A Visible trade

This first section records the value of exports and imports of tangible goods – those things we can see being loaded and unloaded at ports and airports. Foodstuffs, oil, machinery, road vehicles, chemicals, electrical goods and raw materials are important items in the visible trade of the UK. The difference between the values of exports and imports of visible items is known as the *balance of trade* or the *visible balance*.

B Invisible trade

Invisible trade is the buying and selling of services and the main items are shown in Table 23. They include incomes earned by UK firms from selling transport, insurance, financial and other services to overseas residents and expenditures by UK residents on services supplied by overseas firms. Another important item is the interest, profits and dividends earned on UK investments abroad and the corresponding incomes paid abroad on foreign-owned investment in the UK. Until recent years there has been a substantial surplus on this item, but the situation has changed because of the increased earnings of foreign-owned oil companies operating in the North Sea.

The government purchases services overseas for the upkeep of embassies and consulates although there is a corresponding inflow of foreign currency from overseas governments maintaining diplomatic services in the UK. The main reasons for the deficit on government account are the provision of services for troops stationed abroad and the payments of the UK contributions to the EEC budget. Private transfers refer to the funds sent back to their homelands by immigrants in the UK and emigrants from the UK.

C   The balance on current account

If the balances on visible trade and invisible trade are added together we have the balance of payments on current account. This is an important figure because it tells us whether a country is paying its way in the world as a trading nation. The current account is said to be favourable if total receipts exceed total payments. A deficit on visible trade may not represent a problem if it is offset by a surplus on invisible trade. The UK, for example, has had a deficit on visible trade for most years during the past century, but in many of these years the traditional surplus on invisible trade more than offset the adverse balance on visible trade. In the 1970s a worsening of the visible trade deficit led to some serious deficits on the current account. The development of North Sea oil, however, led to an improvement in the visible balance during the late 1970s and should continue to do so during the 1980s.

D   Investment and other capital flows

Flows of payments between countries take place when governments, firms and households make loans to, or purchase assets in, other countries. The capital transactions in the balance of payments are those which give rise to a subsequent flow of income in the opposite direction. For example, if a UK citizen buys shares in an overseas company, there will be an outward flow of foreign currency when the shares are bought (i.e. a capital transaction) but in the following years there will be an inward flow of foreign currency in the form of interest and profits (i.e. an invisible transaction). Capital transactions may take the form of *real* investment, that is the purchase of real assets such as factories, mines and oil refineries or *portfolio* investment where financial assets such as shares and bonds are purchased.

Some of these capital transactions represent short-term investments where money moves from one country to another and is placed in bank deposits or is used to buy short-term securities such as Treasury bills. These transactions take place when holders of short-term balances are seeking higher interest rates or wish to protect their wealth against a possible fall in the external value of a currency.

E   Balancing item

This is *not* the item which 'balances the balance of payments'. It is the sum of all the errors and omissions in the account. The collection of information on all the transactions between residents of a country and the rest of the world is an enormous task and the information obtained by the authorities is most unlikely to be complete. If the balancing item is positive it means that the unrecorded inflow of foreign currency has exceeded the unrecorded outflow; if it is negative, unrecorded outflows must have exceeded unrecorded inflows.

264

Table 23 UK balance of payments, 1980 (£ million)

A Visible trade

Exports	47 376		**Visible balance**
Imports	46 199		+1 177

B Invisible trade

Government	+1 356		
	−3 934	−2 578	
Sea transport	+3 854		
	−3 704	+150	
Civil aviation	+2 233		
	−1 781	+452	
Travel	+2 991		
	−2 724	+267	
Financial services		+1 560	
Other services	+4 259		
	−2 137	+2 122	
Interest/profits	+8 014		
	−8 100	−86	**Invisible balance**
Private transfers	+756		
	−1 083	−327	+1 560

C Current balance

	+2 737

D Investment and other capital flows

Foreign investment in UK private sector	+2 564	
Foreign investment in UK public sector	+413	
UK private investment overseas	−6 870	**Capital transactions**
Official long-term capital	−56	
Other capital transactions	+2 459	−1 490

E Balancing item

	−55

F Balance for official financing (total currency flow)

	+1 192

G Official financing

Transactions with the IMF	+180	
Other short-term borrowing (+) and lending (−)	−1 081	
Changes in reserves (additions −), (drawings on +)	−291	−1 192

Source: *Economic Trends*, HMSO, March 1981.

F Balance for official financing

When the balance on current account, the balance on capital account and the balancing item are added together the total represents the balance for official financing or the *total currency flow*. This total is the net result of all the flows of income and expenditure arising from ordinary trade transactions and capital movements. It is most unlikely that this total will be zero. It would be a remarkable coincidence if the net result of many thousands of independent decisions by UK residents and overseas residents to do business with each other (i.e. to buy and sell, borrow and lend), resulted in an outflow of foreign currency which was exactly equal to the inflow. The overall account will show a surplus or a deficit.

G Official financing

This final section of the balance of payment account shows how the monetary authorities (the Bank of England) have dealt with the overall deficit or surplus. There are two main ways in which they can act.

a   A surplus may be added to the nation's foreign currency reserves; a deficit may be financed by running down the reserves.

b   A deficit may be financed by borrowing from the International Monetary Fund (IMF) or from foreign central banks; a surplus may be used to repay any outstanding debts to these institutions. This section of the balance of payments sometimes causes problems because, at first sight, the plus and minus signs appear to be misleading. For example, 'additions to the reserves' is shown with a minus sign while 'borrowing from the IMF' will be shown with a plus sign. In Table 23 we see that the authorities had to deal with a surplus of £1192 million. Since this surplus has a plus sign, the account can only be balanced by showing the ways in which the surplus was disposed of by using minus signs. Some of the surplus was added to the foreign currency reserves (£291 million) and this transaction has a minus sign since this money went *out of* the balance of payments account and *into* the reserves. Some of it was used to repay foreign debts (£1081 million). The first item in this account refers to an allocation of SDRs to the UK from the IMF (see page 276).

Interpreting the balance of payments account

The balance of payments is described as 'favourable' or 'unfavourable' depending on whether there is an overall surplus or deficit. Merely looking at the overall balance or even the balances on the separate sections, however, can give a misleading impression. It has been noted that the current balance tells us whether the country has been paying its way in the world, but a series of deficits on current account may or may not be a serious matter.

A country in deficit on its current account may be running the deficit because it is importing capital equipment, raw materials and foreign expertise in order to develop its industries. The current deficit may be offset by a surplus on the capital account, in the form of loans from abroad. If these loans are being used to finance improvements in the country's industrial structure, the country's export performance should improve in future years and enable it to earn enough foreign currency to pay off its debts. It would, however, be a serious matter if the current deficit was being incurred to finance the growth of consumption of imported goods.

A developed country may have a deficit on its current account which is more than offset by a surplus on its capital account. It will have a surplus on its over-all balance of payments and, at first sight, this will appear to be a favourable situation. But the inflow of capital may well have consisted of short-term funds attracted to the country by high interest rates. Unlike long-term investment, these funds can be quickly withdrawn by the foreign holders should they wish to do so. A large-scale withdrawal of foreign-owned funds could quickly trans-form the surplus on the capital account into a deficit.

A further point is that a surplus on the balance of payments can hardly be described as favourable if it is being achieved by imposing serious restrictions on imports, or because there is heavy unemployment which is reducing the de-mand for imports (as was the case with the UK in 1980–81). There is a more detailed discussion of balance of payments problems in Chapter 29.

The foreign trade of the UK

The UK is extremely dependent on foreign trade. About 40 per cent of the population's food and a large proportion of the raw materials used by industry have to be imported. In 1980 exports of goods and services were equal to about 25 per cent of the Gross National Product.

In the exports of manufactures, the UK, in recent years, has done less well than her major competitors. The UK's share of the value of the main manufac-turing countries' exports fell from 16 per cent in 1960 to about 9 per cent in 1979. This was due to the fact that the volume of UK exports increased at an annual average rate of 5 per cent, this was only about one-half the rate achieved by the main manufacturing countries as a whole and about one-third the rate for Japan.

Changes in the commodity composition of exports have been very small in recent years. The share of manufactured goods has increased slightly while the share of basic materials has declined. There has been a steady decline in the share of textiles and an increase in the share of chemicals in total exports. Over the next decade the possibility of exporting North Sea Oil and the diminishing dependence on imported oil should have a beneficial effect on the UK's visible trade balance.

The most striking change in the geographical distribution of UK exports in recent years has been the switch away from the traditional Commonwealth markets and a growing dependence on the markets in Western Europe. Ex-ports to Western Europe accounted for about 34 per cent of UK exports in 1960 but by 1980 this share had grown to nearly 60 per cent. This is much in line with developments in world trade as a whole, because trade between industrialized countries has been the fastest growing sector of world trade. The other important development is the growing importance of the markets in the oil-exporting countries.

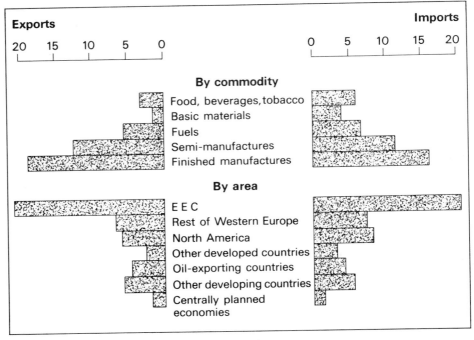

Fig. 22.3   UK visible trade, 1980 (£ billion)

Source: *British Business*, HMSO, 27 February 1981.

The commodity pattern of imports has changed quite radically in recent years. Although the total value of imports of food, beverages and tobacco has been increasing, the share of these commodities in total imports has been falling. The same is true of raw materials. On the other hand, the share of finished manufactures in total imports has been rising (from 22 per cent in 1960 to 36 per cent in 1980). A rise in the imports of manufactures is not undesirable providing there is a corresponding rise in the exports of these goods. Britain, however, must import large amounts of food and raw materials and thus requires a substantial surplus on trade in manufactures. A disturbing feature of UK visible trade is the fact that during the 1970s the import volume of finished manufactures increased three times as fast as the export volume of finished manufactures.

The geographical distribution of the sources of imports has changed in a similar manner to that for exports. Western Europe now supplies about 60 per cent of UK imports and there has been a substantial fall in the share of imports coming from Commonwealth countries. There has also been a large percentage increase in the value of imports to the UK from Japan.

23 Foreign exchange rates

Generally speaking a firm supplying goods or services to customers in other countries will require payment in the currency of its own country. An American firm will demand payment in dollars, a French firm in francs and so on. Hence buyers in international trade need to obtain the currencies of the countries with which they are doing business. This means that a highly developed system of international trade can only function if there is a market where one currency can be exchanged for another. This is the role of the foreign exchange market.

Exchange rates and prices

The amount of foreign currency received for any exported good or service and the amount of home currency paid for an imported good or service depend upon:

a the price charged by the suppliers in their own currency;
b the rate of exchange – the rate at which one currency exchanges for another.

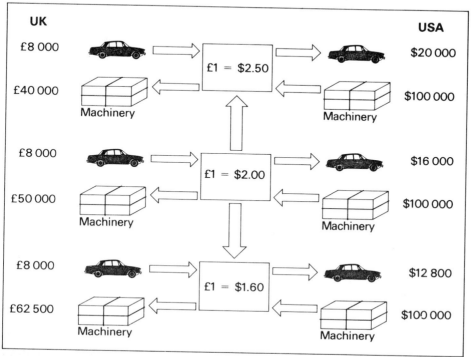

Fig. 23.1 Price effects of changes in the exchange rate

It is most important to understand how changes in the rate of exchange affect export and import prices. Fig. 23.1 shows how changes in the rate of exchange influence the prices of goods traded between the UK and the USA.

An explanation of Fig. 23.1

If we assume that, initially, the rate of exchange is £1 = $2.00 then the British motor car which is priced by the supplier at £8000 will cost the American importer $16 000. The American machinery priced at $100 000 will cost the UK importer £50 000.

1 *If the external value of the pound now rises to £1 = $2.50*, the UK exports to the USA become dearer in the American market while the American exports to the UK become cheaper in the British market. Thus, a rise in the external value of the pound increases the prices of exports (in foreign currency) and reduces the prices of imports (in home currency).

2 *If the value of the pound falls to £1 = $1.60*, we find that the motor car exported from the UK to the USA becomes cheaper in the American market, but the American exports of machinery become dearer in the UK market. Thus, a fall in the external value of the pound reduces the prices of British exports (in foreign currency) but raises the prices of imports (in home currency).

Exchange rates in a free market

In a free market the rate of exchange is determined by the market forces of supply and demand. Where these conditions apply the exchange rate is said to be *floating* or *flexible*. In the explanation which follows we shall assume that the value of the pound is determined in a free market, that is, it is floating.

The demand for pounds

In the foreign exchange market, pounds will be demanded by overseas residents (households and firms) who are, (a) willing and able to buy British goods, (b) demanding services supplied by British firms, and (c) wanting to invest in Britain, that is, they wish to buy British property in the UK, to buy shares in UK companies or to make loans to British residents.

For all these purposes overseas residents will need pounds and they will demand these pounds by offering other currencies in exchange for them. It can be seen, therefore, that an increase in UK exports will increase the demand for pounds.

The supply of pounds

The supply of pounds in the foreign exchange market will depend upon British residents', (a) demands for goods produced in other countries, (b) demands for services supplied by overseas firms, and (c) willingness and ability to invest abroad.

For these purposes UK residents must obtain foreign currencies. Banks, acting on their behalf, will buy these currencies in the foreign exchange market and pay for them with pounds. Thus, an increase in UK imports will increase the supply of pounds in the foreign exchange market.

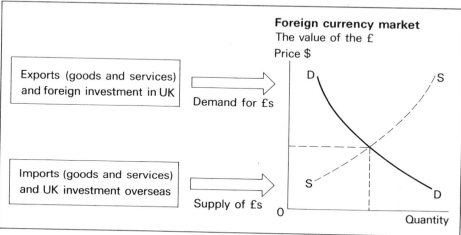

Fig. 23.2

Fig. 23.2 may be used to illustrate the way in which the external value of a currency is determined in a free market.

An increased demand for exports and/or an increase in foreign investment in the UK means that the demand for pounds by overseas residents is increasing. The demand curve in Fig. 23.2 will move to the right and the external value of the pound will rise, that is, its price in terms of other currencies will increase. A fall in the demand for exports will have the opposite effect.

An increased demand for imports and/or an increase in UK investment abroad means that the supply of pounds in the foreign exchange market is increasing; UK residents are offering more pounds in exchange for foreign currencies. The supply curve in Fig. 23.2 will move to the right and the value of the pound will fall.

When a currency is floating, a fall in its value is described as *depreciation*, while an increase in its value is described as *appreciation*.

Advantages and disadvantages of floating exchange rates

In theory, an advantage of a floating exchange rate is that it will automatically correct any tendency for the balance of payments to move into surplus or deficit. The following sequence of events shows how this automatic correction is supposed to work.

271

1   Assume the UK balance of payments is initially in equilibrium (no surplus or deficit).
2   Assume now that export values remain unchanged, but an increased demand for imports tends to move the UK balance of payments into deficit.
3   This increased demand for imports will increase the supply of pounds in the foreign exchange market.
4   The external value of the pound will fall and, as shown in Fig. 23.1, this will make exports cheaper and imports dearer.
5   The changes in the relative prices of exports and imports will increase the volume of exports and reduce the volume of imports and the balance of payments will be brought back into equilibrium.

The reader should be able to reason out the sequence of events which would follow an increase in exports and show how the tendency towards a balance of payments surplus might be eliminated by changes in the exchange rate.

In practice it may not work out like this because the supplies of exports and imports may be slow to adjust to the price changes. For example, if the prices of exports fall, it may take some considerable time before the increased quantities demanded can be supplied. There are also problems associated with the elasticities of demand for exports and imports. A 10 per cent fall in the prices of export will not increase the amount of foreign currency earned unless the quantities demanded increase by more than 10 per cent. A further problem is that a depreciation of the pound increases import prices and, since the UK imports a large amount of foodstuffs and raw materials, this has the effect of raising the cost of living and the costs of production in many industries.

A disadvantage of the system of floating exchange rates is the fact that it greatly increases the risks and uncertainties in international trade. For example, a Lancashire manufacturer of cotton cloth may be quoted a firm dollar price by his American supplier, payment due, say, in three months. He will still not be certain of the costs of his cotton because he does not know what the dollar–pound exchange rate will be when he comes to make payment. If he is quoted \$500 for a bale of cotton and the exchange rate stands at £1 = \$2.50, a bale of cotton will cost him £200. If, however, by the time he comes to make payment, the exchange rate has moved to £1 = \$2.25, a bale of cotton will cost him £222.22. Speculators remove some of this uncertainty by operating a *forward exchange market* where they guarantee to supply foreign currency at some future date at a price agreed now.

A free market invariably attracts speculators and the foreign exchange market is no exception. Speculators will buy currencies whose value is expected to rise with a view to reselling them when they have appreciated in value. They will sell currencies whose value is expected to fall, hoping to repurchase them later at a lower price. For example, suppose the pound sterling stands at £1 = \$2.50 and is expected to fall in value. A speculator exchanges £10 000 for \$25 000. The value of the pound now falls to £1 = \$2.35. If the \$25 000 is now exchanged for pounds, the speculator will receive £10 638.3 and make a profit of £638.3 (minus certain costs for converting the currencies). Had the pound appreciated, of course, a loss would have been made.

The reader should be able to work out a simple example showing the possibilities of making capital gains when a currency is expected to appreciate.

A perfectly free market in foreign currency is not likely to be found in the real world. Even when currencies are said to be floating, governments tend to intervene in the market to smooth out undesirable fluctuations. The central bank is responsible for this type of intervention and the way it operates is explained in the next section.

Fixed exchange rates

For many years after the Second World War most countries operated a system of fixed exchange rates. The external value of a currency was fixed in terms of the dollar and the value of the dollar itself was fixed in terms of gold. In effect, therefore, the values of the currencies were fixed in terms of gold. The 'fixed' rate was not absolutely rigid. The value of a currency was allowed to vary within a narrow band of 1 or 2 per cent on each side of the 'fixed' rate or parity. For example, if the value of the pound were 'fixed' at £1 = \$2.50, a permitted deviation of 2 per cent would allow it to vary between £1 = \$2.55 and £1 = \$2.45. These limits are often described as 'the ceiling' and 'the floor'. Central banks were responsible for maintaining the values of their currencies within the prescribed bands. They are able to do this by acting as buyers or sellers of the currency in the foreign exchange market. For this purpose each central bank must have a fund containing supplies of the home currency and foreign currencies. In the UK this fund is held in the Exchange Equalization Account which is managed by the Bank of England.

The way in which the central bank can use its fund of currencies to influence the exchange rate can be explained by making use of Fig. 23.3 overleaf. Let us assume that the value of the pound has been fixed at A and, initially, the market is in equilibrium at this exchange rate. The permitted band of fluctuation is PP^1 and the value of the pound must be held within these limits. A large increase in imports now causes an increase in the supply of pounds in the foreign exchange market. The supply curve moves from SS to S^{1}S^1 causing a surplus of pounds at the 'fixed' rate (A). If no intervention takes place, the external value of the pound will fall to B which is below the permitted 'floor'. The central bank will be obliged to enter the market and buy pounds. In doing so it will shift the demand curve to the right and raise the value of the pound until it is once again within the agreed limits. In Fig. 23.3 intervention by the Bank of England has raised the exchange rate to C.

When the Bank of England is buying pounds, it will be using up its reserves of foreign currencies; when buying pounds it exchanges foreign currencies for pounds. 'Supporting the pound', that is, increasing the demand for pounds, therefore leads to a fall in the nation's foreign currency reserves. In the opposite situation where an increased demand for pounds tends to lift the value of the pound above the permitted 'ceiling', the central bank will hold down its

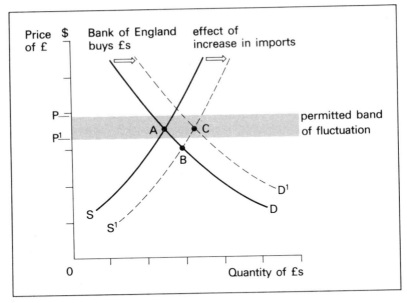

Fig. 23.3

value by selling pounds. This will increase the supply of pounds and lower the exchange rate. When the central bank is selling pounds it will be increasing its holdings of foreign currencies.

The main argument for a fixed exchange rate is the same as that against a floating rate. A fixed rate removes a major cause of uncertainty in international transactions. Traders can quote prices which will be accepted with some degree of confidence; buyers know that they will not be affected by movements in the exchange rate. The risks associated with international trade are lessened and this should encourage more trade between nations and more international borrowing and lending.

Devaluation and revaluation

When a country which is operating a fixed exchange rate experiences a serious and persistent balance of payments deficit, its central bank will have to intervene in the foreign exchange market in order to prevent a fall in the exchange rate. The central bank's activities, as explained earlier, will cause the country's foreign exchange reserves to fall. Although the foreign currency reserves can be increased by borrowing abroad, these loans will have to be repaid and there is a limit to the amount a country may borrow overseas. A country in this situation will probably have to devalue its currency; it will adopt a new and lower exchange rate. For example, in 1967, the pound was devalued from £1 = $2.80 to £1 = $2.40.

Devaluation, like depreciation explained earlier, makes exports cheaper in terms of foreign currency and imports dearer in terms of home currency. Other countries, of course, may retaliate by devaluing their own currencies. In that case, the relative prices of imports and exports may remain unchanged. Whether devaluation is successful in dealing with the deficit problem depends upon:

a   whether or nor the increase in quantities of goods sold abroad more than offsets the fall in their foreign currency prices;

b   how the dearer imports affect the costs of production at home;

c   whether industry is capable of meeting the increased demands for exports.

If a country has a persistent surplus on its balance of payments, the external value of its currency will tend to appreciate. If the country is operating a fixed exchange rate, the central bank will have to intervene and prevent any rise in the exchange rate. It will sell the home currency in the foreign exchange market (i.e. increase its supply) and in doing so it will be building up its foreign currency reserves. While this may seem to be a desirable state of affairs, it can lead to a serious imbalance in the distribution of international liquidity (see next section). One remedy for this problem is *revaluation*; the country moves to a new and higher exchange rate. This will tend to remove the surplus by making exports dearer in foreign markets and imports cheaper in the home market. Since a balance of payments surplus is usually seen as an indication of successful economic management, surplus countries may be reluctant to undertake revaluation.

The International Monetary Fund (IMF)

The IMF was set up as a result of an agreement made at Bretton Woods in the USA in 1944 and it began operations in 1947. It now has some 138 members including all the major countries of the world with the exception of the USSR and some other communist countries. Its main purpose is to encourage the growth of world trade as a means of raising the real income of member countries. It aims to achieve its objectives by:

a   promoting regular meetings and consultations between member countries' so as to encourage international monetary cooperation;

b   encouraging members to adopt stable exchange rates;

c   assisting and urging countries to make their currencies freely convertible;

d   providing financial assistance to countries in balance of payments difficulties so that such countries do not have to use trade restrictions as a means of dealing with their problems.

International liquidity

All nations hold reserves of gold and foreign currencies. These reserves are often described as international liquidity, that is, financial assets which are generally acceptable in the settlement of international debts. The major reserve currencies are those of the leading industrialized countries, the dollar being by far the most important currency.

Nations need these reserves (a) as working balances to finance their overseas trade, (b) to help stabilize their currencies in the foreign exchange market (e.g. the Exchange Equalization Account), and (c) to finance balance of payments deficits while attempts are made to deal with the causes of the deficits. One of the functions of the IMF is to increase the supply of international liquidity.

Each member of the IMF has a quota, the size of which depends upon its national income and its importance as a trading nation. Each member must pay into the Fund an amount equal to 75 per cent of its quota in its own currency and 25 per cent in foreign currencies. There are, however, plans to change this requirement so that a country may pay the whole of its quota in its own currency. Thus, the Fund holds a large supply of national currencies and members may draw on this pool of foreign currencies when they are in balance of payments difficulties. Strictly speaking members do not 'borrow' from the Fund, they 'buy' the foreign currency they need by making payments in their own currencies. The amount of foreign currency any member may purchase depends upon the size of its quota; the larger the quota, the greater its purchasing rights. A limited amount of assistance is available from the Fund without any conditions being imposed, but further drawings are conditional upon the Fund's approval. The IMF may insist that the country seeking assistance pursues economic policies which the Fund thinks are necessary for the removal of that country's economic difficulties. The main purpose of the IMF's assistance is to prevent countries resorting to the use of tariffs, quotas and exchange control as methods of dealing with their problems. The assistance provided by the IMF is of a short-term nature; members are expected to repay the foreign currencies they have borrowed within three to five years, but this period may be extended in certain circumstances.

The rapid growth of world trade during the 1960s and the widespread nature of inflation, and especially the huge increases in the price of oil during the 1970s, have all contributed to the need for a major increase in the supply of international liquidity. The very large deficits incurred by some countries placed an enormous strain on the resources of the IMF. In 1970 the IMF made its first allocation of *Special Drawing Rights* (*SDRs*). These are entirely new reserve assets created by the IMF and, although they cannot be traded on any market, they can be transferred between central banks in exchange for currencies needed to deal with balance of payments problems. SDRs are allocated to member countries in proportion to their quotas and the aim is to increase these allocations so that, in time, the SDR will become a major reserve asset in the world's monetary system. The value of the SDR is a weighted average of the exchange values of sixteen major currencies.

Convertibility

One of the aims of the IMF is to make currencies freely convertible so that holders of one country's currency may freely exchange it for the currency of another country. The reason why this is an important aim of the IMF is the fact that international trade is greatly restricted unless currencies are freely convertible. Fig. 23.4 helps to demonstrate the advantages of *multilateral* trade over *bilateral* trade. Under multilateral trade, each country does not have to balance its trade with each of its trading partners; it need only be concerned with balancing its total exports and total imports. Under a system of bilateral trade, each country has to balance its trade with each of the countries with which it trades.

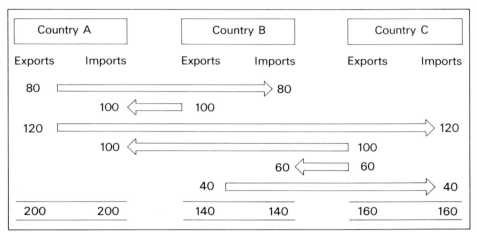

Fig. 23.4   Multilateral trade

In Fig. 23.4 we can see that each country's *total* trade is in balance, but no two countries have balanced trade with each other. Overall balance is achieved because each country's currency is convertible. For example, A has a deficit with B and a surplus with C. It can use its surplus with C to finance its deficit with B by converting its excess earnings of C's currency into B's currency.

If currencies are not convertible, trade must be carried out on a bilateral basis and each country must strike a trade balance with each of its partners. Total trade will be less than it would be if currencies were convertible. This can be demonstrated by using Fig. 23.4. Country A's imports from B must be reduced to 80 because its purchases from B will now be limited to the amount of B's currency it can earn by exporting to B. Similarly B's imports from C will have to fall to 40.

Exchange rates

The IMF system was based on the view that fixed (or very stable) exchange rates are beneficial to the growth of world trade. The system, which operated for many years, obliged member countries to maintain the external values of their currencies within a narrow band around some fixed rate. Initially the limits of this band were 1¼ per cent of the fixed rate although this was later changed to 2½ per cent. This system was operated until the early 1970s when world-wide inflation and the huge increases in the price of oil placed many members in serious balance of payments difficulties. Member countries became very reluctant to carry out the large and frequent devaluations (and revaluations) which would have been necessary under the system of fixed exchange rates. They chose instead to move to the system of floating exchange rates. Since 1975 most of the world's major currencies have been floating although, in most cases, the central banks have been operating in the foreign exchange market to offset short-term fluctuations and pressures brought about by speculation. The system is, in fact, a kind of *managed* flexibility.

The International Bank for Reconstruction and Development (The World Bank)

The IBRD or World Bank is a sister institution to the IMF, set up at the same time and having the same membership. Its functions, however, are quite different. Whereas the IMF exists to provide short-term assistance to help members with balance of payments problems, the World Bank exists to provide long-term loans to help countries with their development programmes. Although its capital is subscribed by member countries, it is also empowered to borrow in the world's capital markets and the member countries guarantee its borrowings.

In the early years of its existence much of its assistance went to countries whose economies had been seriously damaged by the effects of war. These loans were to help with reconstruction. Since the recovery of the industrialized nations, World Bank loans have gone mainly to developing countries. In addition to its financial help, the World Bank also provides developing countries with the services of all kinds of experts to advise and assist them with their development programmes.

24 Free trade areas and common markets

In addition to the international organizations working for the removal of restrictions on international trade, the post-war period has seen the creation of many regional trading blocs. The basic idea of these organizations is for a group of nations, preferably at the same stage of economic development, to join together for the purpose of removing restrictions on trade between themselves. Nations are attracted to the idea by the prospects of the economic advantages of having much larger 'home' markets but, in many cases, there is also a strong political motive. The formation of closer economic ties between countries is seen as a necessary first step to the creation of a political union.

International economic linkages between groups of countries may take many different forms, but the main types are, free trade areas, customs unions and common markets.

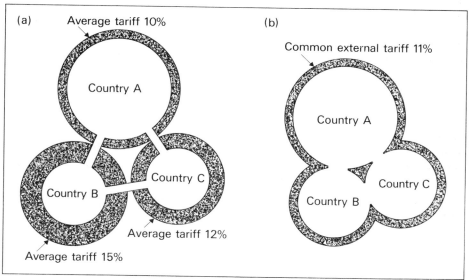

Fig. 24.1(a)   A free trade area

Fig. 24.1(b)   A customs union

1   Free trade areas

Countries which are members of a free trade area agree to remove all tariffs, quotas and other barriers to trade between themselves. As far as trade with the rest of the world is concerned, each member is free to set its own tariffs or quotas. Free trade is limited to those goods which are produced within the member countries. This is a very necessary rule otherwise there would be a large-scale diversion of trade. This can be illustrated by making use of Fig. 24.1. Assume that, in the diagram of the free trade area (Fig. 24.1(a)), the rates of external tariff are those which apply to motor cars. A non-member country exporting cars could route its exports to countries B and C through Country A. Its cars would enter countries B and C after paying duty at the rate of 10 per cent instead of 15 per cent and 12 per cent. In order to avoid this type of trade diversion, most free trade areas have regulations which insist that goods exported from one member country to another only qualify for duty-free entry if something like 50 per cent of the value of the goods has been produced in the exporting country.

The European Free Trade Association (EFTA) came into being in May 1960. Its original members were, Austria, Denmark, Norway, Portugal, Sweden, Switzerland and the United Kingdom. Finland signed an agreement of association in 1961 and Iceland became a member in 1970. It was formed to allow free trade in industrial goods between member states. By 1966 all tariffs and quotas on industrial products had been removed. When they joined the European Community in 1973 the UK and Denmark left EFTA and the remaining members signed a free trade agreement with the EEC.

2 Customs unions

The members of a customs union agree to remove all restrictions on trade between themselves *and* erect a common external tariff on imports from the rest of the world. This means that goods entering the customs union meet the same tariff barriers whichever country they enter. The common external tariff (see Fig. 24.1(b)) removes the problem of trade diversions which are associated with free trade areas.

3 Common markets

A common market is a customs union with several additional features. In addition to the removal of the restrictions on trade between members and the setting up of a common external tariff, a common market also allows for the free movement of the factors of production (labour, capital and enterprise) within the community. It also provides for the freedom of residents to supply such services as banking, insurance, wholesale and retail distribution anywhere within the customs union. A common market also requires members to have common policies on such matters as social security, taxation, transport, agriculture and competition. This close association of the member countries calls for the setting up of what are known as *supra-national* bodies. These are the institutions which supervise the workings of the community and make sure that the various rules and regulations are being observed by all member countries.

The economic arguments – free trade areas and customs unions

For

1 The removal of trade barriers allows member countries to increase total output by means of greater specialization. This argument is based on the theory of comparative advantage.

2 The fact that the industries in member countries will be operating in a greatly enlarged home market will enable the more successful to achieve much greater economies of scale.

3 Free trade between members will subject the industries in member states to greatly intensified competition and this might lead to more efficient production.

4 The prospect of gains from selling in a greatly enlarged market might stimulate firms in the community to undertake more investment. It might also encourage other countries (e.g. USA and Japan) to invest in the community.

Against

1 Free trade areas and customs unions may discriminate against the rest of the world. For example, suppose there are three countries A, B and C, all of which place tariffs on imports. Countries B and C both export footwear, but Country B is the more efficient and lower-cost producer. Country A imports footwear from Country B.

   Countries A and C now form a free trade area (or customs union) so that goods from Country C enter Country A duty free. Country A now imports footwear from Country C because the removal of the tariff has made imports from Country C cheaper than those from Country B (which are still subject to a tariff). In this case, trade has been diverted away from the more efficient producer.

2 Free trade areas and customs unions may encourage the members to be inward-looking. They may concentrate on developing trade between themselves and tend to neglect the interests of producers and consumers outside the community.

3 The existence of a common external tariff means that a member country loses the freedom to vary its trade barriers with the rest of the world. It cannot, for example, raise its tariffs as a means of dealing with a balance of payments deficit.

There are several free trade areas and customs unions established in different parts of the world, notably in Latin America, the Caribbean and Africa. The Council for Mutual Economic Assistance (known as Comecon) is an organization which aims to strengthen the trading links between the USSR and the communist countries of Eastern Europe. But by far the most important example of international economic integration is the European Economic Community.

The European Economic Community (EEC)

There are in fact three European communities.

1 *The European Coal and Steel Community (ECSC)* began work in 1952 and established a common market in coal and steel.
2 *The European Atomic Energy Community (Euratom)* began work in January 1958 and aims to promote the peaceful uses of atomic energy.
3 *The European Economic Community (EEC)* was set up by the Treaty of Rome in 1957 and began work on 1 January 1958.

All these bodies have the same governing institutions. We shall be mainly concerned with the EEC (the Common Market).

The founder members of the European Community were Belgium, France, Germany, Italy, Luxembourg and the Netherlands. On 1 January 1973, Denmark, Ireland and the United Kingdom joined the Community. Greece became a member on 1 January 1981. The Community has a total population of about 270 million. Its combined Gross Domestic Product is almost as great as that of the USA and it is the world's largest exporter and importer.

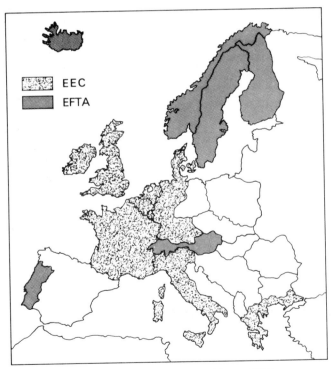

Fig. 24.2   West European trading blocs, 1981

Aims

The aims of the EEC as set out in the Treaty of Rome include the following:

a   the elimination of tariffs, quotas and other trade barriers between members;

b   the establishment of a common external tariff;

c   the abolition, between members, of obstacles to the freedom of movement of persons, services and capital;

d   the establishment of common policies in agriculture and transport;

e   the establishment of common policies on monopolies and restrictive practices so that competition in the Common Market is not distorted;

f   the application of procedures by which the economic policies of member states can be coordinated.

The objectives of the EEC go beyond the setting up of a common market; a closely knit economic and political union is the ultimate objective.

Development

The first step, the formation of a customs union, was achieved fairly easily and quickly. The original six members had removed restrictions on trade between themselves by July 1968 and had also replaced their national tariffs by a common external tariff. The three newer members, the United Kingdom, Ireland and Denmark had achieved the same objectives by July 1977. The external tariff has been gradually reduced in GATT negotiations; in late 1979 its average level was 6 per cent as against the United States' 7.1 per cent and Japan's 9.7 per cent.

The movement towards a common market also required the removal of barriers to the free movement of people, services and capital. Since 1969, nationals of the Community members, have been able to go to any other member country to look for and accept a wage-earning job. On wages, working conditions, social security rights, trade union rights and access to housing, they must be treated equally with nationals of the host country. There has been considerable difficulty in trying to arrange for the free movement between the members of people in the professions where precise qualifications are demanded (e.g. law and medicine). Restrictions on the mobility of some services such as banking, insurance, retailing and real estate have been removed. The elimination of restrictions on the movement of capital has proved difficult.

How the European Community works

The Community has four main institutions, each with its own civil service.

1   The Commission

The role of the Commission is to draft policies and present them to the Council of Ministers for decision. It also has to see that the approved policies are carried out by member governments and is largely responsible for the day-to-day running of the Community. There are fourteen Commissioners appointed by member governments, but they are not in Brussels to represent their national governments; their job is to represent the interests of the Community as a whole.

2 The Council of Ministers

This is the important decision-taking body. The Council takes decisions on policies submitted to it by the Commission. The members, one from each country, directly represent their national governments.

3 The European Parliament

Members of this parliament are directly elected by the citizens of member countries. Its main task is to act as a watchdog on the activities of the Commission and the Council of Ministers. It has the right to be consulted on most of the Commission's proposals before the Council of Ministers can take a decision on them. The European Parliament can dismiss the Commission on a two-thirds majority vote of confidence.

4 The Court of Justice

The Court consists of ten judges and is completely independent of the other institutions. Its main function is to decide whether any country is in breach of the treaties which established the Community. Individuals, institutions, and member governments can appeal to the Court.

There is a large number of other institutions which have been set up to carry out the policies of the Community. Among the more important of these are the following.

The European Investment Bank was formed to provide financial assistance for investment projects mainly in the poorer areas of the Community. It does, however, provide long-term loans for modernization in other areas and for the launching of entirely new projects.

The European Regional Development Fund is designed to provide aid additional to that supplied by member governments for areas suffering from higher than average unemployment.

The European Social Fund is primarily concerned with the problems of redundancy brought about by changes in demand and new technology. It provides financial help for retraining workers made redundant and for the resettlement of such workers.

The European Agricultural Guidance and Guarantee Fund

This fund accounts for the greater part of the Community's expenditure. It is the main instrument for carrying out the Common Agricultural Policy (CAP). The Guidance section of the Fund provides grants for structural improvements such as the merging of farms into larger units, farm modernization, improved drainage, afforestation and so on.

The Guarantee section of the Fund is responsible for setting prices for the main agricultural products. The Fund supports prices in a guaranteed price range. It fixes a minimum price to protect the interests of farmers and a maximum price to protect the interests of consumers. Between these two limits the price is free to fluctuate. The Fund holds the price of a commodity between these limits by:

a   intervening in the market as a buyer or seller;
b   varying the import duties on foreign foodstuffs.

The examples below explain how these measures work.

If a surplus develops which tends to push the market price below the guaranteed minimum price, the authorities can take the following actions.

1   Intervene in the market to purchase the surplus for stockpiling. By increasing the demand they will lift the market price above the lower limit.
2   Raise import duties (or levies as they are called) to reduce imports into the Community.
3   Reduce supplies in the Community markets by granting subsidies on exports.

If a shortage arises which is tending to raise the market price above the agreed maximum price, the authorities can (a) increase market supply by releasing stocks, (b) increase home supplies by lowering the import duties.

In order to ensure that the Community is self-sufficient in the production of many foodstuffs, guaranteed minimum prices have been set at levels which have encouraged increases in production and in some cases this has led to the accumulation of large surpluses.

The Community's Budget

The Community has its own Budget to finance the policies agreed by member states. Revenues are obtained from:

a   levies on agricultural imports;
b   customs duties on other commodities entering the Community;
c   a contribution from each member state equal to a maximum value of a VAT rate of 1 per cent (not 1 per cent of the country's VAT revenue). VAT is explained in Chapter 25.

The Community's expenditure is devoted mainly to the support of agriculture (about 76 per cent of the total in 1980). Among the other items of expenditure are the financing of social policies (e.g. the retraining of workers), investment in the poorer regions of the Community, the provision of aid to developing countries, and the administrative costs of running the Community.

Test paper 9

Short-answer questions

Questions 1, 2, 3 and 4 refer to the following situation.

	Units of Commodity A		Units of Commodity B
With 10 units of resources Country X can produce	100	or	100
With 10 units of resources Country Y can produce	80	or	50

1 What is the opportunity cost of producing 1 unit of A (a) in Country X, (b) in Country Y?

2 What is the opportunity cost of producing 1 unit of B (a) in Country X, (b) in Country Y?

3 Assume (a) each country has 100 units of resources, (b) there is no trade between them and (c) each country devotes half its resources to each industry. What is the total output of each commodity?

4 Now assume that trade between these countries becomes possible. Country Y specializes completely in the production of A. Arrange an allocation of resources in Country X so that the total output of both commodities is greater than it was before trade became possible.

5 International trade is said to bring benefits in the form of:
   a greater specialization leading to higher productivity;
   b a greater variety of goods becoming available to the citizens of the trading countries.
   Indicate two other possible gains from international trade.

6 In what ways are the economic effects of quotas and tariffs (a) similar, and (b) different?

7 'While tariffs may be successful in reducing a country's imports they may also lead to a fall in the country's exports.' Explain.

8 The prices of a country's exports rise, on average, by 10 per cent, while the prices of its imports rise, on average, by 8 per cent. Have the terms of trade moved favourably or unfavourably?

9 'When UK residents buy shares in an American company there is an immediate adverse effect on the balance of payments, but, in the longer term, there could be favourable effects on the balance of payments.' Explain (a) the adverse effects and (b) the longer-term favourable effects.

10 Which trading area accounts for more than one-half of the UK's total exports and total imports?

11 What has been the most important change in the composition of UK imports in recent years?

12 What is the *main* distinction between a free trade area and a customs union?

13 The table below contains the main items in a country's balance of payments account. They are arranged in random order.

Services sold to overseas residents	350
Visible exports	(a)
Balance of payments on current account	+50
Visible imports	600
Services purchased abroad	(b)
Visible balance	−100
Foreign investment in home industry	120
Balancing item	+120
Investment overseas	100
Balance for official financing (total currency flow)	(c)

What are the missing figures at (a), (b) and (c)?

14 *i* 'An increase in the value of imports caused a further fall in the value of the pound in the foreign exchange market.'
ii 'An increase in the value of imports obliged the Bank of England to support the pound in the foreign exchange market.'
Which type of foreign exchange system is referred to (a) in quotation (i) and (b) in quotation (ii)?

15 If the pound depreciates from £1 = \$2.0 to £1 = \$1.80 what happens to,
a the foreign currency prices of UK exports?
b the foreign currency prices of UK imports?

16 What is the difference between *depreciation* and *devaluation*?

True or false?

17 a An improvement in the terms of trade means that the volume of exports has increased relative to the volume of imports.
b Even if one country is more efficient than another in all economic activities, both countries may, under certain circumstances, gain from increased specialization and trade.
c The balance of payments always balances.
d In most years since the Second World War, the UK has had a surplus on visible trade and a deficit on invisible trade.
e The total value of the UK's trade with the Commonwealth countries is greater than the value of her trade with Western Europe.
f The main aim of GATT is to help countries in balance of payments difficulties by providing them with financial assistance.
g When the pound depreciates, foreign goods become more competitive in the UK.

h The Exchange Equalization Account holds reserves of sterling and foreign currencies.

i An increase in UK imports will increase the supply of pounds in the foreign exchange market.

j In the EEC, the Council of Ministers is the main policy-making body.

Multiple-choice questions

18 Which of the following forms of protection will *not* lead to an increase in prices in the home market?

   1   tariffs

   2   quotas

   3   subsidies to home producers

   A   1, 2 and 3

   B   1 and 2 only

   C   2 and 3 only

   D   1 only

   E   3 only

19 Which of the following will improve the UK balance of invisible trade?

   1   more foreign concerts by British 'pop' groups

   2   more foreign tourists visiting Britain

   3   increased profitability of British-owned enterprises located abroad

   A   1, 2 and 3

   B   1 and 2 only

   C   2 and 3 only

   D   1 only

   E   3 only

20 When the pound depreciates against the dollar,

   1   the dollar prices of UK imports fall

   2   the dollar prices of UK exports fall

   3   the sterling prices of UK imports rise

   A   1, 2 and 3

   B   1 and 2 only

   C   2 and 3 only

   D   1 only

   E   3 only

Questions 21 and 22 refer to the following statements.

   A   the difference between the volumes of exports and imports

   B   the difference between the values of exports and imports

   C   the rate at which exports exchange for imports

   D   the rate at which one currency exchanges for another

21 Which of the above describes the terms of trade?

22 Which of the above describes the balance of trade?

23 Which of the following is a feature of the EEC but *not* of EFTA?
A the removal of tariffs on trade between members
B the removal of quotas on trade between members
C the establishment of rules and regulations governing trade between members
D the setting up of a central bank to control the money supply in all member countries
E the establishment of a common tariff on trade with non-member countries.

24 Which of the following is *not* a function of the IMF?
A to work for the full convertibility of national currencies
B to provide financial assistance to members with balance of payments problems
C to encourage stability of exchange rates
D to negotiate a general lowering of barriers to international trade
E to promote international monetary cooperation

Data-response questions

25 The question is based on the following statement.

A country which runs a deficit on *the current account of* its balance of payments is consuming more than it is producing.

Countries importing more goods and services than they export need to run a surplus on the capital account of the balance of payments. Some of this capital is supplied by private investment from overseas, but much of it now takes the form of public borrowing by governments.

Servicing this debt adds heavily to the outflows on the current account of the balance of payments.

a (First paragraph) Would the statement in this paragraph be true if the words in italics were omitted?
b (Third paragraph) Explain how the current account is affected by the existence of a large overseas debt.

26 In a country, imports account for about 20 per cent of total expenditure. The country has a serious balance of payments deficit, but is reluctant to tackle the problem by using measures such as tariffs and quotas. It decides instead to use fiscal and monetary measures to reduce total demand in the home market.

Total expenditure in the economy is £10 000 million per annum. The government aims to reduce imports by £500 million per annum.
a By how much will total expenditure have to be reduced?
b Why is this likely to be an unpopular policy?
c What are the likely reasons for the government being unwilling to use tariffs and quotas?

25 Public finance

Public finance deals with the ways in which the government sector obtains its income and the ways in which that income is spent. In this chapter we shall be concerned with those items of public expenditure which are financed by:

a   taxation levied by the central government;
b   rates levied by local authorities;
c   national insurance contributions;
d   borrowing by central and local government;
e   other sources of government income such as interest on loans, dividends on publicly-owned shares, licence fees and so on.

This means that the government sector is taken to mean the central government and the local authorities. As far as the nationalized industries are concerned, only their borrowings from the state will be treated as public finance. The income and expenditures on their trading activities and their borrowings from other sources will not be classified as public finance.

Public expenditure

The expenditure of money raised from the sources listed above is carried out by the central government and local authorities in the proportions shown in Fig. 25.1. In the UK, total public expenditure is a relatively large figure and amounts to about 45 per cent of the Gross Domestic Product.

Current and capital spending

Official statistics divide public spending into two main categories, current spending and capital spending. The current spending of government covers the costs of the day-to-day operation of the public services. It includes such items as the salaries of civil servants, teachers, doctors, the police, local government officers and so on. It also includes the costs of fuel, lighting, heating, transport, food and all the other goods and services 'consumed' by the public services.

Capital spending consists of direct investment in physical assets such as schools, hospitals, roads, local authority housing, and public baths, together with the loans and grants for investment purposes made to the nationalized industries and to privately-owned enterprises. In 1980–81, about 89 per cent of total public spending was devoted to current expenditure and about 11 per cent to capital transactions.

Fig. 25.1   Public expenditure, UK, 1981–82

Source: *Economic Progress Report*, HMSO, 1981.

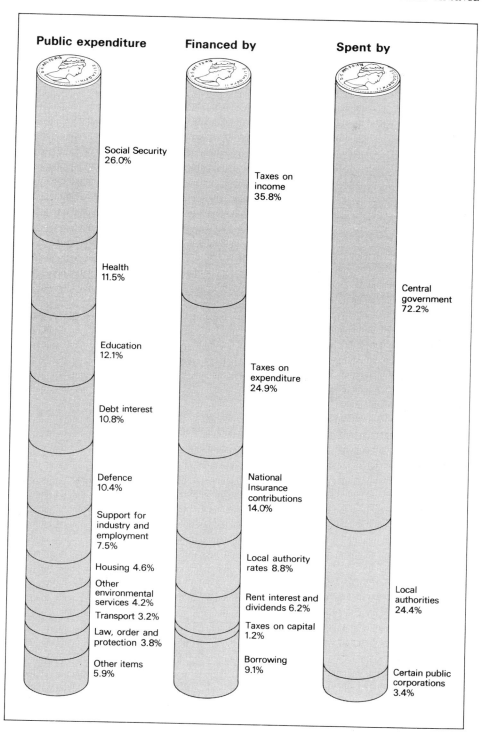

Public expenditure

Social Security
26.0%

Health
11.5%

Education
12.1%

Debt interest
10.8%

Defence
10.4%

Support for
industry and
employment
7.5%

Housing 4.6%

Other
environmental
services 4.2%

Transport 3.2%

Law, order and
protection 3.8%

Other items
5.9%

Financed by

Taxes on
income
35.8%

Taxes on
expenditure
24.9%

National
Insurance
contributions
14.0%

Local authority
rates 8.8%

Rent interest and
dividends 6.2%

Taxes on capital
1.2%

Borrowing
9.1%

Spent by

Central
government
72.2%

Local
authorities
24.4%

Certain public
corporations
3.4%

Real and transfer expenditures

A great deal of the spending which is classified as public expenditure is not spent directly by public authorities; it is passed on to households and firms in the form of money grants. In other words it consists of transfer payments. The more obvious examples of such transfer payments are the social security payments such as unemployment benefit, supplementary benefits, old age pensions and widows' pensions. Interest on the national debt, investment grants, subsidies and students' grants are other examples of transfer payments. In all these cases money which is classified as public expenditure is actually spent on goods and services by households and firms in the private sector.

Expenditure by central and local government on goods and services (i.e. the *real* or direct spending) accounts for about one-half of total public spending.

The sources of income

Fig. 25.1 shows how the public authorities obtain their income. It can be seen that the greater part of the revenue is obtained by taxation. In this connection it should be noted that rates are a form of taxation levied by the local authorities on property owners and national insurance contributions are also a form of taxation. When total expenditure exceeds the revenues from taxation and other sources (e.g. interest and dividends), the difference must be obtained by borrowing. Fig. 25.1 shows that borrowing financed about 9 per cent of public expenditure in 1981–82.

The purposes of public finance

The planned total of public expenditure for the period 1981–82 was about £105 000 million. This is a huge sum of money and both the manner in which the money is raised and the way in which it is spent will have important economic effects. It is possible to classify very broadly the main functions of public finance.

1 The provision of essential public services

This is the oldest function of government. There are certain services which are essential for the security of the state and for the social and economic development of the community which cannot be effectively supplied by private enterprise. These are services such as the upkeep of Parliament, defence, law and order and diplomatic representation abroad. Although everyone benefits from them, it is not possible to measure how much any individual 'consumes' of such services and they cannot, therefore, be sold on the open market; even if they could, it would not be possible to deny the benefits of these services to someone who refused to buy them. The only practical way of providing citizens with these kinds of facilities and benefits is for the state to supply them and to cover the costs from taxation.

There are other goods and services which people want and are willing and able to pay for, but which cannot be provided on a satisfactory basis by means of the price mechanism. The provision of roads, the lighting and paving of streets, the maintenance of public parks and open spaces in the cities are examples of amenities which, in virtually all societies, are provided by the state and financed by taxation. The price mechanism (a toll system) is often used to cover the costs of major bridges or motorways which have relatively few controlled entry and exit points.

2 Social policy

In the UK the largest single element of public expenditure comes under the heading of *social services*. Some of this expenditure takes the form of social security benefits which are designed to help those most in need and to ensure as far as possible that everyone enjoys an adequate minimum standard of living.

Other large items of public spending which form part of the government's social policy are the education and health services. These are provided on a universal basis and not according to people's ability to pay for them; they are supplied free of charge or for very low payments which bear no relation to the costs of the services. The state also allocates large sums of money to help people with the costs of housing.

By making these social services available to all citizens, the state is helping to bring about a much greater equality of opportunity in society. If good health services and a good education were privileges which were only available to the rich, there would be a situation where some people had much better opportunities in life than others. The public provision of social services does not remove the inequalities of opportunity but it does greatly reduce the extent of that inequality.

By providing social services on a universal basis the government is also helping to reduce the inequalities of income in the community. The spending on these services is financed by taxation and, if the tax system is arranged so that the better-off citizens pay proportionately more of their income in taxation, then by making such things as health services and education available to all, the state is, in effect, transferring income from the higher-income groups to the lower-income groups.

3 Industrial policy

The extent to which public money is used to influence the structure, location and performance of industry was described in some detail in Chapter 13. This is an important part of government economic policy.

4 Influencing the whole economy

The income and expenditure of the government sector are now so large that changes in the rates and structure of taxation and in the levels of public spending can have a great influence on the whole economy. Thus, the government may deliberately manipulate its spending plans and the levels of taxation so as to bring about changes in the nation's economic performance. More is said about this later in the chapter.

Taxation

1 Purposes and principles

A tax is similar to a fine in that it involves a compulsory transfer of money to the government. Taxes may be levied on income, wealth and expenditure. The following is a brief summary of the main purposes of taxation.

a   To raise the revenue required to pay for the various services provided by government.

b   To regulate the amount of total spending in the economy. For example, if the government thinks the level of total demand is excessive and likely to lead to inflation, it will increase taxation so as to reduce total spending.

c   To reduce inequalities in the distribution of wealth and income by placing heavier tax burdens on the better-off sections of the community.

d   To protect certain industries from foreign competition in the home market (tariffs are a form of taxation).

e   To discourage the consumption of a particular commodity.

The principles on which a tax system should be based are really a matter of political judgement, but there does seem to be a wide measure of agreement on certain basic principles. These are listed below.

Equity

The principle here is one of equality, that is, equality of sacrifice. Taxes should be related to the ability to pay. It seems generally agreed that the rich should pay more than the poor, but how much more? Most countries seem to have accepted the idea that some form of progressive tax is the most equitable way of taxing income and wealth. With this type of tax, the higher-income groups pay a greater percentage of their income in tax.

Certainty and simplicity

Taxpayers should know how much tax they have to pay, when it is to be paid and how it must be paid. A tax system should be sufficiently simple for the average taxpayer to understand the way in which his or her tax liability is assessed.

Convenience

Taxes should be collected in a convenient form and at a convenient time. The Pay As You Earn (PAYE) system of tax collection is probably the most convenient in general use. Under this system income tax is collected by deductions from weekly wages or monthly salaries. An earlier system where people received a demand for an annual income tax payment on their earnings in the previous year was a very inconvenient system.

Economy

Taxes should be inexpensive to collect and assess; the costs of collection should not be a relatively high percentage of the total tax yield.

2   Different types of taxes

Taxes may be very broadly classified into direct and indirect taxes. *Direct taxes* are those which are levied on income and wealth and they are described as direct because the burden of the tax falls on the person who is responsible for paying it. The most obvious example of a direct tax is income tax. *Indirect taxes* are levied on different forms of expenditure and in this case the person responsible for paying the tax may pass on some or all of the burden of the tax in the form of higher prices. For example, the value added tax (VAT) and the duties on petrol, tobacco and alcohol, are paid by manufacturers and traders, but the burdens are usually borne by the consumers in the form of higher prices. This is seen in Fig. 25.2 which shows how a simple value added tax works.

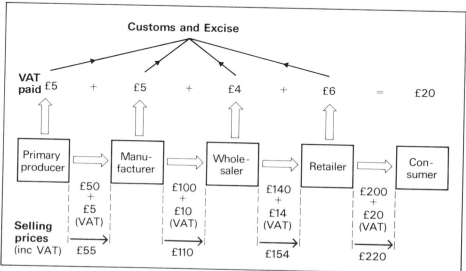

Fig. 25.2   A 10 per cent value added tax

In the example shown in Fig. 25.2 a tax of 10 per cent is levied on the value added at each stage of production. Each firm calculates the VAT on its selling price, deducts from this figure the amount of VAT it paid on its purchases and then pays the difference to the tax authorities. Thus, the manufacturer's net selling price is £100; the VAT on this figure is £10. This firm, however, has paid £5 VAT on its purchases so that the amount of tax it actually pays is £10 minus £5. Note that the whole of the VAT which has been charged on the production of this commodity is passed on to the consumer in the final price.

Proportional taxes

A tax is proportional when all taxpayers pay *the same percentage* of their income, wealth or expenditure in taxation. For example, if income tax were a proportional tax, the higher-income groups would pay more tax than the lower-income groups, but for both groups the percentage of income removed by taxation would be the same. Examples of proportional taxes in the UK are VAT and the tax on profits (Corporation Tax).

Progressive taxes

A tax is progressive when those with higher incomes or more wealth pay *proportionately more* in tax than those with lower incomes and less wealth. As income (or wealth) increases, the rates of taxation increase. For example, the first £5000 of taxable income may be taxed at 30 per cent, the next £1000 at 35 per cent, the next £1000 at 40 per cent and so on. As mentioned earlier, this form of tax is held to be the most equitable type for taxing income and wealth because it distributes the tax burden according to people's ability to pay. Some critics argue, however, that this form of taxation acts as a disincentive to effort, to enterprise, and to people's willingness to accept higher-paid jobs which carry more responsibility. Their argument is based on the fact that progressive taxes take larger and larger slices out of *increases* in income so that *net* increases in pay (i.e. after tax) are very much less than the gross increases in pay. In the UK, personal income tax is a progressive tax.

Regressive taxes

A regressive tax works in exactly the opposite way to a progressive tax. The percentage of income and wealth taken in taxation diminishes as income and wealth increase. Thus the first £5000 of income may be taxed at 30 per cent, the next £1000 at 25 per cent, the next £1000 at 20 per cent and so on. It is most unlikely that any present-day tax would be structured in this way because it would be generally regarded as most inequitable, but flat-rate taxes tend *to act* regressively. Flat-rate taxes are those where the amount of tax is a fixed sum per article or per person (e.g. 50p per litre, or 30p per kilogram). The amount of tax paid in such cases is not related to the purchaser's wealth or income so that the tax paid will represent a greater sacrifice for the lower paid than the higher paid.

Table 24 provides arithmetic examples of the ways in which these different forms of taxation would operate if they were levied on income.

Table 24

Taxable income	A proportional tax			A progressive tax		A regressive tax	
	Tax payable	Tax as % of income	Tax payable	Tax as % of income	Tax payable	Tax as % of income	
£ 4 000	£ 800	20	£ 800	20	£1 600	40	
£ 5 000	£1 000	20	£1 250	25	£1 750	35	
£ 6 000	£1 200	20	£1 800	30	£1 800	30	
£ 7 000	£1 400	20	£2 450	35	£1 750	25	
£ 8 000	£1 600	20	£3 200	40	£1 600	20	
£ 9 000	£1 800	20	£4 050	45	£1 350	15	
£10 000	£2 000	20	£5 000	50	£1 000	10	

The Budget

On Budget Day the Chancellor of the Exchequer presents a financial statement giving details of the government's income and expenditure for the financial year just ended, together with forecasts of the same items for the year ahead. Budget Day is usually between 1 April and 5 May because the powers to collect income and corporation taxes must be renewed by Parliament within one month of the end of the financial year (i.e. 5 April). There is only one main Budget each year, but economic difficulties have sometimes led to 'mini-Budgets' being presented in the autumn or winter.

Deficits and surpluses

The Budget is more than a simple balance sheet showing how the government intends to spend its income and how it intends to obtain that income. It is an extremely important instrument of economic policy. In the past, the Chancellor's job was seen to be one of 'balancing the Budget', that is, making sure that the government's income from taxation was sufficient to cover government expenditure. This is not the case today when governments will deliberately aim at a Budget deficit or surplus depending upon the economic circumstances.

If the economy is working well below capacity and unemployment is widespread, the government may well plan for a Budget deficit where its expenditure exceeds its income (mainly taxes). By this means it will put more purchasing power into the economy than it takes out, and total spending will increase. This increase in social spending will lead to an increased demand for goods and services and unemployment will fall. The difference between revenue and expenditure will be financed by borrowing.

If the economy is operating at full employment and total spending is exceeding the value of total output at current prices, the excess demand will tend to cause inflation. It is also likely to lead to a rise in imports and problems with the balance of payments. Under these circumstances, the Chancellor will aim at a Budget surplus and will plan to remove more money from the economy in the form of taxation than is returned to it in the form of public spending. Total demand, therefore, will fall. A fall in total demand will reduce the upward pressure on prices and it will also reduce the demand for imports.

The Consolidated Fund and the National Loans Fund

The income and expenditure of the central government are handled through a number of funds, but the Budget is concerned with two major funds, both of which are managed by the Bank of England.

The Consolidated Fund handles the revenue from taxation and the other current revenue shown in Table 25. Expenditure from this fund comes under two headings. About 90 per cent of the expenditure is devoted to what are known as *Supply Services*. Estimates of these expenditures have to be placed before Parliament and voted upon annually. In addition to the Supply Services there are expenditures on Standing Services. These expenditures do not require an annual parliamentary vote and consist of such items as a contribution towards the cost of the interest of the national debt, contributions to the EEC Budget, payments to the Royal Family and the salaries of judges.

The National Loans Fund handles the government's borrowing and lending transactions. The revenues of this fund consist of interest on government loans and the repayment of such loans, the contribution towards interest on the national debt from the Consolidated Fund, and any profits from an increase in the note issue. The outgoings from the National Loans Fund include the payments of interest on the national debt, and the loans to public corporations, local authorities and private industry. This fund also deals with any surplus or deficit on the Consolidated Fund. If there is a deficit on the Consolidated Fund it will be financed by a loan from the National Loans Fund; if there is a surplus, it will be transferred to the National Loans Fund and help to finance that fund's expenditures. A deficit on the National Loans Fund itself represents an overall Budget deficit and must be financed by borrowing (see Table 25). A surplus may be used to repay part of the national debt.

The Budget Statement (Table 25)

1 The Inland Revenue Department

This department collects taxes levied on income and capital. These are the taxes previously described as direct taxes.

Source: *Financial Statement and Budget Report 1982–83*, HMSO.

[1] These figures include only the expenditures which are within the responsibilities of the Secretaries of State for Scotland, Wales and Northern Ireland.

Table 25   The UK Budget – estimates 1982–83 (£ million)

The Consolidated Fund

Revenue		Expenditure	
Inland Revenue		*Supply Services*	
Income tax	30 775	Defence	13 945
Corporation tax	4 850	Overseas services	1 605
Capital gains tax	600	Support for industry	6 660
Petroleum revenue tax	4 330	Roads and transport	2 019
Capital transfer tax	465	Housing	2 318
Stamp duties	810	Law, order, protection	2 475
Other taxes	50	Education, science, arts	2 850
Total inland revenue	41 880	Health and personal social	
Customs and Excise		services	10 260
VAT	14 750	Social security	11 768
Oil	5 100	Rate Support Grant	16 087
Tobacco	3 525	Scotland[1]	2 988
Spirits, wine, beer	3 275	Wales[1]	1 168
Betting and gaming	550	Northern Ireland[1]	1 103
Car tax	600	Other services	6 128
Other excise duties	20	Total Supply Services	81 374
Customs duties and levies	1 330	*Standing Services*	
Total customs and excise	29 150	Payment towards interest	
Vehicle excise duties	1 854	on national debt	5 175
National insurance surcharge	3 443	Payments to EEC	2 820
Total taxation	76 327	Other standing services	1 522
Broadcast receiving licences	754	Total Standing Services	9 517
Interest and dividends	321		
Other revenue	5 493		
Total revenue	82 895	*Total expenditure*	90 891

(Deficit on Consolidated Fund = 7 996)

The National Loans Fund

Receipts		Payments	
Consolidated Fund		National Debt:	
contribution to interest		interest	11 467
on national debt	5 175	management	133
Interest on loans and profit		Consolidated Fund deficit	7 996
on the note issue	6 425	Loans:	
Borrowing by National Loans		nationalized industry	721
Fund	9 632	other public corporations	1 242
		local and harbour	
		authorities	− 300
		others	− 27
Total receipts	21 232	*Total payments*	21 232

1 Income tax

This tax is easily the largest single source of government income. It is a progressive tax ranging (in 1982) from 30 per cent on the lowest bands of taxable income to 60 per cent on the highest. The tax is not levied on gross income. There are various allowances such as a married person's allowance and allowances for such expenses as interest payments on mortgages. These allowances are not taxable. Thus,

Gross income − allowances = taxable income

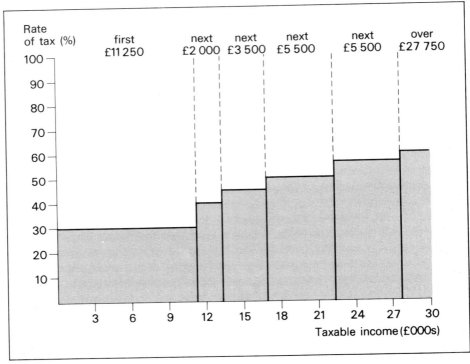

Fig. 25.3   UK income tax, 1981–82

2 Corporation tax

This is a tax which is levied on the gross profits of companies. The current rate (1982) is 52 per cent, but small companies are subject to a reduced rate of tax.

3 Capital gains tax

A capital gain or loss arises when someone disposes of property. If property is sold for a higher price than that at which it was bought, the difference is described as a capital gain and this gain is taxable at a rate of 30 per cent (in 1982). Capital losses can be offset against capital gains when liability for tax is being assessed. The tax applies on the disposal of all types of property, land, buildings, works of art, stocks and shares and so on. There are important exemptions for such things as one's own home, private motor cars, insurance policies, winnings from gambling and gains on government securities.

4 Capital transfer tax

This tax is more commonly known as the *gift tax*. It is a tax levied whenever wealth is transferred from one person to another as a gift. It applies whether the transfer occurs during the donor's lifetime or on his or her death. It is a steeply progressive tax rising to a maximum of 75 per cent (in 1982). Important exemptions from the tax include transfers between a husband and wife and transfers of less than £3000 in any one year.

5 Petroleum revenue tax

This tax is levied on profits from extracting oil and gas under licence in Britain and from its continental shelf. In effect this means the North Sea oilfields.

6 Stamp duties

There are certain legal documents, such as those which transfer the ownership of property, which must bear stamps. The value of the stamps normally varies according to the value of the property being transferred.

2 The Customs and Excise Department

This department collects the taxes on expenditure (i.e. indirect taxes).

1 Value added tax (VAT)

VAT is levied on a very wide range of goods and services. The manner in which it operates is illustrated in Fig. 25.2. It is calculated as a percentage of the value added at each stage of production and the current rate (1982) is 15 per cent. Certain classes of goods and services are given exceptional treatment, being either (i) exempt (ii) zero rated.

When goods and services are exempt, traders do not have to charge VAT on their sales, but they cannot claim back any VAT which has been charged at previous stages of production. Exemption applies to land (including rents), all forms of insurance, letter and parcel post, betting and gaming, finance, education and health services.

Zero rating means complete relief from VAT. In this case, when goods supplied are zero rated, they are not subject to VAT and, additionally, any VAT already paid on inputs used in making the goods can be reclaimed. Exports, food, young children's clothing and footwear, books, newspapers, fuel, construction, passenger transport, drugs and medicine on prescription are some of the important items which are zero rated.

2 Excise duties

These are taxes levied on certain home-produced and imported goods and services. The main subjects of this form of taxation are tobacco, hydrocarbon oils, and alcoholic drink. Excise duties on these three commodities are very important sources of government revenue. In addition, most forms of gambling are liable to taxation.

3   Car tax
This is a special tax on new motor cars and caravans which applies in addition to VAT.

4   Customs duties
These duties are generally described as protective duties since their main purpose is to protect home industry rather than to raise revenue. The income from customs duties and import levies is payable to the EEC.

5   Other sources of revenue

Vehicle excise duties
These include the licence fees payable by all motor vehicle operators and the driving licence fees.

National insurance surcharge
This surcharge or tax is levied on the national insurance contributions paid by employers. It goes into the Exchequer Account and not into the National Insurance Fund (see page 303).

Licences
Most of the income under this heading is derived from broadcast receiving licences, although there is a small income from gun, game and dog licences included under 'other revenue'.

3   Consolidated Fund expenditure

The expenditure items require little further explanation. A point to note is the fact that a large proportion of government expenditure on such services as education, police, housing and roads is contained in the item listed as the Rate Support Grant. This is the government grant to local authorities which covers a part of the costs of the many services they provide. The figure given for Social Security in the Budget Statement does not represent total public spending on this item because a large part of the spending on social security benefits comes from the National Insurance Fund which is not part of the Budget account.

4   The National Loans Fund

The payments under this heading are self-explanatory. The deficit from the Consolidated Fund is transferred to the National Loans Fund which has the responsibility for providing funds to cover this deficit. Since the National Loans Fund lends to both the public and private sectors it has a considerable income in the form of interest on its loans. Table 25 shows that government income was expected to fall well short of its expenditure in 1982–83 and the National Loans Fund would have to borrow a substantial sum to cover the deficit.

5 National insurance contributions

A major source of government income which does not appear in the Budget Statement is the revenue from national insurance contributions payable by employers, employees and the self-employed. This revenue is paid into the National Insurance Fund and is earmarked for payments of various national insurance benefits such as unemployment pay and retirement pensions. National insurance contributions do not cover all the social security benefits and they are supplemented by funds from general taxation to the extent shown in the Budget Statement. For the year 1981–82 the estimated income from national insurance contributions was £17 000 million.

The national debt

The account for the National Loans Fund in Table 25 shows that estimated government outlays for 1982–83 exceed revenue by £9 600 million. This overall deficit must be financed by borrowing. The national debt is the cumulative total of such borrowings. A large part of the debt is the result of wars, the financial burdens of which were too great to be financed wholly out of taxation. In 1981 the UK national debt stood at £113 300 million. The government borrows in a variety of ways, but most of the money borrowed is obtained from the sale of various types of government IOUs or 'promises to pay' which are described as government securities or gilt-edged securities. Some of these securities, such as National Savings Certificates and Premium Bonds, are widely purchased by the general public. One part of the national debt, described as the 'floating debt', consists of short-term borrowings financed by the sale of Treasury bills which have a life of ninety-one days. The greater part of the debt, however, consists of long-term securities which are repayable after periods ranging from one or two years up to twenty-five years and carry a fixed rate of interest. Most of these securities are marketable in the same way as shares in a public company. The dealings in government securities account for a large part of the total activity on the Stock Exchange.

The National Loans Fund account in Table 25 shows that the annual interest payment on the national debt is now one of the largest items of government expenditure. The fact that the national debt is gradually increasing does not necessarily mean that the debt is an increasing burden. It all depends on what is happening to the nation's ability to meet the interest charges. In other words, it depends upon the rate at which the national income is growing. Just as a person with a rising income can afford a larger mortgage so a country with a rising national income is able to support a larger national debt. If the national income is rising faster than the national debt, then, other things being equal, the burden of the debt is decreasing.

The greater part of the national debt, that is, the money which the government has borrowed from UK residents, is owed by the people collectively (i.e. the state) to the people individually. We are, in fact, borrowing from ourselves. The interest payments, therefore, are transfer payments from one group within the community (i.e. taxpayers) to another group (i.e. the holders of securities).

There is one part of the debt which does represent a real burden on the community and that is the part held by residents of other countries. The interest payments and the repayments of capital to overseas holders of the debt are made in foreign currencies. These currencies must be obtained by exporting goods and services. In order to pay our debts to foreigners we must give up part of our real income.

Fiscal policy

A reference was made earlier in the chapter to the deliberate manipulation of government income and expenditure as a means of controlling the economy. When a government carries out changes in expenditure and in taxation as a means of achieving economic and social objectives, it is said to be using fiscal policy (*fiscus* was the name for the public treasury in Ancient Rome). Set out below is a brief account of the instruments of fiscal policy, the way they work (or are expected to work) and the objectives of the various measures.

1 Changes in the taxation of income

An increase in these taxes will have a direct effect on the amount of spending in the economy. An increase in direct taxes will reduce disposable income (i.e. people's ability to spend) and total demand will be reduced. The extent of the fall in total spending, however, depends upon the level of real incomes. In an affluent society, an increase in income tax may lead to a fall in saving as well as a fall in spending. People may be unwilling to lower their standard of living and will try to maintain their expenditure by reducing the amount they save. Nevertheless, an increase in income tax will lead to some fall in total demand.

A reduction in the rates of income tax will increase disposable income, but some of this increased income will be saved and it is unlikely that spending will increase by the full extent of the increase in disposable incomes.

An increase in the tax on profits may reduce the incentive to invest, especially in the more risky enterprises, while a cut may encourage investment.

One effect of increasing the rate of income tax may well be to encourage claims for higher wages. Workers may take this action as a means of resisting any fall in their disposable incomes.

2 Changes in the taxation of expenditure

Changes in indirect taxes may also be used as a means of influencing the level of total demand in an economy. A general increase in expenditure taxes will raise the prices of goods and services. If disposable incomes remain unchanged, the increase in prices will reduce the quantities demanded of those commodities which are subject to taxation. Similarly, a reduction in indirect taxation will lead to lower prices and an increase in the quantities demanded. One serious problem associated with an increase in indirect taxes is the fact that the increased prices will affect the Index of Retail Prices and, under present conditions, this is almost certain to lead to claims for compensating increases in wages and salaries.

3 Taxes on wealth and capital

The main purpose of these taxes is to reduce the inequalities in the distribution of wealth. A major problem with all forms of wealth tax is that of estimating the value of the goods to be taxed. Wealth is held in a wide variety of forms – land, buildings, works of art, jewellery, stocks and shares and so on. There will be no problem in assessing the value of wealth held in the form of money balances or in shares which are quoted on the Stock Exchange, but some real problems can arise in valuing other forms of wealth. A work of art or a piece of jewellery may not have been sold for many years and shares in private companies will have no market valuation since they are not traded in the open market.

Taxes on wealth and capital fall on the results of *past* efforts and are likely, it is argued, to be much less discouraging to effort and enterprise than taxes on income, which fall on *present* efforts. They might, however, reduce such incentives where people's motive for working (especially in their later years) is to accumulate wealth which they wish to pass on to their sons and daughters. On the other hand, many people believe that taxes on wealth[1] and capital will make the owners of property more anxious to move their wealth out of 'non-productive' forms such as antiques, pictures, rare stamps etc., and into more productive forms (industry and commerce). Owners of wealth will only be able to protect the value of their property if it is held in the form of income-earning assets. For example, a person with net wealth valued at £100 000 held in the form of non-income earning assets, would have to pay £10 000 per annum in

[1] The UK taxes wealth when its ownership is transferred. It does not have an annual wealth tax although the Labour government (1974–79) announced its intention to introduce such a tax.

tax if the rate of wealth tax were 10 per cent. An annual wealth tax would gradually reduce this person's wealth and its value could only be maintained if it were held in the form of assets earning an income of at least 10 per cent per annum.

Taxes on wealth and capital may encourage people to spend rather than save and holders of wealth may prefer to 'consume' their wealth rather than have it taken from them in taxation.

4 Changes in government spending

If the rates of taxation remain unchanged, an increase in public spending will increase total demand in the economy, but the effects will depend very much on the form which the increased spending takes. If the government increases its expenditure by improving social security benefits such as pensions and supplementary benefits, total demand will increase immediately, and by almost the full amount of the increase in benefits, because the recipients will generally belong to the lower-income groups and the extra income will be devoted almost entirely to consumption spending. If the government decides to increase its spending on capital projects such as new roads, hospitals, schools etc., the effect on total demand will not be felt for some considerable time because these programmes take a long time to get under way; there is a fairly long period of time required for planning, surveying, arranging contracts and so on.

Increased public spending on services such as education, health, care of the aged and the handicapped, refuse collection etc., will create many new jobs because these services are labour-intensive. Government spending in the form of investment grants will tend to encourage expansion in capital-intensive industries and hence create relatively few jobs in the short run.

If an increase in government spending is not financed by an increase in taxation, the government must borrow. An increase in government borrowing means an increase in the demand for loans and this could lead to an increase in the rate of interest. Other borrowers, such as industry and home-buyers, will find themselves paying higher rates of interest.

The greatest problems associated with changes in public spending as an instrument of fiscal policy arise when the government wishes to cut public expenditure. It may believe that such a step is necessary when there are inflationary pressures in the economy or when it wishes to reduce government borrowing and is reluctant to increase taxation. A reduction in public spending will have a direct effect on the total demand for goods and services, but such a policy is difficult to carry out. The Conservative government elected in 1979 embarked on such a policy but encountered strong political opposition in its attempts to cut public spending. There are various ways in which a government might try to implement such a policy.

Reduced spending on services such as health and education will not only reduce total income, it will tend to cause a significant increase in unemployment because, as pointed out earlier, these services are labour-intensive. In any case, cuts in these services will be strongly resisted. In theory, it is possible to reduce public expenditure on social security benefits, but public opinion would strongly oppose a policy which placed major burdens on the poorer members of society.

Defence spending may also be cut but problems might arise because of the government's commitments to international agreements (e.g. NATO).

A very likely target for reductions in public spending are the capital programmes such as the building of roads, local authority housing, schools and hospitals, the modernization of the rail network and the construction of new airports. The immediate effects of these reductions in public spending would be a fall in aggregate demand and increased unemployment in the construction industries. The longer-term effects would be that the national stock of social and industrial capital would be less than it would have been had the cuts not taken place.

Local government finance

Expenditure

Local authorities are responsible for about one-quarter of total public expenditure. The main categories are set out in Table 26. By far the largest item of current spending is education. Other major services provided by the local authorities include the police and fire services and a variety of environmental services such as sewage, refuse disposal, parks, public baths and so on. Personal social services include provision for the elderly, the handicapped, the mentally ill and children in care. Other items include subsidies on housing and local transport, grants to students and interest on local authority debt.

The largest single item of capital spending is housing and this reflects the fact that the provision of houses to rent is a major responsibility of local government.

Income

1   Grants from the central government
Some of these grants are specific, that is, they are allocated for a particular purpose such as the cost of the police service. The bulk of the grant aid, however, is in the form of a general grant known as the Rate Support Grant which the authority can spend as it wishes.

2   Rates
Rates are local taxes levied on the occupiers of property. There are two determinants of the amount paid in rates, the rateable value and the rate poundage.

Table 26 Revenue and expenditure of local authorities, UK, 1980 (£ million)

Payments   **Receipts**

Current account

Education, libraries, arts	9 074	Current grants from central government	13 275
Local environmental services	1 779	Rates	8 300
Law, order, protection	2 592	Trading surpluses	131
Personal social services	2 007	Rents	3 059
Roads and lighting	1 077	Interest	683
School meals, milk	480	Other receipts	1 100
Other programmes	1 461		
Administration	513		
Total consumption	18 983		
Subsidies (housing, transport)	984		
Grants:			
Education	861		
Other	232		
Interest on debt	4 229		
Total current spending	25 289		
Current surplus	1 259		
	26 548		26 548

Capital account

Education, libraries, arts	593	Current surplus	1 259
Local environmental services	626	Capital grants from central government	337
Law, order, protection	95	Other receipts	41
Personal social services	103	Borrowings from central government and other sources	2 526
Roads and lighting	427		
Housing	1 532		
Trading services	219		
Other items	226		
Capital grants and lending	342		
	4 163		4 163

Source: *National Income and Expenditure*, HMSO, 1981.

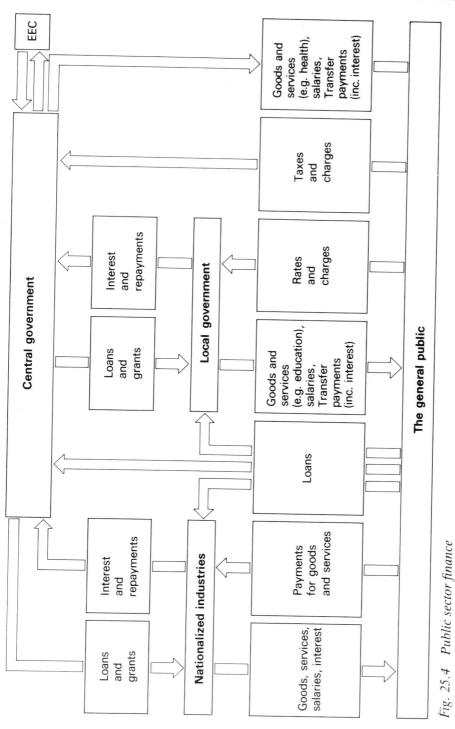

Fig. 25.4 Public sector finance

The rateable value of a property is assessed by valuers from the Inland Revenue Department. It is based on their estimate of the annual rent which the property would command were it to be let on the open market. The rate poundage is, in effect, the rate of taxation; it is the amount per pound of rateable value which the occupier is obliged to pay. Thus, if the total rateable value of all property in an area is £100 million and the authority wishes to raise £80 million in revenue from the rates, it will levy a rate of 80 pence in the pound. The occupier of a house with a rateable value of £300 will be called upon to pay 300 × 80p = £240 in rates for that year.

3   Other income
Additional income is obtained from the rents of council houses, the various fees charged for amenities such as public baths, car parks and recreational facilities, any surpluses arising from trading activities such as local transport, and interest on loans.

4   Borrowing
The borrowings of local authorities must be authorized by Parliament, but loans may be obtained from a variety of sources. Local authorities borrow from the government through the Public Works Loan Board or in the open market by the issue of local authority bonds.

Fig. 25.4 summarizes the financial relationships between the general public and the major institutions in the public sector.

Test paper 10

Short-answer questions

1 Which of the following are transfer payments?
(a) the salaries of policemen, (b) old age pensions, (c) students' grants, (d) insurance premiums on government property.

2 Which *two* of the following are the major sources of the public sector's revenue?
(a) taxes on income, (b) taxes on expenditure, (c) national insurance contributions, (d) local rates.

3 Which of the following is the largest item of public expenditure?
(a) education, (b) health, (c) social security.

4 How does the government borrow the money it requires in order to cover a Budget deficit?

5 How does the UK government apply the principle of equity in its taxation of income?

6 Why are some taxes described as *indirect* taxes?

7

Taxable income (£s)	(i) Tax payable (£s)	(ii) Tax payable (£s)
3000	300	150
4000	600	200
5000	1000	250
6000	1500	300
7000	2100	350

What type of income tax is being levied (a) in column (i), (b) in column (ii)?

8 Why are the flat-rate taxes on tobacco and alcoholic beverages described as regressive?

Questions 9 and 10 are based on the following tax table.

Taxable income	Rate of tax
first £2000	nil
next £1000	10%
next £2000	15%
next £3000	20%

A woman's gross annual income is £5500. Her various allowances against tax amount to £2500.

9 How much tax will she pay on her annual income?

10 If she received a pay increase of £1000 per annum, by how much would her *net* income increase?

11 More than four-fifths of the UK government's revenue from taxation is derived from three direct taxes and four indirect taxes. Name these taxes.

12 Why is a large part of the UK national debt described as a *deadweight debt*?

13 'Since a regressive income tax takes a smaller proportion of higher incomes, it provides a great incentive for people to work harder and more efficiently.' Why, then, do governments not use such a tax?

14 'The prudent household will plan its expenditures according to its income. In preparing his Budget, the Chancellor does exactly the opposite.' Explain.

15 What form of increased government expenditure is likely to have the largest and most immediate impact on consumer spending?

16 What proportion (approximately) of the current spending of local authorities is financed by grants from the central government?

True or false?

17 **a** In the UK, total public spending on goods and services is equal to about 45 per cent of the national income.

b A person paying taxes automatically acquires rights to certain goods and services.

c A proportional income tax leaves the distribution of income unchanged.

d In the UK, the main taxes on income are personal income tax and corporation tax.

e Value added tax is passed on at each stage of production and the whole of the tax *is collected* at the final stage.

f A Budget deficit will tend to increase the level of total demand.

g The excise duties which raise the largest amounts of revenue are levied on goods with elastic demands.

h A large national debt which is held by a small proportion of the population will tend to increase the inequality in the distribution of income.

Multiple-choice questions

18 Which of the following is *not* a source of central government revenue?
   A interest on loans
   B licence fees
   C telephone rentals
   D national insurance contributions
   E dividends on shares

19 Which of the following is a transfer payment?

  A teachers' salaries
  B purchases of drugs for the national health service
  C rental payments on schools' television sets
  D salaries of tax inspectors
  E investment grants

20 When a tax is levied on a commodity, it will have least effect on the market price when the elasticity of demand for the commodity is

  A 0
  B ½
  C 1
  D 2
  E ∞

21 The question relates to the following economic activities.

  1 the production of electricity
  2 house building
  3 the production of motor cars

  Which of the above is/are subject to VAT?

  A 1, 2 and 3
  B 1 and 2 only
  C 2 and 3 only
  D 1 only
  E 3 only

22 Which of the following is/are true of a progressive tax?

  1 it takes more from the higher-income groups than from the lower-income groups
  2 as income increases so does the average rate of tax
  3 the proportion of income taken in tax increases as income increases

  A 1, 2 and 3
  B 1 and 2 only
  C 2 and 3 only
  D 1 only
  E 3 only

23 In the UK, a Budget deficit is likely to lead to

  1 net borrowing by the National Loans Fund
  2 a fall in total spending
  3 an increase in unemployment

  Which of the above is/are correct?

  A 1, 2 and 3
  B 1 and 2 only
  C 2 and 3 only
  D 1 only
  E 3 only

Data-response question

24 The following passage is adapted from an article on the UK Budget for
1980.

> In the short term the cut in public spending is likely to reduce economic
> activity slightly. This is probably also true of the net effect of the actions
> taken to (i) lower direct taxes and (ii) raise indirect taxes. These are
> very necessary steps, however, if the government is to be successful in
> reducing the extent to which the public sector borrows money. At the
> same time, it is hoped that the measures will improve incentives.
>
> The average increase in the duties on petrol, alcoholic drinks and
> tobacco does not go beyond what is necessary to prevent inflation from
> reducing the real value of the revenue from these duties. It is estimated
> that the immediate impact of these measures will be to increase the In-
> dex of Retail Prices by about 1.1 per cent.

a   Why should the net effect of reducing direct and raising indirect taxes
be a reduction in economic activity?
b   How might the tax changes mentioned improve incentives?
c   What is meant by 'preventing inflation from reducing the real value of
the revenue from these duties'?
d   Explain the effects on the Index of Retail Prices of the tax changes
mentioned in the passage.

26 The economy as a whole

The circular flow of income

The chapters on Money, Banking, and Public Finance explained how the government is able to exert a great deal of influence on economic activities by means of its control over the money supply and by its use of fiscal policy. The way in which government activities affect the economy, however, cannot be fully understood without some knowledge of the way in which different sectors of the economy are linked together. The economic system is obviously a very complex mechanism and at this level we can only examine relationships in a very simplified model of the economy. For this purpose it is necessary to re-introduce the flow diagram used in Chapter 17 to explain the nature of the national income.

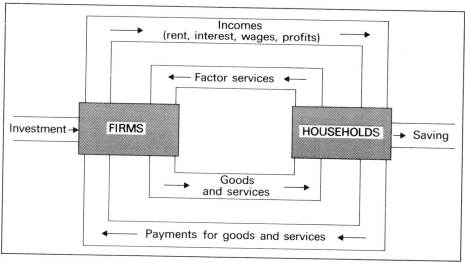

Fig. 26.1

Fig. 26.1 represents a very simple economy which has only two sectors, households and firms. All production is undertaken by firms and the consumer goods and services produced by these firms are purchased by households. These activities give rise to two flows:

a a flow of goods and services from firms to households;
b a flow of payments from households to firms.

In order to produce these goods and services, firms purchase the services of factors of production from households. Payments for the services of labour, land, and capital ultimately go to members of households in the form of wages, rent, interest and profits (we are assuming that firms pay out all profits in the form of dividends). There are, therefore, two further flows:

c a flow of factor services from households to firms;

d a flow of incomes from firms to households.

All these flows are illustrated in Fig. 26.1.

Savings and investment

The flow diagram (Fig. 26.1) does not represent a perfectly 'watertight' system. All the income paid out by firms does not flow back to them in the form of household spending. Some of the income received by households is saved. This saving is described as a *leakage* or *withdrawal* from the circular flow of income, because the decision to save is a decision 'not to spend'. It means that firms are receiving back from households less than they are paying out in the form of income. Now we know that the total value of the incomes (including profits) paid out by firms for factor services is equal to the value of the national output. Therefore, if households save some of their income, demand from households will be less than the value of total output. If this were the whole story, firms would be building up stocks of unsold goods and they would have to cut back on production.

In fact, it is not the whole story because, in addition to the demands from households for consumer goods and services, firms also receive demands for capital goods. The purchase of new capital is described as investment and we shall assume that all investment is carried out by firms. In our simple economy, therefore, the total demand for the national output is made up of two elements, a demand from households for consumer goods and services (C) and a demand from firms for capital goods (I). Thus, Total demand = C + I.

Since investment is a demand for the output of firms which does not arise from the spending of households, it is described as an *injection* into the circular flow of income. An examination of Fig. 26.1 makes it clear that the economy will only be in equilibrium when the rate of leakage (i.e. saving) is equal to the rate of injection (i.e. investment). In other words, there will be no tendency for output and income to change when saving is equal to investment. If the rate at which households plan to save exceeds the rate at which firms plan to invest, leakages will exceed injections and the flow of income in the system will tend to fall. Similarly, if investment exceeds savings, the rate of injection will be greater than the rate of leakage and the flow of income will rise. How and why the level of income changes when investment and saving are not equal may be explained by making use of two arithmetic examples.

Example 1

Assume:

a firms in the economy are producing output at the rate of £100 million per month and hence paying out incomes to factors of production equal to £100 million per month,

316

b   the demand for investment goods (capital) is constant at the rate of £15 million per month,

c   households always save ⅕ of their income.

In this economy, Saving = ⅕ of income = ⅕ of £100m. = £20m. per month

Investment = £15m. per month

Hence,   *Saving > Investment*

Total demand = C (£80m.) + I (£15m.) = £95m. per month

Total supply = Total output = £100m. per month

Hence,   *Total supply > Total demand*

It can be seen that when the rate of saving is greater than the rate of investment, total supply is greater than total demand. Firms will be accumulating unsold stocks at the rate of £5 million per month. They will not go on building up stocks like this and will cut back production. As output falls so will employment and income. *When leakages are greater than injections, output, income and employment will fall.*

Example 2

Assume:

a   firms in an economy are paying out £200 million per month for factor services. This figure includes all profits which are paid out as dividends to households,

b   investment demand is constant at £25 million per month,

c   households always save 1/10 of their income.

In this economy, Saving = 1/10 of income = 1/10 of £200m. = £20m. per month

Investment = £25m. per month

Hence,   *Investment > Saving*

Total demand = C (£180m.) + I(£25m.) = £205m. per month

Total supply = Total output = £200m. per month

Hence,   *Total demand > Total supply*

When the rate of investment is greater than the rate of saving, total demand is greater than total supply. Firms will be running down their stocks in order to satisfy the excess demand. This can only be a short-run measure and firms will tend to increase output. This will cause employment and income to rise. *When injections are greater than leakages, income, output and employment will rise.*

The economy will only be in equilibrium when the total demand for goods and services is equal to the total supply, that is, when leakages (or withdrawals) are equal to injections.

A more realistic economy

The model of an economy described above is a very simple one. It takes account of only two sectors, households and firms. A more realistic model must take account of two other sectors, government and foreign trade. Government activity introduces another leakage in the form of taxation. Taxes withdraw income from the circular flow and reduce the disposable income of households and firms. Government spending on goods and services, on the other hand, represents an injection into the circular flow of income. It is an element of total demand additional to that created by the spending of households and firms.

When a country takes part in international trade, the circular flow of income is subject to a further leakage in the form of imports. Spending on goods and services supplied by foreign firms creates income abroad and not at home and these expenditures represent a withdrawal from the circular flow of income. Exports, on the other hand, create income at home since the demand for home-produced goods and services by overseas residents is additional to that created by the spending of domestic firms, households and government.

The principles outlined earlier are still applicable to this more complex economy. It will be in equilibrium when total demand is equal to total supply, that is, when *total* leakages are equal to *total* injections. If leakages exceed injections, employment and income will fall; if injections exceed leakages, employment and income will rise. The purpose of this elementary treatment of the circular flow of income is to provide some understanding of the economic policies of government. The objectives of government economic policy, the various economic measures used by government to achieve these objectives, and the problems of implementing economic policy, make up the subject matter of the rest of this chapter and of the remaining chapters of this textbook.

Economic policies

Although matters of economic policy arouse great controversy and argument, there is a wide measure of agreement on the aims of economic policy. The disputes are mainly about *how* these aims should be achieved and about which of these aims should be given the highest priority. The principal objectives of government economic policy are:

a   a full and stable level of employment;
b   stable prices;
c   a satisfactory balance of payments position;
d   an acceptable rate of economic growth;
e   a more equitable distribution of income and wealth.

Some of these objectives are discussed in the following chapters, but one of the greatest problems facing governments is the fact that several of these objectives seem to be incompatible. In other words, while it would be relatively easy to achieve any one objective, it seems extraordinarily difficult to achieve several of them at the same time. For example, the government has the power, through the Budget, to inject enough spending into the economy to raise total demand for goods and services to a level which will reduce unemployment to acceptable levels. But this level of demand might be so high as to cause excessive spending on imports and create serious balance of payments problems.

As a further example, the government might find itself having to deal with serious inflationary pressures and be forced to take steps to reduce total demand. It might well succeed in reducing the rate of inflation, but the reduction in total demand might lead to a substantial rise in unemployment.

Instruments of economic policy

The government has a variety of instruments at its disposal for carrying out its economic policies.

1 Monetary measures

The government can influence the level of spending on consumption and investment by controlling the supply of money or the rate of interest. The techniques of monetary policy were explained in Chapter 21.

2 Fiscal measures

The powers to vary the forms and rates of taxation and to change the level and direction of government spending are important instruments of government economic policy. The techniques of fiscal policy were explained in Chapter 25.

3 Public enterprise

The fact that a large sector of the British economy is under public ownership increases the ability of the government to control the economy. It can, for example, stimulate the economy during a depression by increasing investment in the nationalized industries. If excess demand is causing inflation, the government might postpone investment projects in the public sector.

4 Direct controls

The government has powers to use direct controls. Parliament can enact legislation which gives the government statutory powers to control wages, prices, dividends and rents. Other direct controls may take the form of the rationing of consumer goods, restrictions on hire-purchase and the control of building.

5 Persuasion

The success of any national economic policy depends very largely on the extent of the voluntary cooperation of households and firms. The government, therefore, has the tasks of (a) ensuring that the citizens understand the policies it is trying to carry out and (b) getting the active cooperation of firms, trade unions and individuals in making a success of its policies. Large-scale publicity campaigns have become an essential feature of government economic policy. These will include major speeches by ministers; regular meetings between industrialists, trade union leaders and the government; advertising campaigns, exhibitions, conferences and so on.

27 Employment

In recent times the most important responsibilities of government have been to find ways of maintaining a high and stable level of employment and of overcoming the problem of inflation.

Unemployment represents a waste of valuable resources. The output which is not produced while resources are unemployed cannot be made good in the future; there is a permanent loss of real income. The social effects are also a serious matter because people who are out of work suffer a fall in their standard of living and there is also a damaging effect on the morale of workers who are made to feel rejected and unwanted. Policies to deal with unemployment must take account of the fact that there are several types of unemployment.

1 Structural unemployment

This type of unemployment was touched upon when the subject of regional unemployment was discussed in Chapter 12. It develops when a major industry is in permanent decline and is particularly serious when that industry happens to be concentrated in a certain region. The loss of demand for the products of such industries may be due to a variety of reasons. It may be caused by technical progress which produces a new and superior substitute. For example, the development of the oil industry over the past fifty to sixty years led to a serious contraction in the demand for coal. Technical progress also brings about changes in the techniques of production and where these take the form of a large-scale substitution of capital for labour, they will give rise to unemployment even when the output of the industry is not falling. The mechanization of the coal industry and the concentration of the steel industry into a few large capital-intensive plants are examples of technical change reducing the demands for labour in major industries. A further cause of structural unemployment can be the loss of export markets when major industries lose their comparative advantages to other countries. To some extent the British cotton and shipbuilding industries have been affected in this manner.

2 Frictional unemployment

At any given time, frictional unemployment probably accounts for a fairly large percentage of total unemployment. As its name implies, it is associated with the difficulties experienced by workers in moving from one job to another. Occupational and geographical mobility are not perfect and each year very large numbers of people either choose to, or are obliged to, change their jobs. Most of these people do not move immediately from one job to another; there is a time interval during which they are looking for and choosing another job. During this time they will be registered as unemployed. Frictional unemployment arises because the changes in the demands for goods and services and in the techniques of production cause changes in the demand for labour, and the supply of labour cannot adjust quickly to these changes in demand.

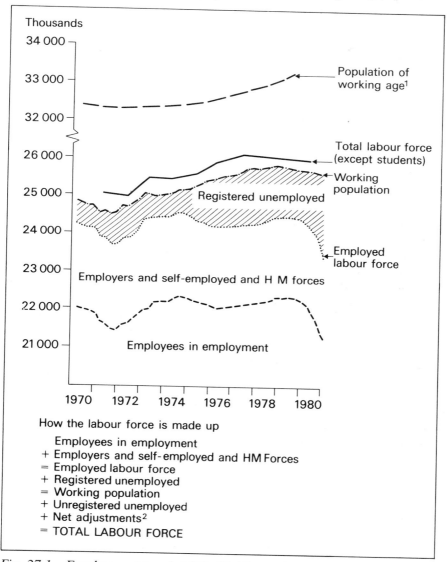

Fig. 27.1   Employment trends 1970–80 (Great Britain)

[1] Defined as males 15 to 64, females 15 to 59. (School leaving age was raised to 16 in 1973.)
[2] Allowance for students with part-time jobs, people with two or more jobs, occupational pensioners, etc.

Source: *Economic Progress Report*, HMSO, July 1981.

3 Seasonal unemployment

In some industries there is a strong seasonal pattern of demand for labour. This is obviously true of tourism, building, and agriculture. In more recent years the extent of these seasonal variations has been reduced. 'Winter breaks' have become more popular and have extended the tourist season, the substitution of capital for labour has reduced the extent of winter lay-offs in agriculture and the use of new materials has reduced the impact of cold weather on building operations.

4 Cyclical unemployment

This term describes the unemployment associated with the trade cycles. Although over the long period, output, employment and real incomes have all risen, this has not been a steady upward trend. Economic activity has proceeded in a series of booms and slumps culminating in the serious and prolonged depression in the 1930s. These fluctuations in the level of output are described as the trade cycle. Since the Second World War these cycles have continued to be a feature of economic activity, but the fluctuations in output and employment have been much smaller than those experienced in the past. Cyclical or general unemployment refers to the unemployment which is due to a fall in the *total* demand for goods and services so that all industries are affected to some extent although some suffer much more severely than others.

Measuring unemployment

In the UK, the official statistics of unemployment record the numbers of people who are out of work and who register themselves as available for work. These figures understate the true extent of unemployment because there will be some people who are out of work and who would take a suitable job if one became available, but who do not place themselves on the unemployment register. One obvious example of the people in this category is provided by those married women who do not qualify for unemployment benefit and who, when they lose their jobs, do not register themselves as unemployed.

The Department of Employment supplies information[1] on the unemployment situation which shows how different groups in the community are affected by unemployment.

1   The official statistics give figures for the numbers unemployed in the different regions, different industries and different occupations. This information gives some indication of the extent of structural unemployment and of

---

[1] In the *Department of Employment Gazette*, published monthly.

the supply and demand conditions in the markets for skilled and unskilled labour.

2 Details are also provided on the duration of unemployment – the length of time various numbers of people have been out of work. For example, if it is found that a substantial proportion of the total unemployed have been out of work for less than six weeks, it indicates that unemployment is mainly of the frictional type. If a large percentage has been out of work for six months or more there is clearly a problem of cyclical unemployment.

3 The *Department of Employment Gazette* also contains tables showing the numbers employed in the different age groups. These are useful in helping to identify other features of the unemployment situation such as (a) whether older people experience more difficulty than younger people in finding jobs when they are made redundant and (b) whether a fall in employment is taking the form of a reduced intake of trainees and causing a relatively large increase in the rate of unemployment among young people.

The unemployment figures give the size of the pool of unemployed persons, but each month there is a massive flow of people into and out of this pool. For example, in the year 1975–76, average unemployment was a little over 1 million, but the number who became unemployed during that year was 4.5 million.

Fig. 27.2 illustrates some features of the duration of unemployment in the UK in July 1981. At this particular time some 54 per cent of the numbers unemployed had been out of work for less than 26 weeks and 22 per cent had been unemployed for more than one year.

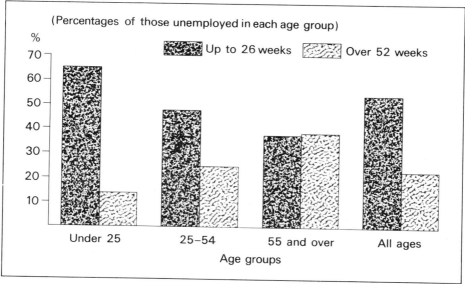

Fig. 27.2   Duration of unemployment by age, UK, July 1981

Source: *Dept. of Employment Gazette*, HMSO, September 1981.

Full employment

Although full employment is a declared aim of government policy, this term does not mean and cannot mean, zero unemployment. Since labour can never be perfectly mobile there will be, at all times, some unemployment of the frictional type. There will also be people in any population who must be classed as unemployables, people who are physically and mentally unable to cope with the disciplines and tensions of work situations.

It is not possible to specify precisely what the term 'full employment' means. A government White Paper on Employment Policy published in 1944 defined full employment as a state which existed when unemployment had fallen to 3 per cent of the labour force. In the first two and a half decades following the Second World War, unemployment averaged much less than 3 per cent. One way of looking at full employment might be to express it in terms of the demand for and supply of labour. Thus, it might be said that full employment exists when the number of vacancies is at least equal to the numbers out of work. This would mean that there were sufficient jobs to occupy the whole labour force, but the jobs were not of the right types or in the right places to create work for those without jobs. But this could still mean that relatively large numbers were unemployed. It seems that full employment must be defined in terms of some unemployment rate which is generally acceptable and this will depend upon the economic conditions and the political attitudes prevailing at the time. When unemployment is being treated as a major political issue we know that full employment does not exist. In the later 1970s, political leaders in the UK were talking about the desirability of 'getting unemployment down to something like 650 000'. This meant that their target for unemployment was a rate of 2½ per cent of the labour force.

Employment policies

Policies to deal with cyclical unemployment

The demand for labour is described as a derived demand. Labour is demanded when the goods and services it produces are demanded. The most serious type of unemployment is that which is due to a low level of aggregate demand, that is, when the total demand for goods and services is not sufficient to buy the output which a fully employed labour force could produce. Our study of the circular flow of income helps us to understand how this situation arises. It means that, at the full employment level of income, the leakages from the circular flow exceed the injections so that income falls and settles down at an equilibrium level which is too low to provide full employment.

In order to raise the level of employment, the government must take steps to increase total spending in the economy. It can use monetary policy, fiscal policy and other measures to increase consumption and investment spending. In other words it will use measures designed to increase the injections into and reduce the leakages from the circular flow of income (see page 317).

1 Fiscal policy

The government will aim at a Budget deficit by reducing taxation and increasing its own spending. A reduction in personal taxation will stimulate consumption spending. A cut in indirect taxes will make goods and services relatively cheaper and increase the quantities demanded. An increase in consumption spending might encourage firms to increase their investment spending as might also a reduction in the tax on profits (i.e. corporation tax).

Increased government spending will also raise the level of total demand. An increase in social security benefits will have an immediate effect on consumption spending because most people receiving these benefits have a high tendency to consume. An increase in investment grants might be used as a means of stimulating private investment and the government could increase investment in the public sector on projects such as new roads, schools, hospitals, airports and so on.

2 Monetary policy

The aim will be to increase total spending by making it easier and cheaper to obtain loans. Thus the government will relax any restrictions on bank lending and take action to bring down the rate of interest. The measures it will use for these purposes have been explained in Chapter 21. If, however, firms and households are very pessimistic about future prospects for the economy, these measures may not be sufficient to persuade them to increase their rates of spending.

The government has powers to vary the conditions of hire-purchase contracts, and, by making them less restrictive, it can bring about an increase in spending. In order to increase aggregate demand it could reduce the size of the minimum deposit and extend the period allowed for repayment.

3 Other measures

Since imports are a leakage from the national flow of income, the government might consider measures to reduce imports in the hope of diverting this demand to home producers. Tariffs may be raised and import quotas reduced, or, if the country is on a fixed exchange rate, the government might decide to devalue. There are problems associated with such measures since other countries are likely to retaliate. Nevertheless, if there are home-produced substitutes available, a reduction of imports would mean an increased demand for the national output. An alternative would be an intensive 'Buy British' campaign.

As a means of alleviating some of the immediate problems arising from the upward trend in unemployment in the 1970s, the UK government introduced several different schemes. Spending on these special employment measures was expected to be about £1000 million in 1980–81.

The Temporary Short-time Working Scheme is open to employers who agree to withdraw an impending redundancy affecting at least ten workers. If employers are prepared instead to introduce short-time working and pay the workers affected for days when they are not working, the state will reimburse the firms to the extent of 50 per cent of normal wages for a period of nine months. In 1980 about 700 000 workers were covered by the scheme.

The Youth Opportunities Programme (YOP) helps unemployed young people by providing training courses and work experience. The state offers tax-free allowances to those taking part in the scheme. In 1981–82 it is planned to offer 440 000 opportunities to youngsters. YOP's training and work-experience schemes usually last for six months.

The Community Enterprise Programme gives priority to those aged eighteen to twenty-four who have been out of work for more than six months and to those aged twenty-five and over who have been unemployed for more than twelve months. The scheme aims to provide full-time temporary employment on projects which benefit the community.

The Job Release Scheme provides financial inducements for people near statutory pensionable age to give up their jobs and make way for unemployed people.

Although large sums of public money are spent on these job-creation schemes, the net cost to the taxpayer is much less than the total of subsidies paid out to finance the schemes. Set against this total cost must be the savings on unemployment benefits and other social security benefits plus the extra tax revenue from those who would otherwise be unemployed.

Policies to combat frictional and structural unemployment

Even when there is a strong demand for labour, there will still be problems of unemployment because of the geographical and occupational immobility of labour. These problems and the policies used to deal with them were discussed under the headings Mobility (pages 52–5) and Regional Policy (pages 109–13). Very briefly, the policy measures are designed to redistribute industry, improve training facilities and provide better information services.

A demand for labour will not, in itself, solve the unemployment problem. It is necessary to ensure that the supply of labour is matched to the demand; workers must be provided with those skills which are in greatest demand. In recent years the UK government has greatly expanded its programmes for industrial and commercial training. But the provision of training facilities is only one aspect of the problem; the incentives to train must also be encouraged. In the late 1970s, when unemployment was relatively high (5 to 6 per cent of the labour force), many industries were reporting serious shortages of skilled labour. While lack of training facilities may have been part of the explanation for this state of affairs, the narrowing of wage differentials between skilled and unskilled workers may well have deterred some would-be trainees for skilled jobs.

Industrial training – government policy

The first comprehensive official action in this area came with the Industrial Training Act of 1964. Under this Act, *Industrial Training Boards* were established to promote training in industries covering a major part of the working population. The boards provide facilities for training and assist individual companies in developing their own training programmes.

Overall responsibility for industrial training lies with the Training Services Division (TSD) of the Manpower Services Commission (MSC). The TSD is responsible for the *Training Opportunities Scheme* (TOPS) which embraces a wide range of training and retraining courses designed to assist unemployed persons, and others who wish to retrain, to acquire some particular industrial or commercial skill. Courses last from four weeks to a year and trainees receive tax-free maintenance grants. Training is carried out in Skill Centres (formerly known as Government Training Centres) of which there are now more than sixty in the UK, in colleges of further education, and in employers' establishments. The TSD also assists firms by running many different courses for management and other personnel (e.g. courses on import and export procedures).

28   Inflation

In recent years inflation has been a world-wide problem, but rates of inflation have differed from one country to another. While some have experienced rates of inflation in excess of 100 per cent per annum, others have succeeded in holding inflation to less than 10 per cent per annum. Fig. 28.1 gives an account of the recent experiences of some major industrialized countries.

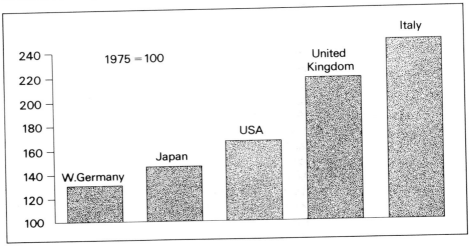

Fig. 28.1   Consumer prices, June 1981

Source: *Dept. of Employment Gazette*, HMSO, June 1981.

Inflation is generally taken to mean a situation where prices are moving persistently upwards. However, in some cases the use of price controls prevents this upward movement of prices. This is described as *suppressed inflation* since the use of price controls indicates that, without them, prices would certainly be moving upwards. We shall concern ourselves with the more usual experience of rising prices. Inflation does not mean that all prices are moving to the same extent; some indeed may be falling. It is the general price level which is rising and the extent of inflation is measured by changes in the Index of Retail Prices.

The effects of inflation

Inflation is considered a problem because many of its consequences are widely regarded as unsatisfactory. One of the problems associated with inflation is its tendency to accelerate. Once inflation has been experienced for some time, people begin to act in anticipation of future price increases. Organized labour will base its wage claims not only on the amount necessary to compensate workers for previous price increases; it will include something to protect workers against future price increases. Firms, when adjusting their prices, will begin to anticipate future as well as current increases in costs. There is, therefore, a danger that the rate of inflation will speed up. There have been occasions when the rate at which prices were rising got completely out of hand. This state of affairs is described as runaway or *hyperinflation*. It occurred in Germany in 1923 when, at one time, prices were doubling every hour. Hungary had a similar experience in 1945 when wages were increased at the rate of 150 per cent *per week* and yet they still lagged behind the rate at which prices were rising.

A further problem is the effects which inflation has on the distribution of income. When prices are rising, real incomes will be falling and people will quite naturally take actions designed to restore their real incomes. The ability of different groups to obtain the necessary adjustments of their money incomes depends upon the strength of their bargaining positions. Some will be more successful than others. Organized groups of workers in strategically important industries such as coal mining, the generation of electricity, or transport, are in a much stronger bargaining position than a group of pensioners. What happens is that inflation causes a redistribution of real income; there are gainers and losers. The gainers are those who can obtain more frequent and relatively larger increases in their money incomes when prices are rising.

People whose money incomes are fixed or relatively fixed are obvious losers. These people will include some pensioners and those who derive income from fixed interest securities or, perhaps, controlled rents.

People in occupations where income is related to the value of output or sales may not suffer any fall in their real incomes. Salespeople, estate agents, architects, surveyors and others often receive commissions or fees which are expressed as a percentage of the value of the goods sold or work carried out. Similarly, many workers have their wages directly linked to the Index of Retail Prices. In all these cases earnings will keep pace with prices.

For most of the post-war period, wages in general have moved ahead of prices, but, as explained above, differences in bargaining strengths have led to a redistribution of income among the wage-earning groups. Whether the fact that some groups have become relatively better off and others relatively worse off is 'fair' or 'unfair' is a value judgement.

A further important feature of inflation is the effect it has on the real value of debts. If a person borrows £1000 for one year and, during the course of that year, prices increase by 10 per cent, the lender is a 'loser'. When the debt is repaid, the money will buy 10 per cent less in terms of goods and services than when it was loaned; its real value will have fallen 10 per cent. In fact, the lender will not suffer to this extent because the borrower will be charged a rate of interest. But the lender could still be a loser if the rate of inflation is greater than the rate of interest. For example, if the lender had charged the borrower a rate of interest of 8 per cent, the borrower would be a gainer; the *real* rate of interest would be −2 per cent. This is one feature of inflation which has greatly benefited the government of the UK (and other governments). The government is by far the largest borrower in the country and, since it borrows mainly by issuing fixed interest securities, the *real* burden of the interest payments has been greatly reduced by inflation.

If the rate of inflation in one country is higher than the rates at which prices are rising in countries with which it trades and competes, its products are becoming less competitive in foreign markets. Imports, on the other hand, will become more competitive in the home market. In such cases inflation is very likely to lead to balance of payments problems.

The causes of inflation

The causes of inflation are very complex and this is a subject on which economists still strongly disagree. There is much argument about whether prices are *pulled* upwards or *pushed* upwards. This has led to the identification of two kinds of inflation, demand-pull and cost-push.

Demand-pull inflation

During the period from 1945 to the mid-1960s when the average rate of unemployment was low (rather less than 2½ per cent), inflation was explained mainly in terms of excess demand. Prices, it was held, were being pulled upwards because of excess demand. Demand-pull inflation is associated with full employment in the following manner.

Suppose the economy is working below full capacity, that is, there are unemployed workers, and land and capital are also lying idle. Now assume that demand rises. This increase in demand will lead to the idle resources being put to work and output will increase. There will be little or no effect on the general price level because the increased demand will be met by an increase in supply. Now suppose that demand continues to increase until the economy is working at full capacity. At this point any further increases in demand cannot be satisfied by increased output and the inevitable result will be that prices begin to rise. In fact some prices will begin to rise even before the economy reaches full employment. This is because some firms will reach full capacity operation while others still have some spare capacity.

Government policy may cause demand-pull inflation. In times of full employment the government may be under great pressure to expand many of the services it provides (e.g. health and education) and to improve facilities such as roads and airports. If it attempts to expand these programmes when economic resources are fully employed, it will create excess demand in the economy unless there is some compensating fall in spending elsewhere due to an increase in saving or an increase in taxation.

Excess demand at times of full employment may also be caused by an increase in investment which is not offset by an increased willingness to save. It may also be due to a large increase in the demand for exports.

Firms faced with increasing demands and encouraged by the higher prices for their goods and services will try to increase their outputs. Since, under conditions of full employment, the factors of production will be in short supply, firms will attempt to attract them from other firms by offering higher rewards (i.e. wages, rents and interest rates). Demand-pull inflation pulls up the prices of factors of production as well as the prices of their products.

Cost-push inflation

Since the mid-1960s, the UK and other countries have experienced much higher rates of inflation than those experienced in the earlier post-war period. But these higher rates of inflation have also been associated with much higher levels of unemployment, and there have been several periods when both the rate of inflation and the rate of unemployment were moving upwards at the same time.

The idea that inflation is due to excess demand does not seem to fit this situation. When unemployment is relatively high and rising, can we say that there is excess demand in the economy? Many economists explain this type of inflation in terms of rising costs pushing up the general price level.

Costs represent the prices paid for the services of the factors of production and we have seen that factor prices may rise when excess demand causes firms to bid up the prices of scarce labour, capital and land. But these factor prices may also rise when there is no excess demand.

The world prices of raw materials may rise and this will raise costs in the UK whatever the state of demand in the economy. The massive increases in the price of oil during the 1970s provide the best example of how external factors may affect domestic costs. Costs and prices may also be pushed upwards by increases in indirect taxes, for example, by increases in tariffs or VAT.

Since wages are the most important element in total costs, wage increases which exceed any increases in productivity have been seen as a major cause of cost-push inflation. Rising unemployment has not seriously weakened the trade unions' demands for higher wages nor their ability to obtain them.

Inflation is not a once-and-for-all increase in prices, it is a continuous process, so that we have to explain why prices continue to rise. When prices move upward, whatever the initial cause, the higher prices will provoke wage demands from workers whose real income has been reduced by rising prices. If, as is likely, the settlement of these demands leads to wage increases greater than the increase in productivity, there will be a further rise in costs and hence a further rise in prices. Once again workers will demand compensating wage increases and so the process will go on. This sequence of events is popularly known as the *wage-price spiral*.

Policies to deal with inflation

Demand-pull inflation

The policy must be designed to reduce total demand in the economy and the government will probably use some or all of the following measures.

1 An increase in taxes on income and expenditure as a means of reducing consumption spending. The extent to which spending falls depends upon the amounts by which people cut saving rather than spending. Any fall in consumption spending is likely to lead to a fall in investment.
2 Cuts in public expenditure. There are, however, serious political problems associated with this policy (see page 306).
3 Increased restrictions on bank lending together with an increase in the rate of interest.
4 A tightening of hire-purchase restrictions.

All of these measures will tend to reduce total demand for goods and services and although they might lower the rate of inflation, they are also likely to cause an increase in unemployment. The increases in indirect taxes which are intended to reduce demand by raising prices might prove to be inflationary. Any increase in the Index of Retail Prices is likely to lead to compensating wage demands.

Cost-push inflation

Governments have not had a great deal of success in framing policies to combat inflation when it is accompanied by a relatively high rate of unemployment. The measures described above which are intended to reduce total demand do not seem appropriate; they will only tend to worsen an already unsatisfactory unemployment situation. Attempts to hold down costs by granting subsidies to producers would probably mean higher taxes. The imposition of price controls when costs are still rising will squeeze profits and may force many firms into bankruptcy. Since, it seems, inflation takes the form of a wage-price spiral, attempts have been made to devise policies which will break this spiral. Many governments have tried to do this with some form of incomes policy.

Incomes policies

These are policies which aim to keep the growth of total income in line with the growth of total output, or, to put it another way, to ensure that money income does not grow faster than real income. If factor incomes do not rise faster than productivity, the cost-push pressures on prices will be greatly reduced. Since wages make up the greater part of total costs, incomes policies tend to give most attention to ways of restricting increases in wages.

The usual procedure is for the government to make an estimate of the likely increase in total output for the year ahead and, on the basis of this estimate, to announce the permitted (or recommended) maximum increase in total income for the next twelve months. This figure is expressed as a percentage increase and is known as the *norm*. For example, the government might announce that it does not wish to see total income rising by more than 5 per cent during the coming year.

There are many problems in trying to make an incomes policy work successfully.

1 In a country where trade unions have enjoyed free collective bargaining for many years, it will be difficult or impossible to make the policy legally enforceable. The success of the policy, therefore, depends upon the government being able to get the voluntary cooperation of a large number of independent trade unions as well as many thousands of firms.

2 It is difficult to 'police' an incomes policy, that is, to make sure that firms are not evading the restrictions and paying their workers more than the norm – especially those firms trying to recruit scarce labour.

3 The fact that increases in wages are limited might act as a disincentive to effort and to attempts to increase efficiency. Workers might feel that there is not much point in improving their performance if there is little chance of getting extra income. If exceptions are made so that increases in productivity are rewarded by wage increases above the norm, workers in occupations where productivity cannot be measured will feel unfairly treated.

4 Trade unions and other groups might interpret the norm as a kind of officially approved *minimum* increase in wages and hence press for rises greater than the norm.

5 An incomes policy aims to limit the annual increase in total and *average* earnings to some given percentage. Firms in growth industries which are short of labour might be permitted to pay more than the norm in order to attract more workers. But, if the increase in average earnings is to be kept to the recommended figure, other firms (e.g. those with surplus labour) must offer less than the norm. Again this will be strongly resented (and resisted) by those workers getting less than the average increase in pay.

6 Trade unions will not surrender their rights to free collective bargaining for an indefinite period. When their rights to bargain freely on behalf of their members have been restricted for one or two years, they are likely to demand the restoration of their freedoms. This will certainly be the case where the incomes policy has permitted only very small increases in income. Once the policy is abandoned, however, there is a tendency for incomes to increase very rapidly as people attempt to 'catch up' or make good the ground they feel they have lost while the incomes policy has been operating. Some economists have likened the end of an incomes policy to the collapse of a dam.

The government will find it difficult to obtain the cooperation of labour in any policy to restrict wage increases unless that policy also includes some provisions to restrict the growth of other incomes – especially dividends and rents. It will also be necessary to include some measures to control the increase in prices otherwise labour will not accept wage restraint. In the UK, incomes policies have sometimes broken down because certain prices which are beyond the government's control (e.g. import prices) have risen sharply and labour has reacted by abandoning wage restraint.

Inflation and the money supply

There has been a growing measure of support for the view that the rate of inflation can only be reduced by controlling the money supply. This view is based on developments of the Quantity Theory of Money. This theory, which goes back at least 200 years, holds that the value of money (i.e. changes in the price level) are caused by movements in the supply of money.

Very simply, the older quantity theory viewed the value of money as being determined in the same way as the value of other commodities, that is, by supply and demand. Other things being equal, an increase in the supply of a commodity will cause its value to fall. The quantity theory held that this was equally true of money.

We must be careful to distinguish between the amount or quantity of *money* and the amount or rate of *spending*. It is the act of spending which affects prices; money which is held but not spent will clearly have no direct influence on the demand for goods and services. The amount of spending which takes place in any given time period depends upon:

a   the quantity of money;

b   the rate at which that quantity of money changes hands i.e. the velocity of circulation.

For example, if the amount of money in an economy is £100m. and, on average, each £1 changes hands four times during the course of a year, then the amount of spending during that year will be £400m.

Many economists (the monetarists) believe that the velocity of circulation is fairly stable so that changes in the money supply will have a direct effect on the level of expenditure. Thus, if the money supply is allowed to grow faster than the output of goods and services, prices are certain to rise.

It is true that inflation is invariably associated with increases in the money supply, but there is considerable disagreement about the relationship. Some economists argue that the increase in the money supply does not *cause* an increase in spending but is *caused by* an increase in the willingness to borrow and spend. The banking system supplies the amount of money which people demand for these purposes. For example, a firm may be forced to concede inflationary wage settlements and in order to meet them may have to borrow from the banks. The money supply will increase, but the increase in the money supply did not cause the higher incomes. It is true that inflation cannot continue unless the money supply increases so as to finance the higher prices and higher incomes.

The controversies surrounding inflation are complex and will continue for a long time. All we can say is that monetarists believe that inflation can only be countered by maintaining a strict control over the money supply.

29 Balance of payments problems

The standard of living in the UK depends very much on the country's performance as a trading nation. It was pointed out in Chapter 22 that the UK is dependent upon imports for nearly one-half of its food and a large proportion of the raw materials used by its industries. These commodities must be paid for in foreign currencies and these currencies must be earned by selling goods and services abroad.

Many modern industries can only achieve low-cost production if they produce on a very large scale. This is true of such industries as those making cars, aircraft, electrical appliances, electronic equipment and chemical products. The UK can only develop and maintain successful industries making some of the newer technical products if these industries have large export markets[1]. The size of the home market is not large enough for the industries to achieve the necessary economies of scale. To some extent this point also applies to important service industries. The economies of scale achieved by UK banking and insurance services are dependent on the existence of large export markets.

In the years since the Second World War there has been a gradual lowering of the barriers to trade and the UK, of course, is now a member of the EEC in which most of the barriers to trade have been removed. This means that British industry is faced with intense competition in both home and overseas markets.

In addition to the increased freedom of movement for goods and services, there has also been a gradual relaxation of the restrictions on the convertibility of currencies and on the movements of money from one country to another. These movements, as explained later, can have serious effects on a country's balance of payments.

The term 'balance of payments problem' invariably refers to the existence of a deficit. A balance of payments surplus is usually regarded as very desirable, but a country experiencing large and persistent surpluses will be causing problems for other countries since its surpluses must be balanced by deficits in other countries.

Causes of balance of payments problems

These problems may be caused by developments at home or abroad.

---

[1] In 1980, a chief executive of the Volkswagen company stated that a company had to have an annual output of at least 2 million cars to survive in world markets.

1 Inflation

This is a major cause of balance of payments problems. If prices at home are rising faster than they are in competitor countries, exports will tend to fall as they become less competitive and imports will increase as they become more competitive.

2 Technical progress

If a country falls behind its competitors in the rate at which it develops or adopts new techniques of production it will tend to lose its markets to products from other countries which are superior in design and performance or produced at lower cost.

3 Immobilities

Even when a country's labour force is capable of producing goods which compete effectively in world markets, balance of payments problems will still arise if capital and labour are slow to move out of industries with poor growth prospects and into industries which are producing goods for expanding markets.

4 A high degree of dependence on imported materials

When the basic source of power was coal, most industrial nations could supply their needs from their own resources. When oil became a major source of energy, many industrial nations found themselves dependent on foreign supplies. When the major oil exporters combined together to form OPEC (Organization of Petroleum Exporting Countries) in order to exercise monopoly powers over the supply of oil, the extent to which they raised oil prices caused serious balance of payments problems for virtually all the nations dependent on oil imports.

5 Capital movements

A deficit on the balance of payments can be caused by unfavourable capital movements as, for example, when the residents of a country decide to invest heavily abroad. This will cause a serious outflow of foreign currency (e.g. to invest in the USA, citizens of the UK must obtain dollars). Similarly, when interest rates are more attractive in foreign financial centres than in London, people holding funds in London may be tempted to withdraw them and transfer them abroad. Again this will cause an outflow of foreign currencies because the deposits in London will be converted into foreign currencies so that they can be invested in other countries.

The kinds of problems caused by a balance of payments deficit depend very much on the type of foreign exchange rate system which the country is using. The explanations which follow are largely a summary of material dealt with in Chapter 23. The examples relate to a particular economy (the UK), but the analysis applies to any economy which finds itself in the circumstances being described.

A balance of payments deficit with a fixed exchange rate

The deficit will reveal itself in the foreign exchange market where the supply of pounds will exceed the demand for pounds and the external value of the pound will tend to fall. But the central bank cannot allow this to happen since it is committed to maintaining a fixed exchange rate. It will, therefore, buy pounds on the foreign exchange market. For these purchases it will use foreign currencies so that its activities will cause the nation's reserves of foreign currencies to fall. If the deficit persists, the authorities may continue to support the pound for some time by borrowing foreign currencies from the IMF and foreign central banks. But these are short-term measures and sooner or later the government will have to take steps to deal with the cause of the deficit. It will almost certainly take action to reduce imports because policies designed to increase exports may take a fairly long time to become effective.

1 Restrictions on imports

The obvious measures are the use of tariffs and quotas to limit imports. These could be made effective, but they will lead to higher prices in the home market and they might cause other countries to retaliate, in which case UK exports could suffer. An alternative is to subsidize home producers, but this will mean higher taxes and, like tariffs and quotas, subsidies infringe the rules of trading agreements such as the EEC and GATT.

2 Restricting home demand

In order to avoid the use of trade barriers, the government might decide to bring about a fall in the demand for imported goods and services by using measures to reduce *total demand* in the home economy (see page 332). If total spending is reduced then spending on imports will be reduced. Again this policy could be made effective, but the cut in total demand will inevitably increase unemployment. One favourable effect might be that the reduced size of the home market might make British firms try harder to increase their export sales.

3 Raising the rate of interest

In order to stem and, perhaps, reverse an outflow of short-term capital, the government might increase the short-term rate of interest. This would make it more profitable to hold funds in London. The disadvantage of such a policy is that UK firms and households will have to pay higher interest charges on their borrowings.

4 Devaluation

This procedure, which aims to reduce imports *and* stimulate exports, was explained in Chapter 23. There are serious problems associated with its use. It will only be successful if the quantities demanded of exports and imports respond in a favourable way to the price changes which devaluation brings about. There is also the danger that other countries may retaliate by devaluing their own currencies. In the case of the UK, the higher costs of imported food and raw materials will also create a problem in the form of higher production costs.

A balance of payments deficit with a floating exchange rate

In theory there should be no balance of payments problem when the external value of a currency is allowed to find its own level in a free market. The forces of supply and demand should move the exchange rate to an equilibrium level at which the value of exports is equal to the value of imports. If the UK balance of payments were moving into deficit, the excess supply of pounds in the foreign exchange market would cause the value of the pound to fall. Imports would then become relatively dearer and exports relatively cheaper (see page 269). The exchange rate would continue to fall until the demand for pounds was equal to the supply of pounds and the balance of payments was in equilibrium.

While these kinds of changes will certainly take place under a system of floating exchange rates, the system may not work as easily and smoothly as the theory suggests. It assumes, for example, that the quantities supplied can respond fairly quickly to the price changes. If the pound depreciates, the prices of UK exports (in foreign currencies) will fall and more will be demanded. But the effects will only be favourable if the demand for exports is elastic and UK industries can meet the increased demand by increasing the supply of exports. If UK firms think that the favourable situation is only temporary, they may be reluctant to expand their capacities and increase their supplies. On the other hand, if resources are immobile, exporting firms wishing to expand may find it difficult to obtain more resources (e.g. skilled labour). The fact that depreciation makes imports dearer could lead to a rapid loss of the price advantages created by the depreciation. The increased prices of imported goods will raise home prices and this could lead to cost-push inflation. This will raise export prices and offset the effects of depreciation on the prices of British goods in foreign markets.

30 Economic growth

Economic growth refers to the growth of the real national income, that is, to an increase in the national output of goods and services. Such an increase may come about in two ways.

1 It may be due to a fall in unemployment when previously idle resources are put to work and the total output of goods and services increases.

2 It may also be brought about by an increase in the nation's capacity to produce. In this case, the full employment output of a country increases.

Economists normally restrict the use of the term economic growth to the kind of changes explained in the second example, because the first example represents a once-and-for-all increase in output. In other words, economic growth is taken to mean the ability of an economy to increase its output even when all its resources are fully employed.

This is an important distinction because there seems to be an almost universal demand for higher living standards. People have come to expect that, materially, they will be much better off than their parents. This demand for continually rising living standards can only be met if there is economic growth as defined in the second example above.

People's expectations of a rising real income are based on the fact that, in the post-war period, many countries have demonstrated that high rates of growth are possible and that such rates can be maintained for many years. In 1976 world output *per head* was 225 per cent higher than the level in 1950. Total world output, of course, grew much faster than this because, during that period, world population had been growing rapidly.

Statistics of economic growth can be misleading in the sense that the annual percentage rates often appear to be very small. We must remember, however, that what seems to be a small annual percentage increase in national output, can, if sustained for several years, bring about major changes in the standard of living in relatively short periods of time. For example, if a country could maintain an annual growth rate of 3 per cent, its gross national product would double in about twenty-four years.

Factors affecting economic growth

The causes of economic growth are complex and we can only indicate some of the things which seem to have a bearing on the rate of economic growth.

1 The rate of investment

Increasing the quantity and quality of the nation's stock of capital is one way of increasing output-per-worker-hour. If workers have more and better capital to work with, their productivity will increase. But a high rate of investment does not seem to guarantee a high rate of growth; much depends on the type of investment and on the way in which the new capital is used.

Investment in newer industries with growing markets is likely to yield larger increases in productivity than investment in older industries with static and declining markets; new capital is much more likely to be fully utilized where the market is growing. Investment which takes the form of piece-meal modernization of older industrial structures is not likely to be so productive as the complete rebuilding of industries when plants of optimum size using the latest techniques and layouts can be built. After the Second World War, West Germany and Japan were able to adopt this second course. Investment in factories, power stations and transport systems will yield much greater increases in output, in the short run, than investment in social capital such as houses, schools and recreation centres.

2 Technical progress

Many economists believe that technical progress is just as important a source of economic growth as increases in the stock of capital. The term 'technical progress' is taken to include such changes as improved techniques of production, the development of new materials, inventions, improvements in the design and performance of machinery, better organization and management, better training facilities and methods, and more efficient means of communication and transport.

3 Economies of scale

It was pointed out in Chapter 6 that increasing the scale of production can often lead to large increases in productivity. This is one explanation for the large number of mergers in recent years. In some industries, the UK government has played an active part in encouraging such mergers.

4 The quality of the labour force

The efficiency of the labour force is obviously a very important factor in determining the rate of economic growth. A healthier working population will clearly be a more productive labour force. Similarly a well-educated labour force will be much more capable of coping with the problems of production than one which has a low level of education. For these reasons expenditure on health and education services can be seen, from a strictly economic viewpoint, as an 'investment in people'. Just as investment in capital goods will raise productivity in future years, so will investment in health and educational facilities. The same will be true of expenditure on industrial and commercial training facilities. Another important point regarding the performance of the labour force concerns the attitudes of the workers. The way in which industry is organized can have a great influence on productivity. If the relations between management and workers are harmonious, productivity will be much higher than where industrial relations are characterized by strife. A great deal of attention is now being paid to this problem and a variety of schemes are being introduced to increase the extent of worker participation in the management of firms.

5 Mobility

In a changing world, a nation's rate of economic growth depends very much on its willingness to accept changes in its economic structure. If productivity is to grow steadily and consistently, (a) resources must be moved into those industries with growing markets, (b) new and more efficient methods of production must be developed and adopted, and (c) working practices must be changed to take full advantage of the newer methods of production.

But these changes are not easy to carry out. Investment in new products and new techniques is often costly and risky. Many firms will have to be convinced that government policies are committed to growth before they will undertake such investment. Many of the necessary changes may be resisted because they call for changes in working attitudes and practices which older workers find difficult to accept. The movement of resources from one activity to another calls for a high degree of mobility in the labour force and for many people this will mean redundancy and retraining. A further objection to technical change arises because much of the new machinery will be of the labour-saving type and will be seen as a threat to workers' jobs. In fact, it may not work out like this. Although a new technology may require less labour per unit of output, if the new techniques produce a product of better quality and at lower cost, total demand will increase and it may happen that more, rather than fewer, workers will be employed.

The benefits of economic growth

Governments are anxious to achieve favourable rates of growth for several reasons.

1   Growth is the key to higher living standards. Increased productivity makes it possible for the community to enjoy, (a) more goods and services for the same number of hours of work, or (b) the same standard of living for fewer hours of work, or (c) some combinations of (a) and (b), that is, a higher material standard of living and more leisure.

2   When real national income per head is increasing, the government will be able to raise more revenue without increasing *the rates* of taxation. If we are all much better off in real terms then the same rates of taxation will still leave us better off *and* produce more revenue for the government. This means that the education, health and other social services can be extended and improved without making any cuts in the community's disposable real income.

3   Policies designed to bring about a more equal distribution of income can be carried out with much less political opposition than when there is little or no growth. When no growth is taking place, one group in society can only be made better off if some other group is made worse off, because income must be transferred from one group to the other. When real income is growing, however, this need not happen, because a greater percentage of *the increase* in real income can be directed towards the lower-income groups (e.g. pensioners).

4   A great deal of political prestige is attached to national rates of economic growth. The publication of 'league tables' showing the growth rates achieved by different countries attracts a lot of publicity and a government's reputation for economic management can be adversely affected if the country has a low place in such a table.

The costs of economic growth

Economic growth has its costs as well as its benefits. We saw in Chapter 3 that capital accumulation (i.e. investment) can only take place if people are prepared to accept sacrifices in term of their *present* standard of living. If the economy is fully employed, the output of capital goods can only be increased by moving resources from the production of consumer goods. Current consumption, therefore, is less than it might have been. While it is true that the increased stock of capital will make possible a greater *future* output of consumer goods, many people may not be prepared to make the sacrifice, especially if the benefits of greater output will not be forthcoming for several years.

There is also a variety of social costs associated with a high rate of growth. It was pointed out in Chapter 5 that the price mechanism does not take full account of the social costs of production. The technical efficiency which makes possible high rates of growth can impose heavy social costs on the community. Some examples are given below.

1   Very large units of transport such as juggernaut lorries and very large jet planes impose costs in the form of noise, pollution and congestion.

2   Very large industrial complexes such as steelworks, chemical plants, power stations and large airports often destroy rural amenities and create heavy pollution.

3   Heavy concentrations of industry increase the extent of urbanization with its problems of congestion and overcrowding.

4   A high rate of economic growth inevitably means a speeding up in the rate of technical and economic change. This calls for increased mobility in the labour force and an increased readiness amongst workers to change their jobs, their place of work or the way they do their jobs. Frequent changes of this nature can be unsettling and unpleasant and can lead to a loss of work satisfaction. Although retraining programmes with adequate financial grants can help to deal with this problem, it is, for many people, a high cost of rapid economic growth.

As against this, it must be pointed out that economic growth increases the ability of a nation to deal with these problems. For example, a rich nation can afford to devote resources to cleaning up the environment while a poor nation cannot devote resources to this task.

Test paper 11

Short-answer questions

Questions 1, 2 and 3 are based on the following table which refers to conditions in a simple two sector economy (i.e. households and firms only). Assume:

i households always save ¼ of income and spend ¾ of income;

ii investment remains constant at £200 million.

In the questions which follow, the economy is assumed to be, initially, at some given level of income. In each case you are asked to say:

a whether, at the given level of income, withdrawals are greater than, less than, or equal to injections;

b whether income, in the next time period, would tend to rise, fall, or remain unchanged.

	Initial level of income	Consumption spending	Saving	Investment	What will happen to income?
1	£600 million	____	____	£200 million	____
2	£800 million	____	____	£200 million	____
3	£1000 million	____	____	£200 million	____

4 The proportion of any increase in income which is spent on consumer goods and services is described as *the marginal propensity to consume*. From the data given below what is the marginal propensity to consume when income rises from £12 000 million to £14 000 million?

Income	Consumption
£12 000 million	£10 500 million
£14 000 million	£11 700 million

5 What type of unemployment is likely to arise when a major industry loses several of its most important markets?

6 If, in a region of the country, there is a significant number of people unemployed, but firms in some industries are unable to obtain the type of labour they require, what type of unemployment is present?

7 How is unemployment officially measured in the UK?

8 How might a government use fiscal policy as a means of reducing unemployment?

9 Why are measures designed to increase the mobility of labour an essential part of a full employment policy?

10 What is the main indicator of the rate of inflation in the UK?

11 Why is inflation described as a 'tax on saving'?

12 'During inflation, borrowers gain and lenders lose.' Explain.

13 Why is the *net* cost of employment subsidies less than the gross cost?

14 A famous economist recently described Britain's major economic problem as being one of *underemployment* rather than unemployment. What did he mean by this statement?

15 Inflation is a situation where prices keep on rising. How, then, can inflation said to be caused by a once-and-for-all increase in import prices?

16 Serious and persistent shortages of labour cause employers to bid up wages and these rising wages lead to rising prices. Is this an example of cost-push inflation?

17 How might a government use fiscal policy to deal with demand-pull inflation?

18 a How might a government use its powers to regulate hire-purchase contracts as a means of dealing with inflation?

b What is the main criticism of this particular measure?

19 An incomes policy aims to ensure that the rise in money incomes does not run well ahead of the rise in ____. What is the missing word (or words)?

20 Why is inflation likely to give rise to balance of payments problems?

21 Why is a deficit regarded as a balance of payments problem?

22 A country's exports are doing badly. Industrialists say that the main cause is the relatively high prices caused by inflation at home. Other commentators say that prices are not the main reason for the poor export performance. What other reasons might account for the loss of export markets?

23 Assume the UK is on a fixed exchange rate and is running a deficit in its balance of payments. This deficit causes the (a) ____ pounds to exceed the (b) ____ pounds in the foreign exchange market. In order to maintain the value of the pound, the central bank is obliged to enter the market and use its supply of (c) ____ in order to buy (d) ____.
What are the missing words at (a), (b), (c) and (d)?

24 Assume that the UK is on a fixed exchange rate and it changes the parity of the pound from £1 = $2.50 to £1 = $2.00
a in relation to the $, the £ has been ____.
b in relation to the £, the $ has been ____.
What are the missing words?

25 'If a highly developed country and a low-income country both maintained the same growth rate for several years, the gap between them, in living standards, would continue to widen.' Why?

26 'It is *innovation* rather than *invention* which is critical in deciding the rate of economic growth.' Distinguish between the words in italics.

27 Economic growth leads to a greater output per head. Why then should so many people have serious doubts about whether a rapid growth rate is beneficial?

True or false?

28 a If an economy is saving more than it is investing, it is growing wealthier.

b The proportion of income spent on consumption goods and services tends to increase as income increases.

c Increased spending on imports and increased saving have similar effects on the circular flow of income.

d Other things being equal, an increase in exports will cause national income to increase.

e A policy designed to reduce unemployment by restricting imports is sometimes described as a policy of exporting unemployment.

f During inflation total real income is rising faster than total money income.

g Index-linking is an attempt to maintain the real value of incomes such as wages, pensions and social security benefits.

h An incomes policy tries to reduce the rate of inflation by relating increases in incomes to increases in prices.

i A country must try to achieve a balance on each of the main sections of its balance of payments account.

j Quotas can be used to reduce imports, but they will almost certainly lead to higher prices in the home market.

Multiple-choice questions

29 Which of the following measures would be most likely to raise the level of employment?

A an increase in indirect taxation
B a budget surplus
C a reduction in interest rates
D an increase in corporation tax
E a lowering of tariffs

30 Which of the following is *not* likely to be a feature of inflation?

A borrowers gaining at the expense of lenders
B an increasing surplus on the balance of trade
C a steady fall in the value of money
D an increase in the supply of money
E a steady rise in the rate of interest

Questions 31, 32 and 33 refer to the following economic terms.

A devaluation
B reflation
C depreciation
D revaluation
E deflation

Which of the above describes a policy which aims to,

31 raise the level of total spending in an economy?

32 raise the external value of a currency from one fixed parity to another?

33 reduce the level of aggregate demand in an economy?

34 Which of the following might increase the rate of economic growth?

1 a fall in the numbers unemployed

2 an increase in the activity rate of the population

3 an increase in the proportion of the population in the working age groups

A 1, 2 and 3

B 1 and 2 only

C 2 and 3 only

D 1 only

E 3 only

35 Which of the following might be included in a policy to reduce the inequality in the distribution of income?

1 subsidies on foodstuffs

2 a progressive income tax

3 the imposition of indirect taxes

A 1, 2 and 3

B 1 and 2 only

C 2 and 3 only

D 1 only

E 3 only

Data-response questions

36 **Patterns of household expenditure, UK 1978**

Percentages of expenditure allocated to:

Households with income in the:	housing	fuel, light, power	food	alcoholic drink and tobacco	clothing and footwear	household goods	transport and vehicles	services and miscellaneous	totals of (i), (ii) and (iii)
	(i)	(ii)	(iii)	(iv)	(v)	(vi)	(vii)	(viii)	(ix)
lowest 20%	22	11	30	6	6	11	6	8	63
second 20%	17	8	27	8	8	13	10	9	52
third 20%	15	6	26	9	8	14	13	9	47
fourth 20%	15	5	24	9	9	14	14	10	44
highest 20% of the income distribution	13	4	21	8	10	16	16	12	38

Source: *Economic Progress Report*, HMSO, January 1980.

a How do the government statisticians obtain the kind of information contained in this table?

b Columns (i), (ii) and (iii) all show a marked decline in the proportion of expenditure as income rises. How would you explain this feature of the table?

c Can you account for the large differences in spending patterns revealed in columns (vi), (vii) and (viii)?

d How might the information in this table help the government and businesses in planning for the future?

37 A country on a fixed exchange rate has a persistent balance of payments deficit which, it is believed, is due to the prices of its exports being uncompetitive in most of the more important overseas markets. It is a member of a customs union and is unable, therefore, to use tariffs and quotas as a means of reducing its imports. Furthermore, the country is enjoying very high levels of employment and the government does not wish to take any action which might lead to higher unemployment. The country imports substantial amounts of food and raw materials.

Assume that this country chooses devaluation as a means of dealing with its balance of payments difficulties.

a In what ways might this improve the situation?

b What adverse effects might result?

c What other actions might the government have to take in order to ensure that devaluation does improve the balance of payments situation?

Index